MOON TAN ★

CHINE SS

Talk
Chinese

FOURTH EDITION

常青圖書
Cypress Books

Chinese Express - Talk Chinese (fourth edition)

By Moon Tan and Haitong Wang

Editor: Mei Li
Cover Design: Seagull Design

First published in Great Britain in 2017 by Cypress Book Co. UK Ltd.
Unit 6, Provident Industrial Estate
Pump Lane
Hayes UB3 3NE
United Kingdom
Tel: 0044 (0)20 8848 0572
E-mail: info@cypressbooks.com

Find us at www.cypressbooks.com

ISBN: 978-1-84570-009-6

Printed in China 2017

ABOUT THE AUTHORS

Moon Tan is a lecturer in Chinese at King's College London. She has more than 20 years experience of teaching Chinese as a foreign language in the UK. She is a member of The International Society for Chinese Language Teaching and a member of The British Chinese Language Teaching Society.

Haitong Wang is a lecturer in Chinese for British diplomats at the Foreign and Commonwealth Office and Westminster School. She is also a cross-cultural advisor to international businesses throughout Europe and has taught at London Business School, and at the School of Oriental and African Studies, London University. She has 20 years teaching experience in the UK and holds an MA in Language Studies. She has worked as a presenter for the Chinese Section of the BBC World Service.

PREFACE

Chinese Express - Talk Chinese is designed for English speakers studying Chinese at beginner's level, equivalent to CEFR A1, A2 levels leading to B1 level. It is suitable for university students who choose Chinese as a module, people who join evening courses at universities or community colleges, and students who want a suitable book for self-study.

Chinese Express - Talk Chinese is concise and user friendly; a book which should be as easy for students to study as for teachers to use. It is different from other textbooks insofar as *Pinyin*, Chinese characters and English are used together throughout the whole book. This will suit students who only need to learn listening or speaking as much as those who want to learn reading and writing as well.

Chinese Express - Talk Chinese uses a communicative approach and places emphasis on learning communication skills. 192 key sentences make up the main structure of the book, around which situational dialogues are introduced, covering the most useful situations in real life. Language points are explained in simple English and set out in a logical step-by-step order that is easy to understand. This is designed to give students the opportunity to gain confidence in using the most common vocabulary and grammar relevant to everyday situations.

The authors of this book believe in learning through doing and this plays a very important role in the lessons in Chinese Express. Each lesson includes an assortment of exercises designed to make students think more about the language as they learn it, so that they can understand and respond more confidently when confronted with the same situations in real life.

The authors would like to thank Professor Shiju Zhao and Dr Yinghua Zhai from Wuhan University in China for checking the grammar and giving professional advice. We also would like to thank Robert McCready and Nigel Pamment for their suggestions and support during the writing of this book and for their assistance in proof reading the book. Our special thanks go to Anthony Ward for kindly polishing our English. Finally, we would like to express our gratitude to Zhansheng Xia, Xian Xu and Wenqing Zhang of the Cypress Book Company for their assistance and professional guidance in preparing this book for publication.

LEARNING CHINESE CAN BE GREAT FUN. ENJOY!

Introducing Key Features

Chinese Express - Talk Chinese covers the main Chinese grammar points and is equivalent to university beginner's level. Clear objectives are stated at the beginning of each lesson. These are followed by 7 or 8 Key Sentences, Relevant Vocabulary consisting of about 25 words and 3 or 4 situational dialogues. The whole book introduces around 600 of the most frequently used words in daily life. There are altogether 25 main lessons and 5 summary lessons. MP3 recordings can be used for most parts of the book for listening practice. It takes about 2 hours to cover each lesson, 60 to 70 hours for the whole book. Relevant cultural insights are given with each summary lesson.

Relevant Vocabulary is arranged in two parts. One is the vocabulary which will be used in the situational dialogues, and the other (with*) are alternative words related to the topics which might appear in the exercises. The vocabulary has been logically divided into groups. For example countries, clothes, food etc will all have vocabulary relevant to those topic although some words might not appear in the dialogues. Learners then are able to enlarge vocabulary quickly and form sentences related to their own life.

Key Sentences cover the most commonly used phrases and expressions in daily life as well as the basic grammar points. There are a total of 188 key sentences. Remembering just one sentence every two days, will give a learner sufficient Language skills to be able to communicate in everyday Chinese within a year.

Situational Dialogues have been designed to be simple and cover different situations related to the topics. All the dialogues are in the MP3 so the dialogues can be used as reading or speaking as well as listening exercises.

Language Points have been explained in a very straightforward way by using simple language which tries to avoid long and complicated grammatical words. They are very easy to understand and examples are given to further explain their use in everyday language. The grammar points follow a logical easy-to-difficult sequence so that a beginner will not be confronted by complex language points at an early stage.

Exercises after each of the lessons can either be used during classes or set as homework. There are a variety of exercises to improve listening, vocabulary and grammar as well as speaking. We suggest talking through the answers after each attempt so that students are able to learn from each other. All the answers can be found in the index so that self-learners will be able to easily correct the answers by themselves.

Chinese Characters and *Pinyin* can be found throughout the whole textbook. Learners who want to focus on listening and speaking only will be easily to finish the whole book without any difficulty while those who are interested in Chinese characters will be able to study the characters relevant to each lesson. There are clear stroke orders for 3 or 4 selected characters at the end of each lesson.

Summary Lessons can be found after every 5 lessons. The key grammar points or patterns for the previous 5 lessons are arranged clearly in a chart with examples. These are followed by paragraphs which can be used as separate reading or listening exercises. There are 5 Cultural Insights which will help learners understand Chinese people and their lives in more depth.

CONTENTS

The Sounds of Chinese — *Pinyin*

Traditional Chinese is not phonetic language and the written characters do not bear any resemblance to actual pronunciation. Nor is there any alphabet, so a system of transcribing Chinese phonetics was devised to assist people learning to read words in Chinese. The system is used in this book and is called *Pinyin* (literally meaning 'spell sound'). *Pinyin* was adopted as an official system in the People's Republic of China in 1958, and has since become a standard form used by news agencies as well as educational institutions.

The original Chinese language is based on the character. The phonetic unit of modern Chinese is a syllable; with each syllable usually represented by one character, made up of an initial, a final and a tone in *Pinyin*.

```
                              tone
            Syllable = initial + final
```

The initial is a consonant that begins the syllable, and the final covers the rest of the syllable. The tone is a variation of pitch which is rising, falling or continuing. There are 21 initials, 36 finals and 4 different tones in modern mandarin Chinese. For example: míng (bright) in which m is the initial, ing is the final and í is the 2nd tone mark placed over the main vowel.

Initials

All consonants except two (–n and –ng) used as initials occur at the beginning of a syllable. The following is the complete list of 21 initial consonants followed by a brief pronunciation guide, with reference to English words: 🔊 00-01

b	p	m	f
d	t	n	l
g	k	h	
j	q	x	
zh	ch	sh	r
z	c	s	

b, p, m, f, d, t, n, l, g, k, h, s are pronounced in a similar way to those in English. b, d, g, are unaspirated, while p, t, k are aspirated.

j   like *jee* in *jeep* (unaspirated)

q   like *chee* in *cheese*

x   like *shee* in *sheep* (with the corners of the lips drawn back)

zh   like *j* in *jelly*

ch   like *ch* in *march* (tongue curled back, aspirated)

sh   like *sh* in *rush*

r   like *r* in *road* (with the tongue loosely rolled in the middle of the mouth)

z   like *ds* in *cards*

c   like *ts* in *cats*

Finals

A final is a simple or compound vowel or a vowel plus a nasal consonant. A few syllables may have no initial consonant (e.g. ài: *love*) but every one has to have a vowel. The following table is a complete list of the 36 final vowels or compound vowels, again with a brief pronunciation guide with reference to English words. 🔊 00-02

	i	u	ü
a	ia	ua	
o		uo	
e	ie		üe
er			
ai		uai	
ei		uei (ui)	
ao	iao		
ou	iou (iu)		
an	ian	uan	üan
en	in	uen (un)	ün
ang	iang	uang	
eng	ing	ueng	
ong	iong		

a   like *a* in *father*

o   like *aw* in *saw*

e   like *e* in *her*

i   like *ee* in *see* (i in zi, ci, si, zhi, chi, shi, and ri is pronounced more like a buzz noise, but not a long i like in bǐ)

u   like *oe* in *shoe*

ü   like *eu* in *pneumonia* (occurs only with the consonants j, q, x, n, and l).

ia   like *yah*

ie   like *ye* in *yes*

er   like *er* in *sister* (American pronunciation)

ai   like *y* in *sky* (light)

ei   like *ay* in *day*

ou   like *owe*

an   like *an* in *man*

-ng (final) a nasalized sound like the *ng* in *English*

uei, uen **and** iou **when preceded by an initial, are written as** ui, un **and** iu **respectively**

Tones

Chinese is a tonal language. There are four distinct tones in official Mandarin Chinese; they are called the 1st tone, the 2nd tone, the 3rd tone, and the 4th tone. There are some syllables that do not have any tone mark, and they are called 'neutral tone'. 🔊 00-03

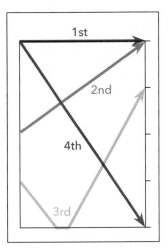

Tones	Mark	Notes
1st	mā	High and level
2nd	má	Starts medium in tone, then rises to high
3rd	mǎ	Starts low medium, fall to the bottom, then rises to high
4th	mà	Starts at the top, then falls sharp and strong to the bottom
Neutral	ma	Flat, with no emphasis

Rules of Spelling

❶ When there is no initial before the final i or ü in a syllable, we add the quasi-initial y before the final, e.g.

i → yi   ü → yu   üe → yue

When there is no initial before compound final started with i in a syllable, we change i into the quasi-initial y, e.g.

iao → yao   iou → you

❷ When there is no initial before a final started with u, we add the quasi-initial w before the final, e.g. u → wu or in place of u (ua → wa, uai → wai)

❸ When a final started with ü is preceded by j, q, x or y, the two dots above ü are dropped, e.g.

ju   qu   xu   xun   yuan

❹ When preceded by initials, the finals iou and uei are shortened as iu and ui respectively while uen is written as un, e.g.

l + iou → liu   h + uei → hui   q + uen → qun

Tone Changes

Each of the four tones, when followed by another, will more or less undertake some changes, but the third tone changes most prominently. Here is a brief account of these changes:

❶ Half-third tone: the 3rd tone loses its final rise when followed by a 1st, 2nd, 4th or a neutral tone syllable, i.e. only the initial falling portion remains.

❷ The 3rd tone changes to the 2nd tone when followed by another 3rd tone syllable, e.g. nǐ hǎo! （你好！）is pronounced ní hǎo! But the syllable is still marked in the 3rd tone.

❸ Bù（不）is 4th tone but it becomes 2nd before another 4th tone. As this is a straightforward rule, bu is marked as second tone when it occurs before a 4th tone in the text, e.g. búcuò（不错）.

❹ Yī（一）is 1st tone as an ordinary number: yī 'one', it becomes 4th tone followed by 1st, 2nd and 3rd, e.g. yìqǐ（一起）, it becomes 2nd when followed by 4th tone, e.g. yíxià（一下）.

Pinyin Practice

1. Pronunciation exercises

❶ Read out the following initials.

b	p	m	f
d	t	n	l
z	c	s	
zh	ch	sh	r
j	q	x	
g	k	h	

❷ Read out the following simple finals.

a　　o　　e　　i　　u　　ü

❸ Contrast the sounds of the initials in each of the following groups.

z	c	s	z	c
j	q	x	zh	ch

s	j	q	x
x	zh	ch	sh

2. Exercises on tones (listen and repeat)

• the first tone

dōngtiān（冬天）	gānbēi（干杯）	gōngsī（公司）
fēijī（飞机）	fēnzhōng（分钟）	kāfēi（咖啡）
jīntiān（今天）	zhēnsī（真丝）	zhōngxīn（中心）

• the second tone

Chángchéng（长城）	Déguó（德国）	Máotái（茅台）
shí nián（十年）	wénxué（文学）	yínháng（银行）

• the third tone

Běijīng（北京）	diǎncài（点菜）	Fǎyǔ（法语）
hěn hǎo（很好）	jiǔbā（酒吧）	kǎoyā（烤鸭）
kělè（可乐）	lǚyóu（旅游）	Měiguó（美国）

• the fourth tone

dàgài（大概）	dànshì（但是）	diànshì（电视）
huìlǜ（汇率）	jièshào（介绍）	kuàilè（快乐）
xiànzài（现在）	zàijiàn（再见）	zuòfàn（做饭）

• the neutral tone

xièxie（谢谢）	bú kèqi（不客气）	méi guānxi（没关系）

• tone changes

kěyǐ（可以） hěn hǎo（很好） shuǐguǒ（水果）

yìdiǎnr（一点儿） yìqǐ（一起） yígòng（一共）

bú rè（不热） bú qù（不去） bú kàn（不看）

• the words with -r ending

nǎr（哪儿） yìdiǎnr（一点儿） wánr（玩儿）

• numbers

líng	yī	èr	sān	sì	wǔ	liù	qī	bā	jiǔ	shí
0	1	2	3	4	5	6	7	8	9	10

3. Dictation exercises

• Listen to these words carefully, and then give tone marks to the following words. 🔊 00-04

ni hao 你好（hello） fandian 饭店（hotel）

fujin 附近（nearby） youming 有名（famous）

yisheng 医生（doctor） laoshi 老师（teacher）

Hanyu 汉语（Mandarin） mingtian 明天（tomorrow）

• Practice on the j, q, x. Listen to the words carefully, and then write down the *Pinyin*. 🔊 00-05

_____ 鸡（chicken） _____ 去（to go） _____ 西（west）

_____ 家（home） _____ 七（seven） _____ 虾（prawn）

_____ 叫（be called） _____ 钱（money） _____ 想（would like to）

_____ 街（street） _____ 请（please） _____ 小（small）

_____ 今天（today） _____ 秋天（autumn） _____ 先生（Mr.）

_____ 经理（manager） _____ 裙子（skirt） _____ 姓名（full name）

• Practice on the z, c, s. Listen to the words carefully, and then write down the *Pinyin*. 🔊 00-06

_____ 早（morning） _____ 菜（vegetable） _____ 三（three）

_____ 在（be at, in） _____ 次（times） _____ 四（four）

_____ 走（to walk） _____ 从（from） _____ 岁（age）

_____ 紫色（purple） _____ 辞典（dictionary） _____ 虽然（although）

• Practice on the zh, ch, sh, r. Listen to the words carefully, and write down the *Pinyin*. 🔊 00-07

_____ 找（look for） _____ 这（this） _____ 中国（China）

_____ 茶（tea） _____ 车（vehicle） _____ 吃（to eat）

_____ 是（to be） _____ 书（book） _____ 什么（what）

_____ 人（people） _____ 日（sun） _____ 认识（to know）

LESSON 1
GREETINGS & FAREWELLS

OBJECTIVES

★ Greeting in formal and informal ways

★ Saying good-bye in different ways

RELEVANT VOCABULARY

Pronouns 🔊 01-01		
你	nǐ	you
我	wǒ	I, me
您*	nín	you (polite)
他	tā	he, him
她*	tā	she, her
们*	men	(used after a personal noun to form a plural)
我们*	wǒmen	we, us
你们*	nǐmen	you (plural)
他们*	tāmen	they, them

🔊 01-02		
好	hǎo	good, well
忙	máng	busy
累	lèi	tired

饿*	è	hungry
吗	ma	(question particle)
呢	ne	(particle for following up question)
不	bù	no, not
很	hěn	very
也	yě	also, too, either

Daily Use Phrases 🔊 01-03

你好	nǐ hǎo	hello
很好	hěn hǎo	very well, very good
早上好*	zǎoshang hǎo	good morning
晚上好*	wǎnshang hǎo	good evening
晚安*	wǎn'ān	good night
谢谢	xièxie	thank you
再见	zàijiàn	good-bye
明天见*	míngtiān jiàn	see you tomorrow
不错	búcuò	not bad, pretty good
怎么样	zěnmeyàng	How are things? How are you?
马马虎虎	mǎmǎhūhū	so-so

Proper Nouns 🔊 01-04

李	Lǐ	Li (a Chinese surname)
李冰	Lǐ Bīng	Li Bing (a Chinese name)
丽丽	Lìli	Lili (a Chinese name)

KEY SENTENCES 🔊 01-05

1. Nǐ hǎo!	你好！	Hello!
2. Nǐ hǎo ma?	你好吗？	How are you?
3. Wǒ hěn hǎo. Nǐ ne?	我很好。你呢？	I'm very well. And you?
4. Nǐ zěnmeyàng?	你怎么样？	How are things going?
5. Wǒ hěn máng.	我很忙。	I am very busy.
6. Xièxie!	谢谢！	Thank you!
7. Zàijiàn!	再见！	Good-bye!

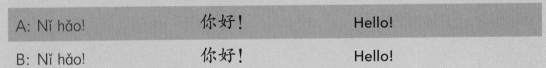

SITUATIONAL DIALOGUES

❶ (On the way to work) 🔊 01-06

A: Nǐ hǎo!	你好！	Hello!
B: Nǐ hǎo!	你好！	Hello!

❷ (Meet a friend at a bus stop) 🔊 01-07

A: Nǐ hǎo ma?	你好吗？	How are you?
B: Wǒ hěn hǎo. Xièxie! Nǐ ne?	我很好。谢谢！你呢？	I'm very well. Thank you! And you?

SITUATIONAL DIALOGUES

9

A: Wǒ yě hěn hǎo.	我也很好。	I'm very well, too.
B: Zàijiàn!	再见！	Good-bye!
A: Zàijiàn!	再见！	Good-bye!

❸ (In the office) 🔊 01-08

A: Lǐ Bīng, nǐ hǎo ma?	李冰，你好吗？	Li Bing, how are you?
B: Búcuò. Nǐ ne?	不错。你呢？	Pretty good. And you?
A: Wǒ yě búcuò. Xièxie!	我也不错。谢谢！	Pretty good, too. Thanks!

❹ (In the office) 🔊 01-09

A: Lìli, nǐ máng bu máng?	丽丽，你忙不忙？	Lili, are you busy?
B: Wǒ bù máng. Nǐ ne?	我不忙。你呢？	I'm not busy. How about you?
A: Wǒ hěn máng.	我很忙。	I'm very busy.
B: Nǐ lèi ma?	你累吗？	Are you tired?
A: Wǒ bú lèi. Nǐ ne?	我不累。你呢？	I'm not tired. How about you?
B: Wǒ yě bú lèi.	我也不累。	I'm not tired, either.

❺ (At a friend's party) 🔊 01-10

A: Lìli, nǐ zěnmeyàng?	丽丽，你怎么样？	Lili, how are things?
B: Mǎmǎhūhū. Nǐ ne?	马马虎虎。你呢？	Just so-so. What about you?
A: Wǒ yě mǎmǎhūhū.	我也马马虎虎。	I'm so-so, too.
B: Lǐ Bīng ne?	李冰呢？	How about Li Bing?
A: Tā hěn hǎo. Xièxie nǐ!	他很好。谢谢你！	He is very well. Thank you!

LANGUAGE POINTS

1. Simple sentence pattern ❶ – *sentence with an adjective*

When adjectives form the predicate, they function as a verb and there is no additional word for 'to be'. For example:

Nǐ hǎo!	你好!	Hello! (Literally: You well.)
Wǒ máng.	我忙。	I am busy. (Literally: I busy.)
Tā lèi.	他累。	He is tired. (Literally: He tired.)

2. Question forms

❶ 'Ma 吗' question: Simply put 'ma 吗' at the end of the statement without changing the word order. For example:

| Nǐ hǎo ma? | 你好吗? | How are you? |

❷ The positive and negative questions: It is formed with the 'verb + not + verb' or 'adj. + not + adj.' construction. For example:

| Nǐ máng bu máng? | 你忙不忙? | Are you busy? |

❸ 'Ne 呢' question: This is used in a follow-up question in a known context without the need to repeat the whole sentence. It is similar to 'and...' or 'how about...'. For example:

| Wǒ hěn hǎo. Nǐ ne? | 我很好。你呢? | I am very well. How about you? |

❹ 'Zěnmeyàng? 怎么样?': It is used as a greeting expression among colleagues, friends, and people who are familiar with each other. For example:

| Nǐ zěnmeyàng? | 你怎么样? | How are you? / How are things going? |

3. Adverbs

Chinese adverbs never go before the nouns, pronouns or at the end of sentences. For example:

| Wǒ yě hěn hǎo. | 我也很好。 | I am very well, too. |

EXERCISES

1. Choose the correct answers

❶ A: Nǐ hǎo!
你 好!

B: a. Wǒ hǎo.   b. Hěn hǎo.   c. Nǐ hǎo!   d. Nǐ ne?
我 好。   很 好。   你 好!   你 呢?

❷ A: Nǐ hǎo ma?
你 好 吗?

B: a. Nǐ hǎo!   b. Wǒ yě hěn hǎo.   c. Nǐ ne?   d. Wǒ hěn hǎo.
你 好!   我 也 很 好。   你 呢?   我 很 好。

❸ A: Nǐ máng bu máng?
你 忙 不 忙?

B: a. Yě máng.   b. Wǒ bù máng.   c. Wǒ hěn lèi.   d. Nǐ ne?
也 忙。   我 不 忙。   我 很 累。   你 呢?

❹ A: Nǐ zěnmeyàng?
你 怎 么 样?

B: a. Nǐ hǎo!   b. Mǎmǎhūhū.   c. Nǐ hǎo ma?   d. Nǐ ne?
你 好!   马 马 虎 虎。   你 好 吗?   你 呢?

❺ A: Wǒ hěn lèi. Nǐ ne?
我 很 累。你 呢?

B: a. Wǒ yě hěn lèi.   b. Nǐ lèi ma?   c. Lèi bu lèi?   d. Bù máng.
我 也 很 累。   你 累 吗?   累 不 累?   不 忙。

2. Translate the following into Chinese

❶ A: Hello, Peter!

B: Hello, Emma!

A: How are you?

B: I'm very well. Thank you. How about you?

A: I'm very well, too. Thanks!

❷ A: Penny, how are you?

B: Just so-so. What about you?

A: I'm so-so, too.

❸ A: Jessica, how are things?

B: Not so bad. What about you?

A: Not so bad, either.

❹ A: David, are you busy?

B: I'm not very busy. And you?

A: I'm very busy.

❺ A: Lucy, are you tired?

B: Yes. I am so tired. What about you?

A: I am so tired, too.

3. Say the following words or phrases in Chinese

❶ hello   **❷** good-bye   **❸** thanks   **❹** good

❺ very good   **❻** not so bad   **❼** so-so   **❽** not very busy

❾ very tired   **❿** thank you

4. Listening comprehension 🔊 01-09

Circle the correct answers according to the phrases you have heard.

❶ a. How are you?	b. Hello!	c. How are things?
❷ a. How are you?	b. Good-bye!	c. Hello!
❸ a. I am very well.	b. Hello!	c. How are things?
❹ a. I am very well.	b. So-so.	c. Not bad.
❺ a. So-so.	b. Not bad.	c. Good-bye!
❻ a. I am very well.	b. Not bad.	c. So-so.
❼ a. Hello!	b. Good-bye!	c. See you tomorrow.
❽ a. See you tomorrow.	b. Good-bye!	c. How are things?

5. Classroom activities

With a classmate, find three ways to greet each other and reply.

6. Chinese characters learning

nǐ	ノ 亻 亻 你 你 你 你						
你	你	你	你	你	你		
hǎo	く 女 女 女ˊ 好 好						
好	好	好	好	好	好		
ma	丨 口 口 口ˊ 吗 吗						
吗	吗	吗	吗	吗	吗		

LESSON 2
NAMES
& TITLES

OBJECTIVES

★ Meeting Chinese people for the first time

★ Introducing people

★ Addressing Chinese people

RELEVANT VOCABULARY

Titles 🔊 02-01		
先生	xiānsheng	Mr., gentleman, husband
小姐	xiǎojie	Miss., young lady
太太	tàitai	Mrs., lady, wife
女士*	nǚshì	Ms.

Relations 🔊 02-02		
朋友	péngyou	friend
男朋友*	nán péngyou	boyfriend
女朋友*	nǚ péngyou	girlfriend
同事*	tóngshì	colleague
同学*	tóngxué	classmate
老师*	lǎoshī	teacher

🔊 02-03

请问	qǐngwèn	may I ask, excuse me
请	qǐng	please
问	wèn	to ask
您贵姓	nín guìxìng	What's your surname? (polite)
贵	guì	honored, noble, expensive
姓	xìng	surname, be surnamed
高兴	gāoxìng	happy, glad
认识	rènshi	to recognize, to know
叫	jiào	to call, to be called
什么	shénme	what
名字	míngzi	name
是	shì	to be
谁	shéi/shuí	who, whom
这	zhè/zhèi	this
那	nà/nèi	that

Proper Nouns 🔊 02-04

陈	Chén	Chen (a Chinese surname)
王	Wáng	Wang (a Chinese surname)
王丹	Wáng Dān	Wang Dan (a Chinese name)
张	Zhāng	Zhang (a Chinese surname)
张燕	Zhāng Yàn	Zhang Yan (a Chinese name)
林	Lín	Lin (a Chinese surname)
林南	Lín Nán	Lin Nan (a Chinese name)

KEY SENTENCES 🔊 02-05

1. Qǐngwèn nín guìxìng?	请问您贵姓？	Excuse me, may I know your surname?
2. Wǒ xìng Chén.	我姓陈。	My surname is Chen.
3. Hěn gāoxìng rènshi nǐ.	很高兴认识你。	I am very glad to meet you.
4. Nǐ jiào shénme (míngzi)?	你叫什么（名字）？	What's your name?
5. Tā shì shéi?	她是谁？	Who is she?
6. Tā shì wǒ péngyou.	她是我朋友。	She is my friend.
7. Zhè shì Lǐ xiānsheng, Lǐ tàitai.	这是李先生、李太太。	This is Mr. Li and Mrs. Li.

SITUATIONAL DIALOGUES

❶ (At a conference) - formal 🔊 02-06

A: Qǐngwèn nín guìxìng?	请问您贵姓？	Excuse me, may I know your surname?
B: Wǒ xìng Chén. Nín ne?	我姓陈。您呢？	My surname is Chen. And you?
A: Wǒ xìng Lǐ.	我姓李。	My surname is Li.
B: Lǐ xiānsheng, nín hǎo!	李先生，您好！	How do you do Mr. Li!
A: Nín hǎo! Chén xiānsheng.	您好！陈先生。	How do you do Mr. Chen!
B: Hěn gāoxìng rènshi nín.	很高兴认识您。	I am very glad to meet you.

SITUATIONAL DIALOGUES

16

A: Wǒ yě hěn gāoxìng rènshi nín.	我也很高兴认识您。	I am very glad to meet you, too.

❷ **(At a friend's birthday party)-informal** 🔊 02-07

A: Qǐngwèn nǐ jiào shénme míngzi?	请问你叫什么名字？	Excuse me, what is your name?
B: Wǒ jiào Wáng Dān. Nǐ ne?	我叫王丹。你呢？	My name is Wang Dan. And you?
A: Wǒ jiào Zhāng Yàn.	我叫张燕。	My name is Zhang Yan.
B: Nǐ hǎo! Zhāng xiǎojie.	你好！张小姐。	How do you do Miss Zhang!
A: Nǐ hǎo! Wáng xiǎojie.	你好！王小姐。	How do you do Miss Wang!
B: Hěn gāoxìng rènshi nǐ.	很高兴认识你。	I am very glad to meet you.
A: Wǒ yě hěn gāoxìng.	我也很高兴。	I am very glad, too.

❸ **(At a reception)** 🔊 02-08

A: Wáng xiǎojie, nǐ hǎo!	王小姐，你好！	Hello, Miss Wang.
B: Lǐ xiānsheng, Lǐ tàitai, nǐmen hǎo!	李先生，李太太，你们好！	Hello Mr. Li, hello Mrs. Li.
A: Tā shì shéi?	她是谁？	Who is she?
B: Tā shì wǒ péngyou, tā jiào Lín Nán.	她是我朋友，她叫林南。	She is my friend. Her name is Lin Nan.
B: Lín Nán, zhè shì Lǐ xiānsheng, nà shì Lǐ tàitai.	林南，这是李先生，那是李太太。	Lin Nan, this is Mr. Li, and that is Mrs. Li.

SITUATIONAL DIALOGUES

| C: Lǐ xiānsheng, Lǐ tàitai hǎo! | 李先生、李太太好！ | Hello Mr. & Mrs. Li. |
| A&D: Lín xiǎojie hǎo! | 林小姐好！ | Hello Miss Lin. |

LANGUAGE POINTS

1. Simple sentence pattern ❷ – *sentence with a verb*

This kind of sentence is the same as in English. The sentence pattern is: Subject + Verb + Object. For example:

Wǒ xìng Chén.	我姓陈。	My surname is Chen.
Tā jiào Lín Nán.	她叫林南。	She is called Lin Nan.
Zhè shì Lǐ xiānsheng.	这是李先生。	This is Mr. Li.

2. 'Nín guìxìng? 您贵姓？'

This is a respectful and polite way of asking the name of a person. It is only used for second parties and it is wrong to say 'tā guìxìng 她贵姓'.

3. Question with a question word

Chinese question words can be placed anywhere in a sentence. The question words simply occupy the same slot in the sentence as the information sought in the reply. For example:

| Nǐ jiào shénme? | 你叫什么？ | What is your name? |
| Tā shì shéi? | 他是谁？ | Who is he? |

To answer this kind of question, simply use the answer to replace the question word.

Questions	Answers
Tā jiào shénme? 他叫什么？	Tā jiào Lǐ Bīng. 他叫李冰。
Zhè shì shéi? 这是谁？	Zhè shì wǒ péngyou. 这是我朋友。
Nà shì shéi? 那是谁？	Nà shì Wáng xiǎojie. 那是王小姐。

4. Addressing Chinese people

Chinese people always put their surnames before the titles.

Surnames	Titles
Wáng 王	xiānsheng 先生
Zhāng 张	tàitai 太太
Lín 林	xiǎojie 小姐
Lǐ 李	nǚshì 女士

EXERCISES

1. Answer the following questions in Chinese

❶ Nǐ xìng shénme?
你 姓 什 么？ _____

❷ Nǐ jiào shénme?
你 叫 什 么？ _____

❸ Nín guìxìng?
您 贵 姓？ _____

❹ Tā shì shéi?
她 是 谁？ _____

❺ Zhè shì bu shì Lǐ lǎoshī?
这 是 不 是 李 老 师？ _____

2. Translate the following into Chinese

❶ My surname is Jones.

❷ I am called Helen.

❸ My friend's name is Lisa.

❹ Miss Wang is my friend.

❺ Mr. Li is also my friend.

❻ I'm glad to meet you.

❼ What is your name?

❽ Excuse me, is she Miss Zhang?

❾ May I know your surname?

❿ What is this?

3. Match the Chinese with the English

❶ xiānsheng
先 生

a. this

❷ tàitai
太太

b. to be called

❸ xiǎojie
小 姐

c. who

❹ péngyou
朋 友

d. Mr.

❺ xìng
姓

e. glad, happy

❻ jiào
叫

f. that

❼ shéi（shuí）
谁

g. friend

❽ gāoxìng
高 兴

h. surname, be surnamed

❾ zhè
这

i. Miss

❿ nà
那

j. Mrs.

4. Listening comprehension 🔊 02-09

Mark true (T) or false (F) according to the short dialogues.

❶ Her surname is Yang. 　　　(　)

❷ Her name is Lin Xiaohong. 　　(　)

❸ He is not Wang Feng. 　　　(　)

❹ His surname is also Zhao. 　　(　)

❺ His surname is Liu. 　　　　(　)

5. Classroom activities

Get to know each other in the class, and introduce two of your friends or classmates.

6. Chinese characters learning

wǒ 我	´ 二 手 手 我 我 我
	我 我 我 我 我

tā 他	ノ イ ⼧ 他 他
	他 他 他 他 他

tā 她	し 女 女 如 如 她
	她 她 她 她 她

men 们	ノ イ ⼧ 们 们
	们 们 们 们 们

NATIONALITIES & LANGUAGES

OBJECTIVES

★ Talking about countries and cities

★ Discussing the languages you can speak

RELEVANT VOCABULARY

Countries and Places 🔊 03-01		
国	guó	country, state
英国	Yīngguó	Britain
法国	Fǎguó	France
美国	Měiguó	USA
德国	Déguó	Germany
奥地利	Àodìlì	Austria
中国*	Zhōngguó	China
俄罗斯*	Éluósī	Russia
日本*	Rìběn	Japan
意大利*	Yìdàlì	Italy
西班牙*	Xībānyá	Spain
伦敦	Lúndūn	London
巴黎	Bālí	Paris
纽约	Niǔyuē	New York

汉堡	Hànbǎo	Hamburg
北京*	Běijīng	Beijing
上海*	Shànghǎi	Shanghai
香港*	Xiānggǎng	Hong Kong
台湾*	Táiwān	Taiwan

Languages 🔊 03-02

语	yǔ	language
英语	Yīngyǔ	English language
法语	Fǎyǔ	French language
汉语*	Hànyǔ	Mandarin Chinese
文*	wén	Language, culture, character
中文*	Zhōngwén	Chinese (language)
英文*	Yīngwén	English (language)
法文*	Fǎwén	French (language)

🔊 03-03

人	rén	person, people
说	shuō	to speak, to say
介绍	jièshào	to introduce
一下	yíxià	a bit, briefly
哪	nǎ/něi	which
哪儿	nǎr	where
地方	dìfang	place
从……来	cóng...lái	to come from...

从	cóng	from
来	lái	to come
对	duì	correct
都	dōu	both, all

Proper Nouns 🔊 03-04

艾玛	Àimǎ	Emma
皮特	Pítè	Peter

KEY SENTENCES 🔊 03-05

1. Wǒ shì Yīngguórén.	我是英国人。	I am British.
2. Wǒ cóng Lúndūn lái.	我从伦敦来。	I am from London.
3. Wǒ shuō Yīngyǔ.	我说英语。	I speak English.
4. Wǒ lái jièshào yíxià.	我来介绍一下。	Let me introduce briefly.
5. Nǐ shì nǎ guó rén?	你是哪国人？	What is your nationality?
6. Nǐ shì shénme dìfang rén?	你是什么地方人？	Where are you from?
7. Wǒmen dōu shì Měiguórén.	我们都是美国人。	We are all American.

SITUATIONAL DIALOGUES

❶ (Introducing oneself in the classroom) 🔊 03-06

Wǒ jiào Àimǎ.	我叫艾玛。	I am called Emma.
Wǒ shì Yīngguórén.	我是英国人。	I am British.
Wǒ shì Lúndūnrén.	我是伦敦人。	I am from London.
Wǒ shuō Yīngyǔ.	我说英语。	I speak English.

❷ (Introducing somebody else in the classroom) 🔊 03-07

Wǒ lái jièshào yíxià.	我来介绍一下。	Let me introduce briefly.
Tā jiào Pítè.	他叫皮特。	He is called Peter.
Tā shì Fǎguórén.	他是法国人。	He is French.
Tā shì Bālírén.	他是巴黎人。	He is from Paris.
Tā shuō Fǎyǔ.	他说法语。	He speaks French.

❸ (In the language centre) 🔊 03-08

A: Nǐ shì nǎ guó rén?	你是哪国人?	What is your nationality?
B: Wǒ shì Měiguórén.	我是美国人。	I am American.
A: Nǐ shì shénme dìfang rén?	你是什么地方人?	Where are you from?
B: Wǒ shì Niǔyuērén.	我是纽约人。	I am from New York.
A: Nǐ tàitai yě shì Měiguórén ma?	你太太也是美国人吗?	Is your wife American, too?
B: Duì, tā yě shì Měiguórén. Wǒmen dōu shì Měiguórén.	对，她也是美国人。我们都是美国人。	Yes, she is also American. Both of us are American.

❹ (At the airport) 🔊 03-09

A: Nín cóng năr lái?	您从哪儿来？	Where do you come from?
B: Wǒ cóng Hànbǎo lái.	我从汉堡来。	I come from Hamburg.
A: Nín shì bu shì Déguórén?	您是不是德国人？	Are you German?
B: Bú shì, wǒ shì Àodìlìrén.	不是，我是奥地利人。	No, I am Austrian.
A: Nín shuō Déyǔ ma?	您说德语吗？	Do you speak German?
B: Duì, wǒ shuō Déyǔ.	对，我说德语。	Yes, I speak German.
A: Wǒmen dōu shuō Déyǔ.	我们都说德语。	We all speak German.

LANGUAGE POINTS

1. 'Yíxià 一下'

It normally describes a short continuing action and literally means 'a short while'. It is used to soften a sentence that otherwise might be seen as abrupt. For example 'Wǒ lái jièshào 我来介绍' without 'yíxià 一下', can sound a little bossy and tactless for Chinese people. It is normally only used in spoken language.

| Wǒ lái jièshào yíxià... | 我来介绍一下…… | Let me introduce briefly... |
| Wǒ lái shuō yíxià... | 我来说一下…… | Let me speak briefly... |

2. 'Duì 对'

'Duì 对' literally means 'correct, right', but sometimes can be translated as 'yes'. For example:

| A: Nǐ shì Fǎguórén ma? | A: 你是法国人吗？ | A: Are you French? |
| B: Duì, wǒ shì Fǎguórén. | B: 对，我是法国人。 | B: Yes, I am. |

3. 'Nǐ cóng nǎr lái? 你从哪儿来？'

In Chinese this can mean either 'Where are you from' or 'Where do you come from'.

EXERCISES

1. Say the following in Chinese

❶ What do you call these countries in Chinese?

| China | Britain | USA | France | Russia | German |
| Canada | Japan | Italy | Denmark | Holland | Spain |

❷ What do you call these people in Chinese?

| the Chinese | the British | the French | the Germans |
| the Canadians | the Italians | the Japanese | the Danish |

❸ What are the following languages in Chinese?

| Chinese | English | French | Italian | German |
| Japanese | Arabic | Spanish | Russian | Indonesian |

2. Match the Chinese with the English

❶ nǎ
哪

a. to be

❷ guó
国

b. language

❸ rén
人

c. also, too

❹ yǔ
语

d. both, all

❺ shì
是

e. people, person

❻ shuō
说

f. which

❼ jiào
叫

g. correct

❽ dōu
都

h. country, state

❾ yě
也

i. to speak

❿ duì
对

j. to be called

3. Fill in the blanks with the words or phrases given

A. jiào	B. shì	C. shuō	D. cóng...lái	E. xìng
叫	是	说	从……来	姓
F. nǎ	G. dōu	H. yě	I. shénme	J. yíxià
哪	都	也	什么	一下

❶ Wǒ (　　　　) Měiguórén.
我 （　　　　）美 国 人。

❷ Tā shì (　　　　) dìfang rén?
他 是 （　　　　）地 方 人？

❸ Tā (　　　　) Bālí (　　　　).
他 （　　　）巴 黎 （　　　　）。

❹ Tā (　　　　) Fǎyǔ.
他 （　　　　）法语。

❺ Wǒ lái jièshào (　　　　).
我 来 介绍 （　　　　）。

❻ Wǒ (　　　　) Ānnà.
我 （　　　　）安娜。

❼ Wǒmen (　　　　) shì Yīngguórén.
我 们 （　　　　）是 英 国 人。

❽ Nǐ shì (　　　　) guó rén?
你 是 （　　　　）国 人？

❾ Tā tàitai (　　　　) shuō Fǎyǔ ma?
他 太太 （　　　　）说 法语吗？

❿ Nín guì (　　　　) ?
您 贵 （　　　　）？

4. Translate the following into Chinese

❶ Are you Chinese?

❷ I am not Chinese. I am Japanese.

❸ Do you speak Japanese?

❹ Does he come from Paris?

❺ What's your nationality?

❻ Lucy is not English. She is Canadian.

❼ His wife speaks German.

❽ Where does Matthew come from?

❾ Anna doesn't speak Italian. She speaks Spanish.

❿ We all speak Chinese.

5. Listening comprehension 🔊 03-10

Mark true (T) or false (F) according to the short dialogues.

❶ She is Italian.　　　　(　)

❷ She speaks German.　　(　)

❸ He is British.　　　　(　)

❹ He is not French.　　　(　)

❺ He is from Hamburg.　　(　)

6. Classroom activities

❶ Introduce yourself: your name, your nationality, where you come from and what languages you speak.

❷ Find out more about the person next to you: their name, nationality, what languages they speak, and where they come from.

❸ Introduce one of your classmates.

7. Chinese characters learning

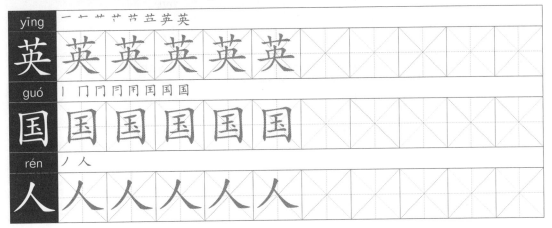

LESSON 4
DAYS
& DATES

OBJECTIVES

★ Talking about year, month, date and day

★ Finding out about birthdays and key dates

RELEVANT VOCABULARY

Numbers 🔊 04-01		
一	yī	one
二	èr	two
三	sān	three
四	sì	four
五	wǔ	five
六	liù	six
七	qī	seven
八	bā	eight
九	jiǔ	nine
十	shí	ten
零*	líng	zero
百*	bǎi	hundred
千*	qiān	thousand

Time Words 1 🔊 04-02

天	tiān	day
今天	jīntiān	today
明天	míngtiān	tomorrow
昨天	zuótiān	yesterday
号	hào	date
日*	rì	date, day (formal), sun
星期	xīngqī	week, day of the week
上星期*	shàng xīngqī	last week
这星期*	zhèi xīngqī	this week
下星期*	xià xīngqī	next week
月	yuè	month
上月*	shàng yuè	last month
这月*	zhèi yuè	this month
下月*	xià yuè	next month
年	nián	year
明年	míngnián	next year
今年*	jīnnián	this year
去年*	qùnián	last year

Festivals 🔊 04-03

春节	Chūn Jié	Spring Festival (Chinese New Year)
圣诞节*	Shèngdàn Jié	Christmas
新年*	xīnnián	new year

04-04

几	jǐ	how many, what (date, time)
去	qù	to go
的	de	(structural particle)
生日	shēngrì	birthday

KEY SENTENCES 04-05

1.	Jīntiān jǐ hào?	今天几号？	What is the date today?
2.	Jīntiān sān hào.	今天三号。	Today is the 3rd.
3.	Míngtiān xīngqī jǐ?	明天星期几？	What day is tomorrow?
4.	Míngtiān Xīngqīliù.	明天星期六。	Tomorrow is Saturday.
5.	Nǐ jǐ yuè jǐ hào qù Zhōngguó?	你几月几号去中国？	When do you go to China?
6.	Wǒ Chūn Jié qù Běijīng.	我春节去北京。	I'm going to Beijing during the Spring Festival.
7.	Wǒ de shēngrì shì yī yuè shíqī hào.	我的生日是一月十七号。	My birthday is on the 17th January.

SITUATIONAL DIALOGUES

❶ (In the office) 🔊 04-06

A: Jīntiān jǐ hào?	今天几号？	What is the date today?
B: Jīntiān sān hào.	今天三号。	Today is the 3rd.
A: Míngtiān xīngqī jǐ?	明天星期几？	What day is tomorrow?
B: Míngtiān Xīngqīliù.	明天星期六。	Tomorrow is Saturday.

❷ (At a ticket office) 🔊 04-07

A: Jīntiān shì Xīngqīwǔ ma?	今天是星期五吗？	Is it Friday today?
B: Bú shì, jīntiān shì Xīngqīsì, míngtiān shì Xīngqīwǔ.	不是，今天是星期四，明天是星期五。	No, today is Thursday. Tomorrow is Friday.
A: Jīntiān shì bu shì jiǔ hào?	今天是不是九号？	Is it the 9th today?
B: Bú shì, zuótiān shì jiǔ hào, jīntiān shì shí hào.	不是，昨天是九号，今天是十号。	No, yesterday was the 9th. Today is the 10th.

❸ (In a travel agency) 🔊 04-08

A: Nǐ jǐ yuè jǐ hào qù Zhōngguó?	你几月几号去中国？	What date are you going to China?

B: Wǒ Chūn Jié qù Běijīng.	我春节去北京。	I'm going to Beijing during the Spring Festival.
A: Chūn Jié shì jǐ yuè jǐ hào?	春节是几月几号？	What date is Chinese New Year?
B: Míngnián Chūn Jié shì yī yuè èrshíjiǔ hào, Xīngqītiān.	明年春节是一月二十九号，星期天。	Next year's Chinese New Year will be on Sunday the 29th January.

❹ (At a friend's home) 🔊 04-09

A: Nǐ de shēngrì shì jǐ yuè jǐ hào?	你的生日是几月几号？	When is your birthday?
B: Wǒ de shēngrì shì yī yuè shíqī hào. Nǐ de ne?	我的生日是一月十七号。你的呢？	My birthday is on the 17th January. What about yours?
A: Wǒ de shēngrì shì sì yuè èrshí hào.	我的生日是四月二十号。	My birthday is on the 20th April.
B: Nǎ nián?	哪年？	Which year?
A: Yī jiǔ bā qī nián.	一九八七年。	1987.

LANGUAGE POINTS

1. The sentence order with time words

❶ Year

To express a particular year, simply say the numbers individually followed by 'nián 年'. For example:

| yī jiǔ bā wǔ nián | 一九八五年 | 1985 |

❷ Month and date

The names of the twelve months are formed by adding 'yuè 月' to each of the numerals from 1 to 12 (i.e. January is 1 yuè, February is 2 yuè, etc). A date is expressed in the same way as the month except one adds 'hào 号' or 'rì 日' to each of the numerals from 1 to 31. E.g. 1st is 1 hào, 12th is 12 hào, and 30th is 30 hào.

❸ Year, month and date

The order a date is expressed in Chinese is the reverse of that used in English. The order is: year, month, and then day. For example:

| yī jiǔ bā wǔ nián shí yuè yī hào | 一九八五年十月一号 | 01/10/1985 |

❹ Weekdays

Weeks are expressed by putting 'xīngqī 星期' before each of the numerals from 1 to 6 (i.e. Monday is xīngqī 1, Tuesday is xīngqī 2, etc). Sunday is written as. 'Xīngqīrì 星期日' or 'Xīngqītiān 星期天'.

Xīngqīyī	星期一	Monday
Xīngqī'èr	星期二	Tuesday
Xīngqīsān	星期三	Wednesday
Xīngqīsì	星期四	Thursday
Xīngqīwǔ	星期五	Friday
Xīngqīliù	星期六	Saturday
Xīngqīrì / Xīngqītiān	星期日 / 星期天	Sunday

2. Question word 'jǐ 几'

When 'jǐ 几' is used to ask about the day and date, it means 'which', rather than 'how many'. For example:

| Jīntiān jǐ hào? | 今天几号？ | What's the date today? (Literally: Today is which date?) |

3. The structural particle 'de 的'

In this lesson, it is used to express possession. For example:

tā de míngzi	他的名字	his name
wǒmen de lǎoshī	我们的老师	our teacher
Lìli de shēngrì	丽丽的生日	Lili's birthday

With close relationships one could leave out the 'de 的'. For example:

| wǒ bàba | 我爸爸 | my dad |
| wǒ māma | 我妈妈 | my mum |

EXERCISES

1. Ask questions about the underlined parts in the following sentences

❶ Jīntiān Xīngqīsì.
今天　星期四。

❷ Zuótiān shì yī yuè èrshíbā hào.
昨天　是一月二十八号。

❸ Jīnnián Chūn Jié shì yī yuè èrshíjiǔ hào, Xīngqītiān.
今年　春节是一月二十九号，星期天。

❹ Tā de shēngrì shì jiǔ yuè liù hào.
他的　生日是九月六号。

❺ Míngtiān shì sì yuè bā hào, Xīngqīwǔ.
明　天是四月八号，星期五。

2. Match the English with the Chinese

❶ Yesterday

❷ Today

❸ Tomorrow

❹ Last week

❺ This week

❻ Next week

❼ Last month

❽ This month

❾ Next month

❿ Last year

⓫ This year

⓬ Next year

a. shàng yuè
　上　月

b. jīnnián
　今年

c. míngnián
　明　年

d. zhèi xīngqī
　这　星期

e. xià yuè
　下 月

f. zuótiān
　昨天

g. qùnián
　去年

h. míngtiān
　明　天

i. xià xīngqī
　下 星期

j. zhèi yuè
　这　月

k. shàng xīngqī
　上　星期

l. jīntiān
　今天

3. Say the following sentences in Chinese

❶ Today is the 11th October.

❷ Tomorrow is Wednesday.

❸ Yesterday was my birthday.

❹ My Mum's birthday is on the 20th December 1964.

❺ My Dad's birthday is on the 17th January 1967.

❻ Bobby's birthday is on the 23rd April 1987.

❼ Christmas Day is on the 25th December.

❽ New Year Day is on the 1st January.

❾ This year Chinese New Year is on the 29th January.

❿ Lili will go to Shanghai next month.

4. Listening comprehension 🔊 04-10

Choose the correct answers according to the short dialogues.

❶ a. 3rd	b. 4th	c. 10th
❷ a. Sunday	b. Wednesday	c. Friday
❸ a. July	b. September	c. January
❹ a. the 12th May	b. the 5th February	c. the 2nd May
❺ a. yesterday	b. today	c. tomorrow

5. Classroom activities

Question your classmates and find out who will be the next one to have his/her birthday and when it is. Find out who is the youngest in your class.

6. Chinese characters learning

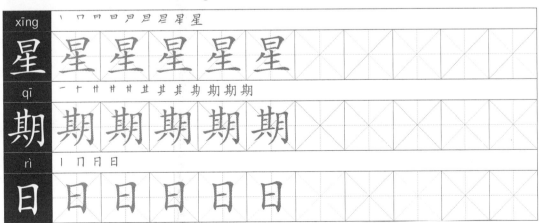

LESSON 5
TIME
& DAILY ROUTINE

OBJECTIVES

★ Describing time and schedules

★ Talking about daily routine

RELEVANT VOCABULARY

Time Words 2 ◑ 05-01		
现在	xiànzài	now, at the moment
点	diǎn	o'clock
分	fēn	minute
一刻	yí kè	a quarter (time)
半	bàn	half
差	chà	less, to (for time)
早上	zǎoshang	(early) morning
晚上	wǎnshang	evening
上午*	shàngwǔ	morning
中午*	zhōngwǔ	noon
下午*	xiàwǔ	afternoon
每	měi	each, every
每天	měi tiān	every day
每年*	měi nián	every year
每月*	měi yuè	every month
每星期*	měi xīngqī	every week

Daily Routine 🔊 05-02

上班	shàngbān	to go to work, to start work
下班	xiàbān	to finish work
起床*	qǐchuáng	to get up
吃*	chī	to eat
早饭*	zǎofàn	breakfast
午饭*	wǔfàn	lunch
晚饭*	wǎnfàn	dinner
上课*	shàngkè	to go to class, to have a lesson
下课*	xiàkè	to finish class
回家*	huíjiā	to return home
睡觉*	shuìjiào	to sleep

🔊 05-03

两	liǎng	two
不客气	bú kèqi	you're welcome
对不起	duìbuqǐ	sorry
没关系	méi guānxi	it doesn't matter
知道	zhīdào	to know
商店	shāngdiàn	shop, store
开	kāi	to open, to start, to operate (a machine, a car)
关	guān	to close, to turn off
门	mén	door

KEY SENTENCES 🔊 05-04

1. Xiànzài jǐ diǎn?	现在几点？	What time is it now?
2. Liǎng diǎn shí fēn.	两点十分。	It is ten minutes past two.
3. Xièxie. / Bú kèqi.	谢谢。/不客气。	Thank you. / You are welcome.
4. Duìbuqǐ. / Méi guānxi.	对不起。/没关系。	Sorry. / It doesn't matter.
5. Nǐ měi tiān jǐ diǎn shàngbān?	你每天几点上班？	What time do you go to work every day?
6. Wǒ bù zhīdào.	我不知道。	I don't know.
7. Shāngdiàn jǐ diǎn kāimén?	商店几点开门？	What time does the shop open?

SITUATIONAL DIALOGUES

❶ (On the way to work) 🔊 05-05

A: Qǐngwèn, xiànzài jǐ diǎn?	请问，现在几点？	Excuse me, what time is it now?
B: Xiànzài liǎng diǎn shí fēn.	现在两点十分。	It is ten minutes past two.
A: Xièxie.	谢谢。	Thank you.
B: Bú kèqi.	不客气。	You are welcome.

❷ (In the language centre) 🔊 05-06

A: Nǐ měi tiān jǐ diǎn shàngbān?	你每天几点上班？	What time do you go to work every day?

B: Zǎoshang bā diǎn yí kè.	早上八点一刻。	8:15 am.
A: Jǐ diǎn xiàbān?	几点下班？	What time do you finish work?
B: Chà yí kè liù diǎn.	差一刻六点。	5:45 pm.
A: Xiànzài jǐ diǎn?	现在几点？	What time is it now?
B: Duìbuqǐ, wǒ bù zhīdào.	对不起，我不知道。	Sorry, I don't know.
A: Méi guānxi.	没关系。	Never mind.

❸ (In front of a shop) ◉ 05-07

A: Shāngdiàn jǐ diǎn kāimén?	商店几点开门？	What time does the shop open?
B: Shàngwǔ jiǔ diǎn.	上午九点。	9:00 am.
A: Jǐ diǎn guānmén?	几点关门？	What time does it close?
B: Wǎnshang liù diǎn bàn.	晚上六点半。	6:30 pm.

LANGUAGE POINTS

1. Telling the time

| yī diǎn | 一点 | 1:00 |
| liǎng diǎn shí fēn | 两点十分 | 2:10 |

sān diǎn yí kè	三点一刻	3:15
sì diǎn bàn	四点半	4:30
chà wǔ fēn jiǔ diǎn	差五分九点	8:55
jiǔ diǎn chà wǔ fēn	九点差五分	8:55

In China many public places use the 24-hour clock. For example:

| shíjiǔ diǎn sānshí fēn | 十九点三十分 | 19:30 |
| èrshí'èr diǎn wǔshíwǔ fēn | 二十二点五十五分 | 22:55 |

2. Order of time words

If the time word is a noun, it goes either before or after the subject; if it is an adverb, it goes after the subject and before the verb. For example:

Wǒ zǎoshang qù xuéxiào.	我早上去学校。	I go to school in the morning.
Zǎoshang wǒ qù xuéxiào.	早上我去学校。	I go to school in the morning.
Wǒ měi tiān qù xuéxiào.	我每天去学校。	I go to school every day.
Wǒ xiànzài qù xuéxiào.	我现在去学校。	I go to school now.

3. 'Rènshi 认识' and 'zhīdào 知道'

Both mean 'to know', but 'rènshi 认识' normally refers to knowing people or Chinese characters, whereas 'zhīdào 知道' is to know a fact or to have heard about someone. For example:

| Wǒ rènshi tā. | 我认识他。 | I know him. (Personally) |
| Wǒ zhīdào tā shì shéi. | 我知道他是谁。 | I know (the fact) who he is. |

(This means that you have heard of this person, know who he is, but you may not know him personally.)

EXERCISES

1. Tell the time in Chinese

❶ 6:00	8:20	13:55 (1:55pm)	3:30
❷ 12:35	11:10	14:20 (2:20pm)	9:45
❸ 5:15	10:05	17:30 (5:30pm)	4:45

❹ 18:08	15:55	19:45 (7:45pm)	2:30
❺ 4:05	12:10	21:15 (9:15pm)	2:35

2. Look and say the time in Chinese

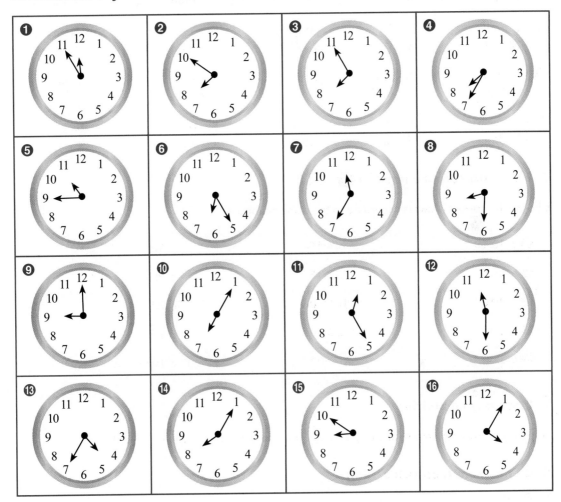

3. Give an account of your timetable in Chinese

❶ _____ get up
❸ _____ go to work / school
❺ _____ finish work / school
❼ _____ read books / newspaper
❾ _____ watch TV

❷ _____ have breakfast
❹ _____ have lunch
❻ _____ go home
❽ _____ have dinner
❿ _____ go to bed

4. Translate the following into Chinese

❶ every day
❹ every year

❷ every month
❺ everybody

❸ every week
❻ every evening

5. Put the following dates in the correct word order

❶ shíjiǔ hào | liù yuè | yī jiǔ qī bā nián | shàngwǔ | Xīngqīyī
19 号 | 6 月 | 1978 年 | 上午 | 星期一

❷ Xīngqīliù | bā yuè | sānshí hào | yī jiǔ wǔ bā nián | xiàwǔ
星期六 | 8 月 | 30 号 | 1958 年 | 下午

❸ shí'èr yuè | bā hào | Xīngqīyī | yī jiǔ bā liù nián | wǎnshang
12 月 | 8 号 | 星期一 | 1986 年 | 晚上

❹ èr líng yī èr nián | Xīngqī'èr | èr yuè | shísì hào | xiàwǔ
2012 年 | 星期二 | 2 月 | 14 号 | 下午

❺ zǎoshang | Xīngqīsān | sānshí hào | bā diǎn | sān yuè
早上 | 星期三 | 30 号 | 8 点 | 3 月

6. Listening comprehension 🔊 05-08

Choose the correct answers according to the short dialogues.

❶ a. 10:10	b. 4:10	c. 10:04
❷ a. 6:15	b. 7:15	c. 9:15
❸ a. 8:10	b. 10:08	c. 7:50
❹ a. 2:30	b. 6:30	c. 9:30
❺ a. 8:00	b. 9:00	c. 10:00

7. Classroom activities

Prepare your own timetable for a day, and find out your language partner's timetable.

8. Chinese characters learning

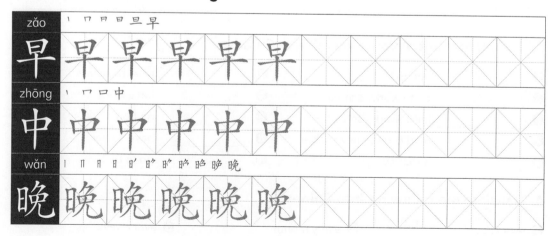

LESSON 6
SUMMARY OF LESSONS 1-5

OBJECTIVES

★ Practicing the vocabulary and grammars from lessons 1-5

★ Cultural insights: Numbers and meanings

KEY PATTERNS

1. Statement sentences

Patterns	Sentences
Subject + adj.	Wǒ máng. 我忙。
Subject + adv. + adj.	Wǒ hěn bàng. 我很棒。
Subject + verb + object	Wǒ shuō Yīngyǔ. 我说英语。

2. Making questions ❶

Patterns	Sentences
Statement + ma 吗?	Nǐ shì Yīngguórén ma? 你是英国人吗?
Statement, noun + ne 呢?	Wǒ shì Yīngguórén, nǐ ne? 我是英国人，你呢?
Verb + bu 不 + verb?	Nǐ shì bu shì Yīngguórén? 你是不是英国人?
Adj. + bu 不 + adj.?	Nǐ máng bu máng? 你忙不忙?
Subject + zěnmeyàng 怎么样?	Nǐ zěnmeyàng? 你怎么样?

3. Making questions ❷

Statements	Questions
Tā jiào Lǐ Bīng. 他叫李冰。	Tā jiào shénme? 他叫什么?
Tā shì wǒ de péngyou. 他是我的朋友。	Tā shì shéi? 他是谁?
Tā shì Zhōngguórén. 他是中国人。	Tā shì nǎ guó rén? 他是哪国人?
Tā cóng Běijīng lái. 他从北京来。	Tā cóng nǎr lái? 他从哪儿来?
Tā shì Běijīngrén. 他是北京人。	Tā shì shénme dìfang rén? 他是什么地方人?
Jīntiān sān hào. 今天三号。	Jīntiān jǐ hào? 今天几号?
Jīntiān Xīngqīliù. 今天星期六。	Jīntiān xīngqī jǐ? 今天星期几?
Shāngdiàn bā diǎn kāimén. 商店八点开门。	Shāngdiàn jǐ diǎn kāimén? 商店几点开门?

RELEVANT VOCABULARY

🔊 06-01

但是	dànshì	but
做	zuò	to do, to make
买	mǎi	to buy
礼物	lǐwù	gift, present
看	kàn	to watch, to see, to look at
电影	diànyǐng	film, movie
请	qǐng	to invite, to treat
饭馆	fànguǎn	restaurant
啊	a	(exclamatory particle)

Proper Nouns 🔊 06-02

普通话	Pǔtōnghuà	Modern standard Chinese
上海话	Shànghǎihuà	Shanghai dialect

STORY TIME

1. Listen to the following story and retell it in Chinese 🔊 06-03

Lìli de shēngrì
丽丽的生日

Wǒ xìng Lǐ, jiào Lǐ Bīng, wǒ shì
我 姓李，叫李冰，我是

Zhōngguórén, cóng Běijīng lái. Wǒ de nǚ
中 国人，从 北京来。我的女

péngyou jiào Lìli, tā yě shì Zhōngguórén,
朋 友 叫丽丽，她也是 中 国人，

dànshì tā bú shì Běijīngrén, tā shì Shànghǎi
但是她不是北京人，她是 上 海

rén. Wǒmen dōu shuō Hànyǔ, Lìli shuō
人。我们 都 说 汉语，丽丽 说

Pǔtōnghuà, yě shuō Shànghǎihuà.
普通话，也说 上 海话。

Míngtiān shì shí yuè wǔ hào, Xīngqīliù, shì Lìli de shēngrì, wǒmen dōu bú
明 天是十月五号，星期六，是丽丽的生 日，我们 都 不

shàngbān. Lìli wèn wǒ: "míngtiān shì wǒ de shēngrì, wǒmen zuò shénme?" Wǒ shuō:
上 班。丽丽问 我："明 天是我的 生日，我们 做 什么？"我 说：

" shàngwǔ jiǔ diǎn shāngdiàn kāimén, wǒ qù mǎi lǐwù. Xiàwǔ liǎng diǎn bàn wǒmen qù
" 上 午九点 商 店开门， 我 去买礼物。下午两 点 半我们去

kàn diànyǐng, wǎnshang wǒ qǐng nǐ qù Fǎguó fànguǎn chī Fǎguó fàn, hǎo bu hǎo?" Lìli
看 电 影，晚 上 我 请你去法国 饭馆 吃法国饭， 好不好？"丽丽

hěn gāoxìng, tā shuō: "hǎo a!"
很 高 兴，她说："好啊！"

2. Read the story again, and then answer the following questions

❶ What is Li Bing's nationality?

❷ Where is Li Bing from?

❸ Who is Lili? Where is Lili from?

❹ Which languages does Lili speak?

❺ When is Lili's birthday?

❻ Are they both working on Lili's birthday?

❼ What will they do on Lili's birthday?

CULTURAL INSIGHTS

Numbers and meanings

Four

The number 4 is an unlucky number in Chinese. The word 'four' is a homonym for the noun 'death' or the verb 'to die'. Therefore, some Chinese people prefer not to live at places that have a number 4 in the address. By the same token, numbers like 14 and 44 are also inauspicious and avoided. Some hotels in China now don't even have a '44th floor' because many Chinese guests would not want to stay on it.

Eight

The number eight, on the other hand, is a very lucky number. It sounds like the word for 'getting rich' in Chinese, especially in Cantonese. Therefore, businesses love to have the number 8 in any part of their address or phone number. They believe that the use of the number 8 will actually bring them good luck and prosperity. In fact, people will pay a premium to buy phone numbers and car license plates that contain 8. So if you see a license plate that has the number 8 for all its numerals, you can be sure the person is a businessman who spent a fortune on it! Similarly, a real estate property with an 8 in its address will be in greater demand.

Playing with numbers

The interesting thing about numbers in Chinese is that you can easily transform a number in to a completely different word by putting them together. It certainly makes memorizing numbers easier. For example, the number 9 is identical to the words 'liquor' or 'wine'. Similarly, the number 8 sounds exactly like the word bar. When combined, the number 98 sounds like the word 'pub'. Moreover, the number 5 can sound like the word 'I' or 'me'. And the number 7 sounds like the verb 'go'. When combined the number 5798 sounds like the phrase 'I go to the pub'!

CHINESE CHARACTERS LEARNING

pǔ	丶 丷 丷 并 并 扩 計 並 普 普 普
普	普 普 普 普 普

tōng	⁷ ⁷ ⁷ 甬 甬 甬 甬 涌 通 通
通	通 通 通 通 通

huà	丶 讠 讠 订 订 讦 话 话
话	话 话 话 话 话

LESSON 7
ADDRESSES & TELEPHONE NUMBERS

OBJECTIVES

★ Finding out and giving addresses

★ Finding out and giving telephone numbers

★ Offering business cards

RELEVANT VOCABULARY

Places 🔊 07-01		
饭店	fàndiàn	hotel, restaurant
房间	fángjiān	room
家	jiā	home, family
大街	dàjiē	avenue
街	jiē	street
大使馆	dàshǐguǎn	embassy
路	lù	road
办公室*	bàngōngshì	office
咖啡厅*	kāfēitīng	café
酒吧*	jiǔbā	bar, pub
卫生间*	wèishēngjiān	toilet
学校*	xuéxiào	school
教室*	jiàoshì	classroom

| 图书馆* | túshūguǎn | library |

Communication 🔊 07-02

电话	diànhuà	telephone
手机	shǒujī	mobile phone
微信	wēixìn	WeChat
地址	dìzhǐ	address
网址	wǎngzhǐ	website

🔊 07-03

住	zhù	to live, to stay
多少	duōshao	how many, how much
在	zài	to be at, to be located, in, on
号	hào	number
名片	míngpiàn	business card
保持联系	bǎochí liánxi	to keep in touch

Proper Nouns 🔊 07-04

长城	Chángchéng	the Great Wall
长城饭店	Chángchéng fàndiàn	Great Wall Hotel
西城区	Xīchéng Qū	Xicheng District
东城区	Dōngchéng Qū	Dongcheng District
长安大街	Cháng'ān Dàjiē	Chang'an Avenue
建国门	Jiànguómén	Jianguomen (place name)
光华路	Guānghuá Lù	Guanghua Road (road name)

KEY SENTENCES 🔊 07-05

1. Nǐ zhù nǎr?	你住哪儿？	Where do you live?/ Where are you staying?
2. Wǒ zhù Chángchéng Fàndiàn yāo líng yāo bā hào fángjiān.	我住长城饭店1018号房间。	I am staying at the Great Wall Hotel, Room 1018.
3. Nǐ de diànhuà shì duōshao?	你的电话是多少？	What is your telephone number?
4. Nǐ jiā zài nǎr?	你家在哪儿？	Where is your home?
5. Zhè shì wǒ de shǒujī hào hé wǒ de wēixìn.	这是我的手机号和我的微信。	This is my mobile number and my WeChat.
6. Bǎochí liánxi.	保持联系。	Keep in touch.
7. Zhè shì wǒ de míngpiàn.	这是我的名片。	This is my business card.

SITUATIONAL DIALOGUES 🔊 07-06

❶ (On the phone)

A: Nǐ zhù nǎr?	你住哪儿？	Where are you staying?
B: Wǒ zhù Chángchéng Fàndiàn yāo líng yāo bā hào fángjiān.	我住长城饭店1018号房间。	I am staying at the Great Wall Hotel, Room 1018.
A: Nǐ de diànhuà shì duōshao?	你的电话是多少？	What is your telephone number?
B: Wǒ de diànhuà shì liù sān yāo jiǔ èr líng sì qī.	我的电话是63192047。	It is 63192047.

❷ **(At a café)** 🔊 07-07

A: Nǐ jiā zài nǎr?	你家在哪儿？	Where is your home?
B: Wǒ jiā zài Xīchéng Qū. Nǐ ne?	我家在西城区。你呢？	My home is in Xicheng District. How about you?
A: Wǒ jiā zài Dōngchéng Qū.	我家在东城区。	My home is in Dongcheng District.
B: Nǐ de shǒujī hào shì duōshao?	你的手机号是多少？	What is your mobile phone number?
A: Wǒ de shǒujī hào shì yāo sān wǔ wǔ èr qī yāo yāo jiǔ yāo yāo.	我的手机号是13552711911。	My mobile number is 13552711911.
B: Zhè shì wǒ de shǒujī hào hé wǒ de wēixìn.	这是我的手机号和我的微信。	This is my mobile number and my WeChat.
A: Bǎochí liánxi.	保持联系。	Keep in touch.

❸ **(At a company reception)** 🔊 07-08

A: Qǐngwèn nín de dìzhǐ?	请问您的地址？	Excuse me, what is your address?
B: Běijīng Cháng'ān Dàjiē shí hào.	北京长安大街10号。	10 Chang'an Avenue, Beijing.
A: Nín de diànhuà shì duōshao?	您的电话是多少？	What is your telephone number?
B: Liù sì èr jiǔ sān wǔ qī bā.	64293578。	64293578.
A: Zhè shì wǒ de míngpiàn.	这是我的名片。	This is my business card.
B: Hǎo, xièxie.	好，谢谢。	Thank you.

SITUATIONAL DIALOGUES

4 (In the office) 07-09

A: Yīngguó Dàshǐguǎn zài nǎr?	英国大使馆在哪儿？	Where is the British Embassy?
B: Zài Jiànguómén Guānghuá Lù shíyī hào.	在建国门光华路11号。	It is at 11 Guanghua Road, Jianguomen.
A: Dàshǐguǎn de diànhuà shì duōshao?	大使馆的电话是多少？	What is the Embassy's telephone number?
B: Duìbuqǐ, wǒ bù zhīdào. Zhè shì tāmen de wǎngzhǐ.	对不起，我不知道。这是他们的网址。	Sorry, I don't know. This is their website.
A: Xièxie.	谢谢。	Thank you.

LANGUAGE POINTS

1. 'Zài 在'

It means 'to be located, to be at; in; on etc'. Note the sentences don't need 'to be' - 'shì 是'. For example:

Wǒ jiā zài Lúndūn.	我家在伦敦。	My home is in London.

2. 'Yī' and 'yāo'

'Yāo' is used when number 'one' occurs in telephone numbers, room numbers, bus and train numbers, etc, once the number is more than two digits, particularly in North China. For example:

Telephone number 119 can be said as yāo yāo jiǔ.

Room number 1018 can be said as yāo líng yāo bā.

EXERCISES

1. Fill in the blanks with appropriate words

❶ Nǐ jiā _____ nǎr?
你 家 _____ 哪 儿 ?

❷ Qǐngwèn _____ zài nǎr?
请 问 _____ 在 哪 儿 ?

❸ Nǐ qù _____ ?
你 去 _____ ?

❹ Lín Nán _____ bàngōngshì ma?
林 南 _____ 办 公 室 吗 ?

❺ Nǐ zài _____ xué Hànyǔ?
你 在 _____ 学 汉 语 ?

2. Ask questions about the underlined parts in the following sentences

❶ Wǒ jiā zài Fǎguó Bālí.
我 家 在 法 国 巴 黎 。

❷ Yīngyǔ xuéxiào zài Běijīng Lù yìbǎi wǔshísì hào.
英 语 学 校 在 北 京 路 154 号 。

❸ Wǒ de diànhuà shì bā liù sì sān èr jiǔ wǔ qī.
我 的 电 话 是 8 6 4 3 2 9 5 7 。

❹ Wǒ de shǒujī hào shì líng líng yāo sān wǔ sì bā jiǔ liù èr.
我 的 手 机 号 是 0 0 1 3 5 4 8 9 6 2 。

❺ Wǒ zhù zài Běijīng Fàndiàn yāo sì èr liù fángjiān.
我 住 在 北 京 饭 店 1 4 2 6 房 间 。

3. Translate the following into English

❶ Qǐngwèn, Zhōngguó Yínháng zài nǎr?
请 问 , 中 国 银 行 在 哪 儿 ?

❷ Xiànzài nǐ qù nǎr?
现 在 你 去 哪 儿 ?

❸ Wǒ tàitai bú zài jiā,　tā zài bàngōngshì.
我 太太不在家，她在 办公室。

❹ Wǒ bàba,　māma zhù zài Shànghǎi.
我 爸爸、妈妈 住 在 上 海。

❺ Wǒmen qù Zhōngguó fànguǎn chīfàn.
我 们 去 中 国 饭馆 吃饭。

❻ Tā Xīngqīliù qù shāngdiàn mǎi dōngxi.
他 星 期六去 商 店 买 东 西。

❼ Qǐngwèn, Xīngbākè kāfēidiàn zài nǎr?
请 问，星巴克咖啡店 在 哪儿？

❽ Wǒ měi Xīngqīsān qù Zhōngwén xuéxiào.
我 每 星 期三 去 中 文 学 校。

❾ Gāo lǎoshī de jiā bú zài Běijīng.
高 老师 的 家 不 在 北 京。

❿ Zhè shì wǒ de diànzǐ yóujiàn dìzhǐ.
这 是 我 的 电子 邮 件 地址。

4. Translate the following into Chinese

❶ My mother is not at home.

❷ My Chinese teacher lives in London.

❸ Where do you live?

❹ Excuse me, where is the toilet?

❺ What is your mobile phone number?

❻ What is your telephone number?

❼ May I ask your e-mail address, please?

❽ Mr. Chen is in his office.

❾ What is your room number?

❿ Where is your home?

5. Listening comprehension 🔊 07-10

Choose the correct answers according to the short dialogues.

❶ a. Beijing Hotel	b. Changcheng Hotel	c. Dongfang Hotel
❷ a. Room 1325	b. Room 1425	c. Room 1245
❸ a. 02078031649	b. 02087031649	c. 02078301649

❹ a. 07981642315   b. 07981463215   c. 07981462315

❺ a. 5 Anjialou Road   b. 55 Anjialou Road   c. 15 Anjialou Road

6. Classroom activities

Question your classmates and fill in the following form.

Surname	
First name	
Nationality	
Date of birth	
Telephone number	
E-mail address	
Home address	

7. Chinese characters learning

shǒu	ノ ニ 三 手
手	手 手 手 手 手

jī	一 十 オ 木 机 机
机	机 机 机 机 机

hào	丶 ㅁ 口 믁 号
号	号 号 号 号 号

LESSON 8
FAMILY
& FAMILY MEMBERS

OBJECTIVES

★ Talking about family members

★ Asking and telling people's ages

RELEVANT VOCABULARY

Family Members 🔊 08-01		
爸爸	bàba	dad / father
妈妈	māma	mum / mother
父亲	fùqin	father
母亲	mǔqin	mother
父母*	fùmǔ	parents
哥哥	gēge	elder brother
姐姐	jiějie	elder sister
弟弟	dìdi	younger brother
妹妹	mèimei	younger sister
女儿	nǚ'ér	daughter
儿子*	érzi	son
孩子*	háizi	child
爱人*	àirén	spouse
丈夫*	zhàngfu	husband

妻子*	qīzi	wife
爷爷*	yéye	grandfather
奶奶*	nǎinai	grandmother
猫*	māo	cat
狗*	gǒu	dog

Measure Words 🔊 08-02

口	kǒu	(measure word for family members)
个*	gè	(general measure word)
只*	zhī	(measure word for animals)

🔊 08-03

有	yǒu	to have, there be
没有	méiyǒu	not have, there is not
多大	duō dà	how old
岁	suì	year (of age)
和	hé	and
年纪	niánjì	age

KEY SENTENCES 🔊 08-04

1. Nǐ jiā yǒu jǐ kǒu rén?	你家有几口人？	How many people are there in your family?
2. Tāmen shì shéi?	他们是谁？	Who are they?
3. Nǐ yǒu dìdi ma?	你有弟弟吗？	Do you have younger brothers?

4. Nǐ mèimei duō dà?	你妹妹多大？	How old is your younger sister?
5. Tā jīnnián shíjiǔ suì.	她今年十九岁。	She is 19 years old this year.
6. Nǐ nǚ'ér jǐ suì?	你女儿几岁？	How old is your daughter?
7. Nǐ fùqin duō dà niánjì?	你父亲多大年纪?	How old is your father?

SITUATIONAL DIALOGUES

❶ (At a friend's party) 🔊 08-05

A: Nǐ jiā yǒu jǐ kǒu rén?	你家有几口人？	How many people are there in your family?
B: Wǒ jiā yǒu sì kǒu rén.	我家有四口人。	There are four people in my family.
A: Tāmen shì shéi?	他们是谁？	Who are they?
B: Wǒ bàba, māma, jiějie hé wǒ.	我爸爸、妈妈、姐姐和我。	They are my dad, my mum, my elder sister and myself.

❷ (At a friend's party) 🔊 08-06

A: Nǐ yǒu dìdi ma?	你有弟弟吗？	Do you have younger brothers?
B: Méiyǒu, wǒ yǒu gēge. Nǐ ne?	没有，我有哥哥。你呢？	No, but I have elder brothers. And you?
A: Wǒ yě méiyǒu dìdi, wǒ yǒu mèimei.	我也没有弟弟，我有妹妹。	I don't have younger brothers either. I have a younger sister.
B: Nǐ mèimei duō dà?	你妹妹多大？	How old is your younger sister?
A: Tā jīnnián shíjiǔ suì.	她今年十九岁。	She is 19 years old this year.

SITUATIONAL DIALOGUES

SITUATIONAL DIALOGUES

❸ (At a friend's party) 🔊 08-07

A: Nǐ jiā yǒu jǐ kǒu rén?	你家有几口人？	How many people are there in your family?
B: Sān kǒu. Wǒ tàitai, wǒ nǚ'ér hé wǒ.	三口。我太太，我女儿和我。	There are three people, my wife, my daughter and myself.
A: Nǐ nǚ'ér jǐ suì?	你女儿几岁？	How old is your daughter?
B: Wǔ suì.	五岁。	She is five.
A: Nǐ fùqin, mǔqin ne? Tāmen duō dà niánjì?	你父亲、母亲呢？他们多大年纪？	How about your father and mother? How old are they?
B: Wǒ fùqin jīnnián wǔshíbā suì. Wǒ mǔqin jīnnián wǔshíliù suì.	我父亲今年五十八岁。我母亲今年五十六岁。	My father is 58 this year. My mother is 56 this year.
A: Tāmen zhù zài nǎr?	他们住在哪儿？	Where do they live?
B: Tāmen zhù zài Shànghǎi.	他们住在上海。	They live in Shanghai.

LANGUAGE POINTS

1. 'Yǒu 有' and 'méiyǒu 没有'

Note that the negative of 'yǒu 有' (*to have*) is 'méiyǒu 没有', never 'bù yǒu 不有'.

2. Measure words

Most Chinese nouns are preceded by a measure word when used in a context involving numbers and specifically with the words 'this' and 'that'. This is similar to 'a <u>cup</u> of tea' or 'a <u>bottle</u> of beer' in English and specifically 'this cup of tea or that bottle of water'. There are about 20 measure words regularly used in Chinese of which 'gè 个' is the most common. Note that some nouns don't require any measure word at all. E.g.: 'yì tiān 一天', 'yì nián 一年'. (See more about measure words in summary lesson 18.)

3. 'Èr 二' and 'liǎng 两'

Both mean 'two', but when the number 'two' comes before a measure word, or before a noun where no measure word is required, 'liǎng 两' is used instead of 'èr 二', For example:

liǎng kǒu rén	两口人	two family members
liǎng ge mèimei	两个妹妹	two younger sisters
liǎng tiān	两天	two days

4. 'Jǐ 几' and 'duōshao 多少'

While both words mean '*how many*', 'jǐ 几' assumes that the answer will be a small number (normally less then 10) and 'duōshao 多少' will be a large number (normally more than 10 or not sure).

'jǐ 几' must always be followed by a measure word while 'duōshao 多少' might be used without a measure word. For example:

How many people are there in your family?

| Nǐ jiā yǒu jǐ kǒu rén? | 你家有几口人? | (assumes a small number) |
| Nǐ jiā yǒu duōshao rén? | 你家有多少人? | (assumes a large number) |

5. Asking someone's age

There are three ways to ask:

a. Nǐ jǐ suì? 你几岁?

Normally used for children under the age of ten.

b. Nín duō dà niánjì? 您多大年纪?

Normally used for older people. Generally the estimated age should be over fifty. The sentence literally means, '*How big is your age record?*' It's a very polite way to ask a person's age.

c. Nǐ duō dà? 你多大?

Used for teenagers and other adults.

EXERCISES

1. Rewrite the following yes/no questions using the positive and negative question form

❶ Nǐ shì Yīngguórén ma?
你 是 英 国 人 吗?

❷ Tā yǒu háizi ma?
他 有 孩子 吗?

❸ Wáng Dān zài jiā ma?
王 丹 在 家 吗?

❹ Zhè shì nǐ de shū ma?
这 是 你 的 书 吗?

❺ Nǐmen xué Hànyǔ ma?
你们 学 汉语 吗?

❻ Nǐ de Hànyǔ lǎoshī shì Zhōngguórén ma?
你 的 汉语 老师 是 中 国 人 吗?

❼ Tā shì nǐ jiějie ma?
她 是 你 姐姐 吗?

❽ Ni de jiā zài Lúndūn ma?
你 的 家 在 伦 敦 吗?

2. Match the Chinese with the English

❶ gēge
哥哥

a. daughter

❷ dìdi
弟弟

b. son

❸ jiějie
姐姐

c. dad

❹ mèimei
妹妹

d. elder sister

❺ háizi
孩子

e. father

❻ fùqin
父亲

f. mother

❼ mǔqin
母亲

g. spouse

❽ àirén
爱人

h. mum

❾ érzi
儿子

i. child

❿ nǚ'ér
女儿

j. elder brother

⓫ bàba
爸爸

k. younger sister

⓬ māma
妈妈

l. younger brother

3. Complete the following questions asking the ages of different family members (Use the two different question formats)

❶ Tā gēge
他 哥哥 _____? (33 years old)

❷ Nǐ nǚ'ér
你 女儿 _____? (8 years old)

❸ Nín fùqin
您 父亲 _____? (67 years old)

4. Translate the following into Chinese

❶ There are four people in my family. They are my wife, my son, my daughter and myself.

❷ How many children do you have?

❸ How old is your son?

❹ Do you have a girlfriend? What's her name?

❺ Is she your wife?

❻ How many elder brothers do you have?

❼ How old is your younger brother?

❽ How old is your mother?

❾ Does your younger sister have a boyfriend?

❿ My son is called Patrick. My daughter is called Grace.

5. Listening comprehension 🔊 08-08

Choose the correct answers according to the short dialogues.

❶ a. four people	b. five people	c. six people
❷ a. yes	b. no	c. she has an elder brother
❸ a. 14	b. 15	c. 16
❹ a. 56	b. 57	c. 58
❺ a. 6	b. 7	c. 8

6. Classroom activities

Talk about yourself and your family in Chinese. Include such information as the number of people in your family, who they are, what their names are, and how old they are.

7. Chinese characters learning

fù	ノ 八 グ 父								
父	父	父	父	父	父				
mǔ	ㄥ 口 口 母 母								
母	母	母	母	母	母				
qīn	、 亠 亠 立 立 辛 辛 亲								
亲	亲	亲	亲	亲	亲				

LESSON 9
WORK & PROFESSIONS

OBJECTIVES

★ Asking about jobs

★ Talking about professions

RELEVANT VOCABULARY

Professions 🔊 09-01		
会计	kuàijì	accountant
护士	hùshi	nurse
秘书	mìshū	secretary
作家	zuòjiā	writer
老师	lǎoshī	teacher
律师 *(N. China)*	lǜshī	lawyer
医生 /大夫 *dài fu*	yīshēng	doctor
学生	xuésheng	student
工程师*	gōngchéngshī	engineer
记者*	jìzhě	journalist
商人*	shāngrén	businessman/woman
职员*	zhíyuán	office worker, clerk
经理* *often*	jīnglǐ	manager
教授* *reaele*	jiàoshòu	professor

公务员*	gōngwùyuán	civil servant

[handwritten: public, person, public affairs]

Work Places 09-02

银行	yínháng	bank
律师行*	lǜshīháng	law firm
医院	yīyuàn	hospital
公司	gōngsī	company
工厂*	gōngchǎng	factory
小学	xiǎoxué	primary school
大学*	dàxué	university
中学*	zhōngxué	secondary school

[handwritten: industry, export, law]

09-03

工作	gōngzuò	work, job
退休 (休息、rest)	tuìxiū	to retire
了	le	(particle)
读书 out loud	dú shū (v.s) kan shu (silent)	to read a book
写书	xiě shū	to write a book
哦	ò	oh

KEY SENTENCES 09-04

1. Nǐ zài nǎr gōngzuò?	你在哪儿工作?	Where do you work?
2. Wǒ zài yínháng gōngzuò.	我在银行工作。	I work in a bank.
3. Nǐ zuò shénme gōngzuò?	你做什么工作?	What do you do for a living?

4. Wǒ shì kuàijì.	我是会计。	I am an accountant.
5. Nǐ fùqin gōngzuò ma?	你父亲工作吗?	Does your father work?
6. Tā tuìxiū le.	他退休了。	He is retired.
7. Xiànzài tā zài jiā dú shū, xiě shū.	现在他在家读书、写书。	He reads and writes books at home now.
8. Nǐ nǚ'ér shì bu shì xuésheng?	你女儿是不是学生?	Is your daughter a student?

SITUATIONAL DIALOGUES

❶ (In the language centre) 🔊 09-05

A: Nǐ zài nǎr gōngzuò?	你在哪儿工作?	Where do you work?
B: Wǒ zài yínháng gōngzuò.	我在银行工作。	I work in a bank.
A: Nǐ zuò shénme gōngzuò?	你做什么工作?	What do you do for living?
B: Wǒ shì kuàijì. Nǐ ne?	我是会计。你呢?	I am an accountant. And you?
A: Wǒ shì hùshi, zài yīyuàn gōngzuò.	我是护士，在医院工作。	I am a nurse. I work in a hospital.

❷ (In the office) 🔊 09-06

A: Nǐ àirén zài nǎr gōngzuò?	你爱人在哪儿工作?	Where does your wife work?
B: Tā zài diànhuà gōngsī gōngzuò.	她在电话公司工作。	She works at a telephone company.
A: Tā zuò shénme gōngzuò?	她做什么工作?	What does she do there?
B: Tā shì mìshū.	她是秘书。	She is a secretary.

❸ (At a café) 🔊 09-07

A: Nǐ fùqin gōngzuò ma?	你父亲工作吗?	Does your father work?
B: Tā tuìxiū le. Xiànzài tā zài jiā dú shū, xiě shū.	他退休了。现在他在家读书、写书。	No, he is retired. He reads and writes books at home now.
A: Ò, tā shì zuòjiā a! Nǐ mǔqin ne?	哦，他是作家啊！你母亲呢?	Oh, he is a writer. How about your mother?
B: Wǒ mǔqin gōngzuò, tā shì xiǎoxué lǎoshī.	我母亲工作，她是小学老师。	My mother is working. She is a primary school teacher.

❹ (At a friend's party) 🔊 09-08

A: Nǐ shì lǜshī ma?	你是律师吗?	Are you a lawyer?
B: Wǒ bú shì lǜshī, shì yīshēng.	我不是律师，是医生。	No, I'm not. I'm a doctor.
A: Nǐ nǚ'ér shì bu shì xuésheng?	你女儿是不是学生?	Is your daughter a student?
B: Tā shì dàxuéshēng.	她是大学生。	Yes, she is a university student.
A: Nǐ érzi ne?	你儿子呢?	How about your son?
B: Tā shì zhōngxuéshēng.	他是中学生。	He is a secondary school student.

LANGUAGE POINTS

1. The sentence order with 'zài 在'

The pattern is:

Subject + zài 在 + place + verb

Tā zài yínháng gōngzuò.	他在银行工作。	He works in a bank.

2. The particle 'le 了'

There are many different grammatical functions of 'le 了'. In this lesson it indicates a change of state. When 'le 了' is used in sentences that describe a present event, it indicates that a new situation has appeared. For example:

Tā tuìxiū le.	他退休了。	He is retired. (He used to work, but not anymore.)
Wǒ è le.	我饿了。	I am hungry (now). (I wasn't hungry before.)

EXERCISES

1. Match the Chinese with the English

❶ yīshēng
医生

❷ hùshi
护士

❸ lǎoshī
老师

❹ xuésheng
学生

❺ shāngrén
商人

❻ lǜshī
律师

❼ mìshū
秘书

❽ zhíyuán
职员

❾ jīnglǐ
经理

❿ kuàijì
会计

a. businessman/women

b. teacher

c. office worker, clerk

d. manager

e. secretary

f. accountant

g. doctor

h. nurse

i. lawyer

j. student

2. Translate the following into English

❶ yīyuàn
医 院

❷ xuéxiào
学 校

❸ gōngsī
公 司

❹ xiǎoxué
小 学

❺ zhōngxué
中 学

❻ dàxué
大 学

❼ gōngchǎng
工 厂

❽ shāngdiàn
商 店

❾ yínháng
银 行

3. Translate the following into Chinese

❶ This is my younger brother, not my elder brother.

❷ What work does your father do for a living?

❸ Where does your mother work?

❹ My father is a lawyer and my mother is a doctor.

❺ My elder brother is an engineer. He works in a German company.

❻ My younger brother is a student. He is studying in a university.

❼ My elder sister is a teacher. She works in a secondary school.

❽ My younger sister is an accountant. She works in a bank.

❾ Both my father and mother are very old. They have retired. (use 'le 了')

❿ My father has retired; my mother has also retired. (use 'le 了')

4. Listening comprehension 🔊 09-09

Mark true (T) or false (F) according to the short dialogues.

❶ He is an accountant. He works in a bank.   (   )

❷ She works in a school.   (   )

❸ She is a doctor.   (   )

❹ He is a lawyer. He is not a teacher.   (   )

❺ He is not working.   (   )

5. Classroom activities

❶ Work in pairs and ask each other where you work, what kind of jobs you do and write down the details.

❷ Talk about your family members, who they are, what they are called, and what jobs they do with your classmates.

6. Chinese characters learning

gōng	ノ 八 公 公								
公	公	公	公	公	公				

sī	丁 丁 司 司 司								
司	司	司	司	司	司				

gōng	一 丁 工								
工	工	工	工	工	工				

zuò	ノ イ イ 竹 竹 作 作								
作	作	作	作	作	作				

LESSON 10
INTERESTS & ABILITIES

OBJECTIVES

★ Talking about hobbies

★ Finding out about abilities

RELEVANT VOCABULARY

Modal Verbs 🔊 10-01		
喜欢	xǐhuan	to like, to enjoy
会	huì	can, be able to
爱	ài	love, to love
可以*	kěyǐ	can, may, alright, OK
应该*	yīnggāi	should

Hobbies 🔊 10-02		
看书	kàn shū	to read
看电视*	kàn diànshì	to watch TV
听音乐	tīng yīnyuè	to listen to music
做运动	zuò yùndòng	to do exercises
运动	yùndòng	sport, exercise
做饭	zuòfàn	to cook
看电影	kàn diànyǐng	to watch film

上网	shàngwǎng	to surf the internet
跑步	pǎobù	to run
打网球	dǎ wǎngqiú	to play tennis
打	dǎ	to play (in a sport or game), to hit
踢*	tī	to kick, to play
足球*	zúqiú	football
篮球*	lánqiú	basketball
游泳*	yóuyǒng	to swim
唱歌*	chànggē	to sing
跳舞*	tiàowǔ	to dance, dance

🔊 10-03

周末	zhōumò	weekend
书	shū	book
东西	dōngxi	things
健身房	jiànshēnfáng	gym
真的	zhēnde	really, truly
非常	fēicháng	very, extremely
常/常常	cháng/chángcháng	often
功夫	gōngfu	kung fu
一点儿	yìdiǎnr	a little
博客	bókè	blog
新闻	xīnwén	news
有时候	yǒushíhou	sometimes

KEY SENTENCES 🔊 10-04

1. Zhōumò nǐ xǐhuan zuò shénme?	周末你喜欢做什么？	What do you like to do at weekends?
2. Tā xǐhuan qù jiànshēnfáng zuò yùndòng.	她喜欢去健身房做运动。	She likes to go to the gym to do exercises.
3. Wǒ huì zuò Zhōngguó fàn.	我会做中国饭。	I can cook Chinese meals.
4. Zhōumò wǒ cháng qù kàn diànyǐng.	周末我常去看电影。	I often go to the cinema at weekends.
5. Wǒ huì yìdiǎnr gōngfu.	我会一点儿功夫。	I can do a little bit of kung fu.
6. Wǒ ài shàngwǎng kàn bókè, kàn xīnwén.	我爱上网看博客，看新闻。	I love to read blogs and watch news online.
7. Zhōumò wǒ yǒushíhou qù pàobù, yǒushíhou hé péngyou qù dǎ wǎngqiú.	周末我有时候去跑步，有时候和朋友去打网球。	At weekends, sometimes I like jogging, sometimes I like to play tennis with friends.

SITUATIONAL DIALOGUES

SITUATIONAL DIALOGUES

❶ (In the office) 🔊 10-05

A: Zhōumò nǐ xǐhuan zuò shénme?	周末你喜欢做什么？	What do you like to do at weekends?

B: Wǒ xǐhuan zài jiā kàn shū, tīng yīnyuè.	我喜欢在家看书，听音乐。	I like to stay at home reading and listening to music.
A: Nǐ tàitai xǐhuan zuò shénme?	你太太喜欢做什么？	What does your wife like to do?
B: Tā xǐhuan qù shāngdiàn mǎi dōngxi, yě xǐhuan qù jiànshēnfáng zuò yùndòng.	她喜欢去商店买东西，也喜欢去健身房做运动。	She likes to go shopping. She also likes to go to the gym to do exercises.

❷ (At a friend's home) 🔊 10-06

A: Nǐ xǐhuan chī Zhōngguó fàn ma?	你喜欢吃中国饭吗？	Do you like eating Chinese food?
B: Fēicháng xǐhuan. Wǒ huì zuò Zhōngguó fàn.	非常喜欢。我会做中国饭。	Yes, very much. I can cook Chinese meals.
A: Zhēnde?	真的？	Really?
B: Zhōumò wǒ cháng zuò Zhōngguó fàn.	周末我常做中国饭。	Yes, I often cook Chinese meals at weekends.
A: Nǐ huì zuò Yīngguó fàn ma?	你会做英国饭吗？	Can you cook English meals?
B: Yīngguó fàn? Wǒ bú huì.	英国饭？我不会。	English meals? I don't know how.

❸ (In the language centre) 🔊 10-07

A: Nǐ ài kàn diànyǐng ma?	你爱看电影吗？	Do you like watching films?
B: Ài kàn. Zhōumò wǒ cháng qù kàn diànyǐng.	爱看。周末我常去看电影。	Yes, I do. I often go to the cinema at weekends.

A: Nǐ xǐhuan kàn shénme diànyǐng?	你喜欢看什么电影？	What kinds of film do you like to watch?
A: Wǒ xǐhuan kàn Zhōngguó gōngfu diànyǐng.	我喜欢看中国功夫电影。	I like to watch Chinese martial arts films.
A: Nǐ huì bu huì Zhōngguó gōngfu?	你会不会中国功夫？	Can you do Chinese martial arts?
B: Huì yìdiǎnr.	会一点儿。	A little bit.

❹ (In a canteen) 🔊 10-08

A: Nǐ wǎnshang chángcháng zuò shénme?	你晚上常常做什么？	What do you usually do in the evenings?
B: Wǒ ài shàngwǎng kàn bókè, kàn xīnwén.	我爱上网看博客，看新闻。	I love to read blogs and watch news online.
A: Nà zhōumò ne?	那周末呢？	How about weekends?
B: Zhōumò wǒ yǒushíhou qù pǎobù, yǒushíhou hé péngyou qù dǎ wǎngqiú.	周末我有时候去跑步，有时候和朋友去打网球。	At weekends, sometimes I like jogging, sometimes I like to play tennis with friends.

LANGUAGE POINTS

1. Modal verbs

Some modal verbs such as 'xǐhuan 喜欢' (like to + verb) and 'ài 爱' (love to+ verb), can be modified by 'hěn 很', meaning 'very much'. For example:

| Tā hěn xǐhuan kàn Měiguó diànyǐng. | 他很喜欢看美国电影。 | He likes to watch American films very much. |
| Wǒ hěn ài chī Zhōngguó fàn. | 我很爱吃中国饭。 | I love to eat Chinese food very much. |

2. 'Cháng 常' and 'chángcháng 常常'

'Cháng 常' is equivalent to 'chángcháng 常常' in most situations.

EXERCISES

1. Fill in the blanks with the words given

A. huì	B. xǐhuan	C. yìdiǎnr	D. fēicháng	E. chángcháng	F. yǒushíhou
会	喜欢	一点儿	非常	常常	有时候

❶ Nǐ（　　　）chī shénme?
你（　　　）吃 什 么?

❷ Nǐ（　　　）shuō Yīngyǔ ma?
你（　　　）说 英 语 吗?

❸ Wǒ（　　　）xǐhuan kàn Měiguó diànyǐng.
我（　　　）喜 欢 看 美 国 电 影。

❹ Zhōumò nǐ（　　　）zuò shénme?
周 末 你（　　　）做 什 么?

❺ Wǒ àirén（　　　）qù Xiānggǎng mǎi dōngxi.
我 爱人（　　　）去 香 港 买 东 西。

❻ Wǒ huì shuō（　　　）Hànyǔ.
我 会 说（　　　）汉语。

2. Translate the following into English

❶ Xīngqītiān wǒ cháng qù túshūguǎn kàn shū.
星 期天 我 常 去图书 馆 看 书。

❷ Wǒ tàitai xǐhuan mǎi dōngxi, bù xǐhuan zuòfàn.
我 太太喜欢 买 东 西,不喜 欢 做 饭。

❸ Zhōumò nǐ xǐhuan zuò shénme?
周 末 你喜欢 做 什 么?

❹ Nǐ huì bu huì shuō Fǎyǔ?
你 会 不 会 说 法语?

❺ Nǐ ài bu ài kàn Zhōngguó diànyǐng?
你爱不爱看 中 国 电 影?

❻ Wǒ huì shuō yìdiǎnr Xībānyáyǔ.
我 会 说 一点儿西班 牙语。

❼ Zhōumò wǒ yǒushíhou qù yóuyǒng, yǒushíhou qù tiàowǔ.
周 末 我 有 时 候 去 游 泳，有 时 候 去 跳 舞。

❽ Míngnián wǒ hěn xiǎng qù Běijīng.
明 年 我 很 想 去 北 京。

3. Translate the following into Chinese

❶ Do you like French films?

❷ I don't like French films.

❸ What kind of films do you like?

❹ I like Chinese films very much.

❺ I enjoy playing basketball and tennis. I also enjoy swimming.

❻ I like swimming, and I don't like tennis.

❼ I don't like to play football, but I like to watch football.

❽ What would you like to drink?

❾ Where would you like to go?

❿ I would like to go to Shanghai next April.

4. Listening comprehension 🔊 10-09

Mark true (T) or false (F) according to the short dialogues.

❶ She likes watching American films.   (   )

❷ She can cook Italian meals.   (   )

❸ She doesn't like shopping.   (   )

❹ He likes eating Chinese food very much.   (   )

❺ He can't cook Chinese meals.   (   )

5. Classroom activities

Give your personal information, including:

• your surname, first name, and nationality

• the country or place you come from

• the language you speak

• your home and your family members

• your job and the place where you work

• things which you like or dislike

6. Chinese characters learning

xǐ	一 十 土 キ 吉 吉 吉 吉 直 喜 喜 喜								
喜	喜	喜	喜	喜	喜				
huān	フ ス ス′ スヘ スケ 欢								
欢	欢	欢	欢	欢	欢				
kàn	一 二 三 手 耂 看 看 看 看								
看	看	看	看	看	看				
shū	フ ㄱ 书 书								
书	书	书	书	书	书				

LESSON 11
INVITATIONS & APPOINTMENTS

OBJECTIVES

★ Inviting people for an event, activity or meal

★ Making an appointment

RELEVANT VOCABULARY

Events 🔊 11-01		
会	huì	meeting
酒会	jiǔhuì	drinks party
聚会*	jùhuì	party
舞会*	wǔhuì	dancing party
晚会*	wǎnhuì	evening party
音乐会*	yīnyuèhuì	concert
招待会*	zhāodàihuì	reception
会议*	huìyì	conference

🔊 11-02		
时间	shíjiān	time
什么事	shénme shì	what's happening
事	shì	things, matter, business
吧	ba	(suggesting particle)

太……了	tài...le	extremely..., too...
太	tài	too, very, extremely
一起	yìqǐ	together
什么时候	shénme shíhou	when (question)
空	kòng	free time
烤鸭	kǎoyā	roast duck
鸭	yā	duck
羊肉	yángròu	lamb
涮羊肉	shuàn yángròu	lamb hotpot (a famous Beijing dish)
肉	ròu	meat

KEY SENTENCES 🔊 11-03

1. Xīngqīwǔ wǎnshang nǐ yǒu shíjiān ma?	星期五晚上你有时间吗？	Will you be free on Friday evening?
2. Wǒ qǐng nǐ lái wǒmen gōngsī de xīnnián jiǔhuì ba?	我请你来我们公司的新年酒会吧？	Can I invite you to come to the New Year drinks party at my company?
3. Wǒmen yìqǐ kāi ge huì ba?	我们一起开个会吧？	Shall we have a meeting together?
4. Shénme shíhou?	什么时候？	When?
5. Duìbuqǐ, Xīngqīwǔ wǒ yǒu shì.	对不起，星期五我有事。	Sorry, I've got things to do this Friday.
6. Zhōumò nǐ yǒu kòng ma?	周末你有空吗？	Will you be free this weekend?

| 7. Wǒ qǐng nǐ chī Běijīng kǎoyā, zěnmeyàng? | 我请你吃北京烤鸭，怎么样？ | I'd like to invite you to eat Beijing roast duck. What do you think? |
| 8. Shénme shíjiān? | 什么时间？ | What time? |

SITUATIONAL DIALOGUES

❶ (On the phone) 🔊 11-04

A: Xīngqīwǔ wǎnshang nǐ yǒu shíjiān ma?	星期五晚上你有时间吗？	Will you be free on Friday evening?
B: Yǒu. Yǒu shénme shì ma?	有。有什么事吗？	Yes. Why, what's happening?
A: Wǒ qǐng nǐ lái wǒmen gōngsī de xīnnián jiǔhuì ba?	我请你来我们公司的新年酒会吧？	Can I invite you to come to the New Year drinks party at my company?
B: Tài hǎo le! Jǐ diǎn?	太好了！几点？	That's great! What time?
A: Wǎnshang liù diǎn.	晚上六点。	Six o'clock in the evening.

SITUATIONAL DIALOGUES

83

SITUATIONAL DIALOGUES

❷ (In the office) 🔊 11-05

A: Wǒmen yìqǐ kāi ge huì ba?	我们一起开个会吧？	Shall we have a meeting together?
B: Shénme shíhou?	什么时候？	When?
A: Zhè Xīngqīwǔ zěnmeyàng?	这星期五怎么样？	How about this Friday?
B: Duìbuqǐ, Xīngqīwǔ wǒ yǒu shì.	对不起，星期五我有事。	Sorry, I've got things to do this Friday.
A: Xià Zhōu'èr ne?	下周二呢？	How about next Tuesday?
B: Xià Zhōu'èr kěyǐ.	下周二可以。	Next Tuesday is OK.

❸ (On the phone) 🔊 11-06

A: Zhōumò nǐ yǒu kòng ma?	周末你有空吗？	Will you be free this weekend?
B: Yǒu.	有。	Yes.
A: Wǒ qǐng nǐ chī Běijīng kǎoyā, zěnmeyàng?	我请你吃北京烤鸭，怎么样？	I'd like to invite you to eat Beijing roast duck. What do you think?
B: Wǒ bù xǐhuan chī kǎoyā.	我不喜欢吃烤鸭。	I don't like roast duck.
A: Chī shuàn yángròu, hǎo ma?	吃涮羊肉，好吗？	How about lamb hotpot?
B: Hǎo. Shénme shíjiān?	好。什么时间？	That's fine. When?
A: Xīngqīliù wǎnshang qī diǎn.	星期六晚上七点。	Saturday evening, seven o'clock.

LANGUAGE POINTS

1. 'Zěnmeyàng? 怎么样？'

In addition to the meaning given in Lesson 1, it is also a very useful phrase which can be put at the end of sentences to express the meaning 'How about...? What's it like?' For example:

| Zhè ge zěnmeyàng? | 这个怎么样？ | How about this one? |
| Wǒmen qù jiǔbā, zěnmeyàng? | 我们去酒吧，怎么样？ | How about going to the pub? |

2. Particle 'ba 吧'

'Ba 吧' at the end of a sentence makes whatever you say more friendly and casual by turning a statement into a rhetorical question. For example:

| Wǒmen qù kàn diànyǐng ba? | 我们去看电影吧？ | Shall we go to the cinema? |

3. 'Tài...le 太……了'

The word 'tài 太' by itself means 'too'. It is normally used in conjunction with 'le 了' to mean 'extremely' or 'very much' in a positive sentence. It can express praise or dissatisfaction. The negative is: 'bú tài... 不太……' without 'le 了'. For example:

Tài máng le!	太忙了！	Extremely busy! / Too busy! (dissatisfaction)
Tài hǎo le!	太好了！	Excellent! / Great! (praise)
Tài xǐhuan le!	太喜欢了！	Like it very much.
Bú tài máng.	不太忙。	Not too busy.
Bú tài hǎo.	不太好。	Not very good.
Bú tài xǐhuan.	不太喜欢。	Not like it very much.

EXERCISES

1. Answer the questions in Chinese

❶ Nǐ měi tiān shénme shíjiān shàngbān?
你 每 天 什 么 时 间 上 班？

❷ Nǐ měi xīngqī jǐ yǒu Hànyǔ kè?
你 每 星 期几有 汉语课？

❸ Zhōumò nǐ cháng zuò shénme?
周 末 你 常 做 什 么？

❹ Nǐ shénme shíhou qù Běijīng xué Hànyǔ?
你 什 么 时候 去 北京 学 汉语？

❺ Wǒ qǐng nǐ qù chī kǎoyā, zěnmeyàng?
我 请 你 去 吃 烤鸭，怎么样？

❻ Jīntiān wǎnshang jǐ diǎn nǐ lái wǒ jiā?
今 天 晚 上 几点 你 来 我 家？

2. Add appropriate verbs before the nouns

	diànshì		fàn		píjiǔ		shāngdiàn		dōngxi
_____	电视	_____	饭	_____	啤酒	_____	商店	_____	东西

	huì		shíjiān		Hànyǔ		Yīngguórén		péngyou
_____	会	_____	时间	_____	汉语	_____	英国人	_____	朋友

3. Translate the following into Chinese

❶ What time can I see you?

❷ When will you be free?

❸ Have you got anything to do tomorrow?

❹ What do you think of the new film? – It's great!

❺ Shall we meet at the pub at 7 o'clock?

❻ Today is my treat. What would you like to eat?

❼ Mr. Chen invited us to his house next Sunday.

❽ Are you doing anything at the weekend?

❾ This week I'm very busy. I have no time at all.

❿ Wednesday is OK. I am not busy.

4. Listening comprehension 🔊 11-07

Mark true (T) or false (F) according to the short dialogues.

❶ She will be free this weekend.   (   )

❷ She loves to go for a Chinese meal.   (   )

❸ He was very busy at the moment.   (   )

❹ She doesn't like roast duck.   (   )

❺ He loves to go to the pub.   (   )

5. Classroom activities

Role play:

You would like to invite your Chinese friend to dinner and to watch a Chinese film which is only on from this Friday until Sunday. He/she is very busy. Try to arrange the evening together.

6. Chinese characters learning

yǒu	一 ナ オ 有 有 有							
有	有	有	有	有				

shí	丨 冂 冂 日 日一 时 时							
时	时	时	时	时				

jiān	丶 丶 门 门 间 间 间							
间	间	间	间	间				

LESSON 12
SUMMARY OF LESSONS 7-11

OBJECTIVES

★ Practicing the vocabulary and grammars from lessons 7-11

★ Cultural insights: Everyday etiquette and customs

KEY PATTERNS

Patterns	Sentences
Noun + zài 在 + place	Nǐ jiā zài nǎr? 你家在哪儿?
Subject + zài 在 + place + verb	Tā zài yínháng gōngzuò. 他在银行工作。
Statement + le 了	Tā tuìxiū le. 他退休了。
Subject + yǒu 有 + object	Wǒ jiā yǒu sì kǒu rén. 我家有四口人。
Subject + méiyǒu 有 + object	Wǒ méiyǒu dìdi. 我没有弟弟。
Subject + number + suì 岁	Tā shíjiǔ suì. 她十九岁。
Subject + modal verb + V. + object	Wǒ xǐhuan hē Zhōngguó chá. 我喜欢喝中国茶。 Wǒ huì zuò Zhōngguó fàn. 我会做中国饭。
Statement, + zěnmeyàng 怎么样?	Wǒmen qù chī Zhōngguó fàn, zěnmeyàng? 我们去吃中国饭，怎么样?
Statement + ba 吧?	Wǒmen qù kàn diànyǐng ba? 我们去看电影吧?
Tài...le 太……了	Tài guì le. 太贵了。

More about usage of 'èr 二' and 'liǎng 两'

Both 'èr' and 'liǎng' mean 'two'. When two comes before a measure word, or before a noun which has no measure word before it, 'liǎng' is used instead of 'èr', as in:

liǎng diǎn	两点	two o'clock
liǎng tiān	两天	two days
liǎng nián	两年	two years
liǎng ge xīngqī	两个星期	two weeks
liǎng ge yuè	两个月	two months

In larger numbers containing the number two, such as 12, 22, 32, 42, 'èr' is used irrespective of whether it is followed by a measure word, as in:

shí'èr diǎn	十二点	12 o'clock
shí'èr tiān	十二天	12 days
shí'èr nián	十二年	12 years
shí'èr ge xīngqī	十二个星期	12 weeks
shí'èr ge yuè	十二个月	12 months

RELEVANT VOCABULARY

🔊 12-01		
还	hái	also, as well
家	jiā	(measure word)
因为	yīnwèi	because
所以*	suǒyǐ	so, therefore
跟	gēn	with, and
外语	wàiyǔ	foreign language
外国	wàiguó	foreign country

STORY TIME

1. Listen to the following story and retell it in Chinese 🔊 12-02

Wǒ men de   Ai hào
我们 的 爱好

Lìli   shēngrì nà tiān, xiàwǔ wǒmen qù kàn Zhōngguó diànyǐng, wǎnshang wǒmen
丽丽 生日那天，下午我们 去看 中 国 电影，晚 上 我们

qù chī Fǎguó fàn, hái gēn péngyou yìqǐ qù jiǔbā hējiǔ,   fēicháng gāoxìng.
去吃法国饭，还 跟 朋 友 一起去 酒吧喝酒， 非 常 高兴。

Lìli   shì yīshēng, zài yì jiā yīyuàn gōngzuò.   Yīnwèi tā hěn máng, tā méiyǒu hěn duō
丽丽是医 生， 在一家 医院 工 作。因为她很 忙，她没有很多

shíjiān gēn wǒ zài yìqǐ.   Zhōumò tā xǐhuan xué wàiyǔ,   tā huì shuō Yīngyǔ hé Rìyǔ,
时间 跟 我在一起。周 末她喜欢 学 外语，她会 说 英语和日语，

yě ài kàn wàiyǔ shū hé wàiguó diànyǐng.
也爱看外语书和外国 电影。

Wǒ bú tài xǐhuan xué wàiyǔ,   wǒ xǐhuan zuòfàn, Zhōngguó fàn, Fǎguó fàn,   Yì-
我不太喜欢 学外语，我喜欢 做饭，中 国 饭、法国 饭、意

dàlì fàn,   Rìběn fàn,   wǒ dōu huì zuò.   Lìli   hé tā de bàba māma dōu ài chī wǒ zuò
大利饭、日本 饭，我都 会做。丽丽和她的爸爸 妈妈都爱吃我做

de fàn.   Jīntiān Lìli   wèn wǒ huì bu huì zuò Yīngguó fàn,   wǒ xiǎng: "Yīngguó fàn?
的饭。今天 丽丽问我会不会做 英国饭，我 想："英 国饭？

Shénme shì Yīngguó fàn ne?"
什 么是英国 饭呢？"

2. Read the story again and then answer the following questions

❶ What did they do in the afternoon of Lili's birthday?

❷ Where did they go in the evening on Lili's birthday?

❸ What does Lili do? Where does Lili work?

❹ What does Lili like to do at the weekend?

❺ What is the writer's hobby?

❻ What kind of things does the writer not like to do?

❼ What kind of dishes can the writer cook?

CULTURAL INSIGHTS

Everyday etiquette and customs

Saying 'Thank you' and 'Sorry'

In daily life 'thank you' and 'sorry' are not used as much as in the West. This is just the same in a Chinese office between employees. Hierarchy exists throughout Chinese society, which including in the working environment. Traditionally, a senior person would not say 'thank you or sorry' to his junior in age or position and the working relationship between them would be formal. For Chinese people, they hardly 'sorry', only when they really have done something wrong.

Gentlemen first

'Ladies first' doesn't apply in China. When you attend a formal/business banquet, by Chinese custom, the waiters will first serve the most senior male by social ranking and age. The most junior female is typically served last. Similarly, when you enter through a door or into an elevator, the most junior staff is expected to open and hold doors while the senior members enter in the order of their social ranking, regardless of whether they are male or female. When two people are of the same rank, then the older person gets the seniority. If you are a female Chinese government official, you are treated as one of the men in a predominantly male profession. No one would open doors for you just because you are a woman; instead, people would give you proper respects according to your rank and seniority.

Gift giving - Don't open gifts in front of others

Gift giving is a staple of Chinese culture. However, unlike in some Western countries, Chinese gifts should be opened in private, not in front of others. From the Chinese perspective, however, people should avoid seeming too eager to receive gifts, and this is why they should refrain from opening gifts in front of the giver. If someone too eager to get gifts, they are perceived as greedy, whereas someone who modestly puts the unopened gift aside for later is deemed more cultured.

Never give a clock as a gift

The word clock is '*Zhong*', which sounds exactly like the word for funeral. Thus, giving someone a clock, or '*Songzhong*' in Chinese sounds exactly like the phrase 'attending someone's funeral'. Due to this similarity, a Chinese person would never give another Chinese person a clock as a gift.

CHINESE CHARACTERS LEARNING

zhōu	ノ 刀 月 冃 用 用 周 周								
周	周	周	周	周	周				
mò	一 二 キ 才 末								
末	末	末	末	末	末				
hěn	ノ ク 彳 彳 彳 彳 彳 很 很								
很	很	很	很	很	很				
máng	丶 丶 忄 忄 忙 忙								
忙	忙	忙	忙	忙	忙				

LESSON 13
TELEPHONING & VISITING

OBJECTIVES

★ Making phone calls

★ Visiting companies

★ Leaving messages

RELEVANT VOCABULARY

Telephone Words 🔊 13-01		
喂	wèi	hello, hey
回电话	huí diànhuà	to call back
打电话*	dǎ diànhuà	to make phone calls
接电话*	jiē diànhuà	to answer the phone
找	zhǎo	to look for, to find
转	zhuǎn	to change to (extension), to pass on
打错了*	dǎ cuò le	wrong number
留言*	liúyán	to leave a message
占线*	zhànxiàn	(line) engaged

🔊 13-02		
位	wèi	(measure word for person-polite)
给	gěi	to give, for
回	huí	to return

一定	yídìng	definitely, certainly
告诉	gàosu	to tell
等	děng	to wait
客人	kèrén	guest
姓名	xìngmíng	full name
接	jiē	to answer the phone, to pick up somebody

Proper Nouns 🔊 13-03

吴	Wú	Wu (a Chinese surname)
京华公司	Jīnghuá gōngsī	(company name)
马修	Mǎxiū	Matthew

KEY SENTENCES 🔊 13-04

1. Qǐngwèn Wú lǎoshī zài ma?	请问吴老师在吗？	Hello, is teacher Wu there, please?
2. Nín shì nǎ wèi?	您是哪位？	Who is calling?/ Who is it?
3. Qǐng tā gěi wǒ huí diànhuà.	请他给我回电话。	Could you please ask him to call me back?
4. Nǐ hǎo, shì Jīnghuá gōngsī ma?	你好，是京华公司吗？	Hello, is this the Jinghua Company?
5. Qǐngwèn nín zhǎo shéi?	请问您找谁？	May I ask who you would like to visit?
6. Wǒ shì Yīngguó dàshǐguǎn de Mǎxiū.	我是英国大使馆的马修。	This is Matthew from the British Embassy.
7. Qǐng děng yíxià.	请等一下。	Wait for a second, please.

SITUATIONAL DIALOGUES

❶ (Phoning somebody) 🔊 13-05

A: Wèi, nǐ hǎo!	喂，你好！	Hello!
B: Nǐ hǎo! Qǐngwèn Wú lǎoshī zài ma?	你好！请问吴老师在吗？	Hello, is teacher Wu there, please?
A: Tā bú zài, nín shì nǎ wèi?	他不在，您是哪位？	He is not in. Who is calling?
B: Wǒ shì Zhāng Yàn. Qǐng tā gěi wǒ huí diànhuà, hǎo ma?	我是张燕。请他给我回电话，好吗？	This is Zhang Yan speaking. Could you please ask him to call me back?
A: Hǎo, wǒ yídìng gàosu tā.	好，我一定告诉他。	OK, I'll definitely tell him.

❷ (Visiting a company) 🔊 13-06

A: Nǐ hǎo, shì Jīnghuá gōngsī ma?	你好，是京华公司吗？	Hello, is this the Jinghua Company?
B: Shì a, qǐngwèn nín zhǎo shéi?	是啊，请问您找谁？	Yes. May I ask who you would like to visit?
A: Wǒ zhǎo Chén jīnglǐ.	我找陈经理。	I would like to see manager Chen.
B: Hǎode. Nín shì nǎ wèi?	好的。您是哪位？	Ok. May I ask who it is?

A: Wǒ shì Yīngguó dàshǐguǎn de Mǎxiū.	我是英国大使馆的马修。	This is Matthew from the British Embassy.
B: Qǐng děng yíxià.	请等一下。	Wait for a second, please.
A: Xièxie.	谢谢。	Thanks.

❸ (Phoning a hotel) 🔊 13-07

A: Nǐ hǎo, Chángchéng Fàndiàn.	你好，长城饭店。	Hello, Great Wall Hotel.
B: Nǐ hǎo, qǐng zhuǎn yāo líng yāo bā hào fángjiān.	你好，请转1018号房间。	Hello, could you put me through to room 1018 please?
A: Kèrén xìngmíng?	客人姓名？	May I ask the guest's name, please?
B: Chén Yàn.	陈燕。	Chen Yan.
A: Duìbuqǐ, méi rén jiē.	对不起，没人接。	Sorry, no one is answering the phone.

LANGUAGE POINTS

'Gěi 给'

Literally 'to give', it also means 'for' or 'to' and is never put at the end of a sentence. For example:

| Wǒ gěi wǒ péngyou mǎi shū. | 我给我朋友买书。 | I will buy a book for my friend. |
| Wǒ gěi wǒ jiějie dǎ diànhuà. | 我给我姐姐打电话。 | I will telephone my sister. |

EXERCISES

1. Answer the following questions

❶ Qǐngwèn nín zhǎo shéi?
请 问 您 找 谁？

❷ Zhāng jīnglǐ zài ma?
张 经理在 吗？

❸ Wèi, shì diànhuà gōngsī ma?
喂，是 电 话 公 司 吗？

❹ Nín shì nǎ wèi?
您 是 哪 位？

❺ Yào liúyán ma?
要 留言 吗？

2. Say the following in Chinese

❶ make a phone call
❷ leave a message
❸ call back
❹ wait a moment
❺ pass on (a message)
❻ (line) engaged

3. Fill in the blanks with appropriate words

❶ Nǐ zhǎo _____?
你 找 _____?

❷ Nín shì _____ wèi?
您 是 _____ 位?

❸ Wáng xiānsheng _____ ma?
王 先 生 _____ 吗?

❹ _____ Běijīng Fàndiàn ma?
_____ 北 京 饭 店 吗?

❺ _____ bu _____ liúyán?
_____ 不 _____ 留言?

4. Translate the following into Chinese

❶ This is Maria speaking.
❷ May I ask who is calling?
❸ Sorry, you have got the wrong number.
❹ Would you like to leave a message?
❺ Have you got a mobile phone?
❻ What is your mobile phone number?

5. Translate the following into Chinese

❶ A: Hello. Is that the Chinese Embassy?

B: Yes. Who do you like to speak to?

A: May I speak to Mr. Wang, please?

B: Sorry. He is not in at the moment.

❷ A: Hello, this is Dongfang Hotel.

B: Can you put me through to extension 1464, please?

A: Hold on a minute, please.

B: Thank you.

A: Sorry, the line is engaged.

6. Listening comprehension 🔊 13-08

Mark true (T) or false (F) according to the short dialogues.

❶ Mr. Zhang is not in. ( )

❷ This is Edward from the American Embassy. ( )

❸ He will call Mr. Zhang again. ( )

❹ This is Changcheng Hotel. ( )

❺ The line is engaged. ( )

7. Classroom activities

Role play:

You have something urgent to tell your Chinese friend. Please make a phone call to her. Unfortunately, she is not in. Leave a message with her flatmate, and ask for her mobile number.

8. Chinese characters learning

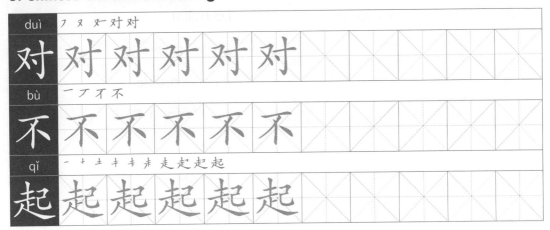

LESSON 14
MONEY & CURRENCY

OBJECTIVES

★ Understanding Chinese currency

★ Exchanging money

★ Finding out the exchange rates

RELEVANT VOCABULARY

Currency 🔊 14-01		
英镑	Yīngbàng	Pound sterling
人民币	Rénmínbì	Chinese currency (RMB)
欧元	Ōuyuán	Euro
美元	Měiyuán	US dollar
日元*	Rìyuán	Japanese yen
卢布*	Lúbù	Russian rouble
块	kuài	yuan (informal)
元*	yuán	yuan
角*	jiǎo	10 cents
分*	fēn	cent
毛*	máo	10 cents (informal)
镑*	bàng	pound

🔊 14-02

想	xiǎng	would like, to think
换	huàn	to change, to exchange
些	xiē	some
钱	qián	money
要	yào	to want, to need, will
百	bǎi	hundred
千*	qiān	thousand
万*	wàn	ten thousand
让	ràng	to let, to allow
汇率	huìlǜ	exchange rate

KEY SENTENCES 🔊 14-03

1. Wǒ xiǎng huàn xiē qián.	我想换些钱。	I'd like to exchange some money, please.
2. Nín xiǎng huàn shénme qián?	您想换什么钱？	What kind of money would you like to exchange?
3. Yì Yīngbàng huàn duōshao Rénmínbì?	一英镑换多少人民币？	How many RMB can I get for one pound?
4. Nín yào huàn duōshao?	您要换多少？	How much would you like to exchange?
5. Ōuyuán zěnme huàn?	欧元怎么换？	How many RMB does one Euro convert to today?
6. Ràng wǒ xiǎngxiang.	让我想想。	Let me think about it.
7. Jīntiān Yīngbàng de huìlǜ shì duōshao?	今天英镑的汇率是多少？	What is the exchange rate of pounds to RMB today?

SITUATIONAL DIALOGUES

❶ (At the airport) 🔊 14-04

A: Xiǎojie, wǒ xiǎng huàn xiē qián.	小姐，我想换些钱。	Miss, I'd like to exchange some money, please.
B: Nín xiǎng huàn shénme qián?	您想换什么钱？	What kind of money would you like to exchange?
A: Yīngbàng. Yì Yīngbàng huàn duōshao Rénmínbì?	英镑。一英镑换多少人民币？	Pounds sterling. How many RMB can I get for one pound?
B: Bā kuài qī. Nín yào huàn duōshao?	八块七。您要换多少？	¥8.7. How much would you like to exchange?
A: Èr bǎi Yīngbàng.	二百英镑。	£200.
A: Gěi nín.	给您。	Here is your money.
B: Xièxie.	谢谢。	Thank you.
A: Bú kèqi.	不客气。	You are welcome.

❷ (In the bank) 🔊 14-05

A: Qǐngwèn, Ōuyuán zěnme huàn?	请问，欧元怎么换？	Excuse me, how much RMB does one Euro convert to today?
B: Yì Ōuyuán huàn qī kuài jiǔ Rénmínbì.	一欧元换七块九人民币。	One Euro converts to ¥7.9.
A: Měiyuán ne?	美元呢？	How about US dollars?
B: Yì Měiyuán huàn liù kuài èr Rénmínbì.	一美元换六块二人民币。	One dollar converts to ¥6.2.
A: Děng yíxià, ràng wǒ xiǎngxiang.	等一下，让我想想。	Wait a moment, let me think about it.

B: Nín xiǎng huàn shénme qián?	您想换什么钱？	What kind of money would you like to exchange?
A: Wǒ xiǎng huàn Měiyuán.	我想换美元。	I'd like to exchange some US dollars.
B: Huàn duōshao?	换多少？	How much would you like to change?
A: Wǔ bǎi Měiyuán.	五百美元。	US $500.

❸ (In the Bank of China) ⏺ 14-06

A: Jīntiān Yīngbàng de huìlù shì duōshao?	今天英镑的汇率是多少？	What is the exchange rate of pounds to RMB today?
B: Yì Yīngbàng huàn jiǔ kuài èr Rénmínbì.	一英镑换九块二人民币。	One pound converts to ¥9.2.
A: Zhēn búcuò.	真不错。	That's not bad.
B: Nín xiǎng huàn duōshao?	您想换多少？	How much would you like to change?
A: Sān bǎi Yīngbàng.	三百英镑。	£300.

LANGUAGE POINTS

1. Chinese currency

It is known as 'Rénmínbì (RMB) 人民币' - the people's currency (RMB). The units of currency are expressed as: yuán 元, 'jiǎo 角', and 'fēn 分'. The largest single unit is 'yuán 元'. There are 10 'jiǎo 角' in one 'yuán 元' and 10 'fēn 分' in one 'jiǎo 角'. In spoken Chinese, 'kuài 块' is used for 'yuán 元', and 'máo 毛' for 'jiǎo 角', but 'fēn 分' remains unchanged.

Formal	Informal	
yuán 元	kuài 块	1 yuán 元 = 10 jiǎo 角 = 100 fēn 分
jiǎo 角	máo 毛	1 jiǎo 角 = 10 fēn 分
fēn 分	fēn 分	

For example:

RMB	Formal	Informal
¥6.00	liù yuán 六元	liù kuài 六块
¥0.50	wǔ jiǎo 五角	wǔ máo 五毛
¥0.08	bā fēn 八分	bā fēn 八分
¥6.58	liù yuán wǔ jiǎo bā fēn 六元五角八分	liù kuài wǔ máo bā (fēn) 六块五毛八（分）

Note that if there is more than one currency term involved in a price the last one can be omitted.

2. Reduplication verbs

As with 'yíxià 一下', reduplication is used to soften a sentence, describing a short action, or a short while. It is normally used in spoken language. For example:

kànkan 看看 = kàn yíxià 看一下 = kàn yi kàn 看一看 - have a look

xiǎngxiang 想想 = xiǎng yíxià 想一下 = xiǎng yi xiǎng 想一想 - think about it

3. 'Ràng 让 + someone + verb'

It means let or allow someone do something. For example:

Ràng wǒ xiǎngxiang.	让我想想。	Let me think about it.
Ràng wǒ lái jièshào yíxià.	让我来介绍一下。	Let me introduce briefly.

EXERCISES

1. Say the following amounts in Chinese using the three monetary units

¥10	¥1.20	¥5.64	¥7.08	¥33.94
¥580	¥99.99	¥382.16	¥40.60	¥5.05
¥0.50	¥2.00	¥4.99	¥119.20	¥49.19

2. Translate the following into English

❶ Wǒ méiyǒu Měiyuán, wǒ yǒu Ōuyuán.
我 没 有 美 元，我 有 欧 元。

❷ Yì Měiyuán néng huàn liù kuài sān máo wǔ Rénmínbì.
一 美 元 能 换 六 块 三 毛 五 人 民 币。

❸ Wǒ qù Zhōngguó Yínháng huàn qián.
我 去 中 国 银 行 换 钱。

❹ Wǒ xiǎng qù Shànghǎi gōngzuò.
我 想 去 上 海 工 作。

❺ Nǐ míngnián qù Běijīng, shì ma?
你 明 年 去 北 京，是 吗?

❻ Wǒmen míngtiān qù Zhōngguó Chéng chī Zhōngguó fàn.
我 们 明 天 去 中 国 城 吃 中 国 饭。

3. Complete the following sentences in Chinese

❶ Chinese money is called _____.
❷ American money is called _____.
❸ Japanese money is called _____.
❹ English money is called _____.
❺ Russian money is called _____.
❻ European money is called _____.

4. Translate the following into Chinese

❶ I am going to the bank.
❷ I'd like to change US dollars.
❸ How many Renminbi does one pound convert to today?
❹ One pound converts to ¥9.1.
❺ How much money would you like to change?
❻ I would like to change $500.

5. Listening comprehension 🔊 14-07

Choose the correct answers according to the phrases you have heard.

❶ a. ¥200	b. ¥100	c. ¥300
❷ a. ¥120	b. ¥220	c. ¥210
❸ a. ¥5.00	b. ¥5.50	c. ¥0.50
❹ a. ¥6.49	b. ¥64.90	c. ¥69.40
❺ a. ¥7.80	b. ¥0.78	c. ¥78.00
❻ a. ¥2.99	b. ¥29.90	c. ¥299
❼ a. ¥0.5	b. ¥0.05	c. ¥5.00
❽ a. ¥39.99	b. ¥33.99	c. ¥3.99

6. Classroom activities

Role play:

You have just arrived in Beijing. You would like to change some Sterling into RMB and HK dollars. Find out what the exchange rates are and decide whether to change now or later.

7. Chinese characters learning

yuán	一 二 テ 元				
元	元	元	元	元	元
jiǎo	′ ′′ ′′ ′′ 角 角 角				
角	角	角	角	角	角
fēn	′ 八 分 分				
分	分	分	分	分	分

LESSON 15
SHOPS
& SHOPPING

OBJECTIVES

★ Asking prices

★ Methods of paying

★ Shopping phrases

RELEVANT VOCABULARY

Stationery ◑ 15-01		
地图	dìtú	map
词典	cídiǎn	dictionary
英汉词典	Yīng-Hàn cídiǎn	English-Chinese dictionary
汉英词典*	Hàn-Yīng cídiǎn	Chinese-English dictionary
杂志*	zázhì	magazine
报纸*	bàozhǐ	newspaper
纸*	zhǐ	paper
笔*	bǐ	pen
铅笔*	qiānbǐ	pencil

Shops and Markets ◑ 15-02		
书店	shūdiàn	bookshop
百货商店*	bǎihuò shāngdiàn	department store

购物中心*	gòuwù zhōngxīn	shopping centre
超市*	chāoshì	supermarket
市场*	shìchǎng	market
中心*	zhōngxīn	centre

Measure Words 🔊 15-03

张	zhāng	(measure word for flat objects)
本	běn	(measure word for books)
斤	jīn	(a traditional unit of weight, equal to 0.5 kg)
支*	zhī	(measure word for pens)

🔊 15-04

多少钱	duōshao qián	how much is it?
怎么卖	zěnme mài	how to sell?
卖	mài	to sell
用	yòng	to use
信用卡	xìnyòngkǎ	credit card
行	xíng	all right, OK
只	zhǐ	only
收	shōu	to accept, to receive
现金	xiànjīn	cash
苹果	píngguò	apple
西瓜	xīguā	water melon
贵	guì	expensive
便宜	piányi	cheap
一共	yígòng	altogether

KEY SENTENCES 🔊 15-05

1. Nín mǎi shénme?	您买什么？	What would you like to buy?
2. Wǒ xiǎng mǎi dìtú.	我想买地图。	I'd like to buy a map.
3. Nín yào jǐ zhāng?	您要几张？	How many would you like to buy?
4. Qǐngwèn, yǒu Yīng-Hàn cídiǎn ma?	请问，有英汉词典吗？	Excuse me, do you have any English-Chinese dictionaries?
5. Wǒ kěyǐ kànkan ma?	我可以看看吗？	Can I have a look, please?
6. Zhè běn cídiǎn duōshao qián?	这本词典多少钱？	How much is the dictionary?
7. Yòng xìnyòngkǎ xíng bu xíng?	用信用卡行不行？	Can I use a credit card?
8. Píngguǒ zěnme mài?	苹果怎么卖？	How much are the apples?
9. Tài guì le. Piányi yìdiǎnr ba?	太贵了！便宜一点儿吧？	Too expensive. Can you make it a bit cheaper?

SITUATIONAL DIALOGUES

❶ (On the way to a bookshop) 🔊 15-06

A: Nǐ qù nǎr?	你去哪儿？	Where are you going?
B: Wǒ qù shūdiàn.	我去书店。	I am going to the bookshop.
A: Mǎi shénme?	买什么？	What do you want to buy?
B: Mǎi dìtú.	买地图。	I'd like to buy a map.

SITUATIONAL DIALOGUES

❷ (In a tourist shop) 🔊 15-07

A: Nín mǎi shénme?	您买什么？	What would you like to buy?
B: Wǒ xiǎng mǎi dìtú.	我想买地图。	I'd like to buy a map.
A: Shénme dìtú?	什么地图？	What kind of map?
B: Běijīng dìtú.	北京地图。	A map of Beijing.
A: Nín yào jǐ zhāng?	您要几张？	How many would you like to buy?
B: Yì zhāng. Duōshao qián?	一张。多少钱？	Only one. How much is it?
A: Liù kuài wǔ.	六块五。	¥6.5.

❸ (In the bookshop) 🔊 15-08

A: Qǐngwèn, yǒu Yīng-Hàn cídiǎn ma?	请问，有英汉词典吗？	Excuse me, do you have any English-Chinese dictionaries?
B: Yǒu.	有。	Yes, we do.
A: Wǒ kěyǐ kànkan ma?	我可以看看吗？	Can I have a look, please?
B: Kěyǐ.	可以。	Yes.

A: Zhè běn duōshao qián?	这本多少钱？	How much is it?
B: Liùshíbā kuài.	六十八块。	¥68.
A: Hǎo, wǒ yào yì běn.	好，我要一本。	OK, I'd like one.
B: Yòng xìnyòngkǎ xíng bu xíng?	用信用卡行不行？	Can I use a credit card?
A: Duìbuqǐ, wǒmen zhǐ shōu xiànjīn.	对不起，我们只收现金。	Sorry, we only accept cash.

❹ (At a market) 🔊 15-09

A: Qǐngwèn, píngguǒ zěnme mài?	请问，苹果怎么卖？	Excuse me, how much are the apples?
B: Liù kuài yì jīn.	六块一斤。	¥6 per half kilogramme.
A: Xīguā ne?	西瓜呢？	How about the water melons?
B: Bā máo qián yì jīn.	八毛钱一斤。	¥0.8 per half kilogramme.
A: Wǒ yào yì jīn píngguǒ hé yí ge dà xīguā.	我要一斤苹果和一个大西瓜。	I would like half a kilogramme of apples and one big water melon.
B: Hǎo. Gěi nín.	好。给您。	OK. Here you are.
A: Yígòng duōshao qián?	一共多少钱？	How much altogether?
B: Yígòng èrshíliù kuài.	一共二十六块。	That's ¥26 altogether.
A: Tài guì le. Piányi yìdiǎnr ba?	太贵了！便宜一点吧？	Too expensive. Can you make it a bit cheaper?
B: Hǎo ba. Gěi èrshíwǔ kuài ba.	好吧，给二十五块吧。	OK, ¥25.

LANGUAGE POINTS

1. '**Xíng bu xíng? 行不行？'**

This is often used at the end of sentences and means 'is it OK'. The similar expression is 'hǎo bu hǎo? 好不好？' and 'zěnmeyàng? 怎么样？'.

2. Asking price

a) Item + duōshao qián? 多少钱？
b) Item + zěnme mài? 怎么卖？

For example:

| Yì běn cídiǎn duōshao qián? | 一本词典多少钱？ | How much is a dictionary? |
| Píngguǒ zěnme mài? | 苹果怎么卖？ | How much are the apples? |

You must put 'qián 钱' with 'duōshao 多少'. 'Duōshao 多少' by itself only means the quantity 'how much/ how many'.

EXERCISES

1. Fill in the blanks with measure words

❶ zhè (　　　) zázhì (magazine)
这 (　　　) 杂志

❷ zhè (　　　) shū (book)
这 (　　　) 书

❸ nà (　　　) huàbào (comic)
那 (　　　) 画报

❹ nà (　　　) zhàopiàn (photo)
那 (　　　) 照片

❺ yì (　　　) yínháng (bank)
一 (　　　) 银行

❻ sān (　　　) shāngdiàn (shop)
三 (　　　) 商店

❼ liǎng (　　　) lǎoshī (teacher)
两 (　　　) 老师

❽ sì (　　　) dìtú (map)
四 (　　　) 地图

❾ wǔ (　　　) xuésheng (student)
五 (　　　) 学生

❿ liù (　　　) cídiǎn (dictionary)
六 (　　　) 词典

2. Fill in the blanks using appropriate words

❶ Zhè běn cídiǎn _____ qián?
这 本词典 _____ 钱？

❷ Nǐmen _____ bu shōu Rìyuán?
你们 _____ 不 收 日 元？

❸ Nǎr _____ chāoshì?
哪 儿 _____ 超 市？

❹ Yòng xìnyòngkǎ _____ ma?
用 信 用 卡 _____ 吗？

❺ Nǐ yào mǎi _____？
你 要 买 _____？

3. Translate the following into Chinese

❶ Go to a bookshop to buy books.
❷ Go to the fishmonger to buy fish.
❸ Go to a bakery to buy bread.
❹ Go to the butcher to buy lamb.
❺ Go to a shoe shop to buy shoes.
❻ Go to a clothes shop to buy garments.
❼ Go to a department store to buy teacups.
❽ Go to a supermarket to buy milk.
❾ Go to a greengrocer to buy vegetables.
❿ Go to a shopping centre to do some shopping.

4. Translate the following into English

❶ Wǒ méiyǒu xiànjīn, wǒ zhǐ yǒu zhīpiào.
我 没 有 现 金，我 只 有 支 票。

❷ Nà ge shūdiàn yǒu hěn duō Yīngyǔ shū.
那 个 书 店 有 很 多 英 语 书。

❸ Wǒ xǐhuan qù gòuwù zhōngxīn mǎi dōngxi.
我 喜 欢 去 购 物 中 心 买 东 西。

❹ Hěn duō xiǎo shāngdiàn bù kěyǐ yòng xìnyòngkǎ.
很 多 小 商 店 不 可 以 用 信 用 卡。

❺ Zhè zhāng dìtú duōshao qián?
这 张 地 图 多 少 钱？

5. Translate the following into Chinese

❶ How much is this dictionary?
❷ Sorry. We only accept cash. We don't accept cheques.
❸ Could you tell me where I can find a shoe shop?
❹ Are there many supermarkets in Beijing?
❺ I'd like to go to a shopping centre on Sunday.

6. Listening comprehension 🔊 15-10

Choose the correct answers according to the short dialogues.

❶ a. bank	b. supermarket	c. bookshop
❷ a. map of Beijing	b. map of China	c. map of London
❸ a. ¥8.50	b. ¥5.80	c. ¥7.80
❹ a. US dollar	b. Pound sterling	c. RMB
❺ a. ¥12.95	b. ¥22.95	c. ¥2.95

7. Classroom activities

Role play:

You are in a small book store. You would like to buy a map of Beijing and a map of China, both in *Pinyin*. Find out if they are available in the store and the prices. You would also like to a buy an English-Chinese dictionary.

8. Chinese characters learning

duō	ノ ク タ タ 多 多							
多	多	多	多	多	多			
shǎo	丨 丬 小 少							
少	少	少	少	少	少			
qián	ノ ト ヒ 乍 牟 钅 钅 钱 钱 钱							
钱	钱	钱	钱	钱	钱			

COLOURS & CLOTHING

OBJECTIVES

★ Describing colours

★ Clothes vocabulary and measure words

★ Buying clothes

RELEVANT VOCABULARY

Clothing 1 🔊 16-01		
服装*	fúzhuāng	garment
衣服*	yīfu	clothing, clothes
大衣	dàyī	overcoat
毛衣	máoyī	jumper, sweater
上衣*	shàngyī	top (clothes)
领带	lǐngdài	tie
衬衫*	chènshān	shirt
西服*	xīfú	suit
T恤衫*	tīxùshān	T-shirt
夹克衫*	jiákèshān	jacket
件	jiàn	(measure word)
条	tiáo	(measure word)

Colours 🔊 16-02

颜色	yánsè	colour
绿（色）	lǜ (sè)	green (colour)
红	hóng	red
黑	hēi	black
蓝	lán	blue
粉	fěn	pink
白	bái	white
紫*	zǐ	purple
黄*	huáng	yellow
灰*	huī	grey
棕*	zōng	brown
深*	shēn	dark (colour)
浅*	qiǎn	light (colour)

🔊 16-03

能	néng	may, can, to have the permission to
试	shì	to try
当然	dāngrán	of course
别的	bié de	other

KEY SENTENCES 🔊 16-04

1. Wǒ xiǎng kànkan nà jiàn dàyī.	我想看看那件大衣。	I'd like to take a look at that overcoat, please.
2. Néng shìshi ma?	能试试吗？	Can I try it on, please?
3. Dāngrán kěyǐ.	当然可以。	Of course you can.
4. Wǒ bù xǐhuan lǜsè de.	我不喜欢绿色的。	I don't like the green one.
5. Yǒu bié de yánsè ma?	有别的颜色吗？	Do you have any other colours?
6. Yǒu piányi de ma?	有便宜的吗？	Do you have any cheaper ones?
7. Yígòng sān bǎi qīshí-liù kuài.	一共三百七十六块。	Altogether that's ¥376.
8. Gěi nín, zhè shì sǐ bǎi kuài.	给您，这是四百块。	Here you are. This is ¥400.

SITUATIONAL DIALOGUES

❶ (In a clothes shop) 🔊 16-05

A: Nín mǎi shénme?	您买什么？	What would you like to buy?

B: Wǒ xiǎng kànkan nà jiàn dàyī. Duōshao qián yí jiàn?	我想看看那件大衣。多少钱一件？	I'd like to take a look at that overcoat, please. How much is it?
A: Jiǔ bǎi jiǔshíjiǔ kuài.	九百九十九块。	¥999.
B: Néng shìshi ma?	能试试吗？	Can I try it on, please?
A: Dāngrán kěyǐ.	当然可以。	Of course you can.
B: Wǒ bù xǐhuan lǜsè de. Yǒu bié de yánsè ma?	我不喜欢绿色的。有别的颜色吗？	I don't like the green one. Do you have any other colours?
A: Yǒu hóng de hé hēi de.	有红的和黑的。	Yes, we have red ones and black ones.
B: Hǎo, wǒ yào yí jiàn hēi de ba.	好，我要一件黑的吧。	OK, I'd like a black one.

❷ (In a department store) 🔊 16-06

A: Qǐngwèn, nà tiáo lǐngdài duōshao qián?	请问，那条领带多少钱？	Excuse me, how much is that tie?
B: Èr bǎi liùshí kuài.	二百六十块。	¥260.
A: Tài guì le! Yǒu piányi de ma?	太贵了！有便宜的吗？	It's too expensive! Do you have any cheaper ones?
B: Yǒu.	有。	Yes, we do.
A: Zhè tiáo lán de duōshao qián?	这条蓝的多少钱？	How much is this blue one?
B: Yì bǎi sānshíwǔ kuài.	一百三十五块。	¥135.
A: Zhè ge hěn piányi.	这个很便宜。	This one is quite cheap.
B: Nín yào yì tiáo ma?	您要一条吗？	Would you like to buy it?
A: Wǒ yào yì tiáo.	我要一条。	Yes, I'd like one.

❸ (In a woollen clothes shop) 🔊 16-07

A: Qǐngwèn, nà jiàn fěn máoyī duōshao qián?	请问，那件粉毛衣多少钱？	Excuse me, how much is that pink jumper?
B: Yì bǎi bāshíbā kuài.	一百八十八块。	¥188.
A: Yǒu bái de ma?	有白的吗？	Do you have it in white?
B: Yǒu.	有。	Yes, we do.
A: Wǒ yào yí jiàn fěn de, yí jiàn bái de.	我要一件粉的，一件白的。	I'd like a pink one and a white one.
B: Yígòng sān bǎi qīshíliù kuài.	一共三百七十六块。	That's ¥376 altogether.
A: Gěi nín, zhè shì sì bǎi kuài.	给您，这是四百块。	Here you are. This is ¥400.
B: Zhǎo nín èrshísì kuài.	找您二十四块。	Here is your ¥24 change.
A: Xièxie.	谢谢。	Thank you.
B: Bú kèqi.	不客气。	You're welcome!

LANGUAGE POINTS

1. 'Néng 能' and 'huì 会'

Both can be translated into 'can' and 'be able to' but 'huì 会' puts more emphasis on the concept of ability and knowledge of a skill. For example:

Tā huì shuō Hànyǔ.	他会说汉语。	He can speak Chinese. (knows how to speak)
Nǐ míngtiān néng lái ma?	你明天能来吗？	Are you able to come tomorrow?

2. Adjective + 'de 的'

It means 'one' or 'ones' when the subjects are understood. For example:

dà de	大的	big one(s)
hǎo de	好的	good one(s)
hóng de	红的	red one(s)
piányi de	便宜的	cheap one(s)

EXERCISES

1. Match the Chinese with the English

❶ hóng qúnzi
红 裙子

a. black overcoat

❷ huáng lǐngdài
黄 领带

b. navy blue jacket

❸ qiǎnfěn máoyī
浅 粉 毛衣

c. white shirt

❹ shēnlǜ kùzi
深绿裤子

d. red skirt

❺ shēnlán jiákèshān
深 蓝 夹克衫

e. brown shoes

❻ bái chènshān
白 衬 衫

f. yellow tie

❼ zōngsè píxié
棕 色皮鞋

g. light pink jumper

❽ hēi dàyī
黑大衣

h. dark green trousers

2. Translate the following into Chinese

❶ two English people ❷ three Chinese books ❸ twelve months

❹ a cup of Chinese tea ❺ four bottles of beer ❻ five pencils

❼ two younger sisters ❽ one elder brother ❾ two children

3. Translate the following into English

❶ Wǒ xiǎng mǎi yí jiàn hóng máoyī.
我 想 买 一 件 红 毛衣。

❷ Qǐngwèn, nà jiàn hēi dàyī duōshao qián?
请 问，那件黑大衣多 少 钱?

❸ Zhè tiáo lǐngdài shì zhēnsī de ma?
这 条 领 带 是 真 丝 的 吗?

❹ Yǒu méiyǒu lǜsè de?
有 没 有 绿 色 的?

❺ Wǒ xiǎng yào nà jiàn qiǎnlánsè de.
我 想 要 那 件 浅 蓝 色 的。

4. Fill in the blanks with the words given

A. huì	B. xiǎng	C. bù néng	D. kěyǐ
会	想	不 能	可以

❶ Shàngwǔ wǒ yǒu shì, (   ) qù dàshǐguǎn.
上 午 我 有 事, (   ) 去 大 使 馆。

❷ Wǒ xiànzài bù (   ) kàn diànshì, (   ) kàn bàozhǐ.
我 现 在 不 (   ) 看 电 视, (   ) 看 报 纸。

❸ Tā bú (   ) shuō Fǎyǔ.
他 不 (   ) 说 法语。

❹ Wǒmen (   ) zài zhèr zuò yíhuìr ma? Dāngrán (   ).
我 们 (   ) 在 这 儿 坐 一 会 儿 吗? 当 然 (   )。

❺ Tā mèimei hěn (   ) dāng yīshēng, bù (   ) dāng lǎoshī.
她 妹 妹 很 (   ) 当 医 生, 不 (   ) 当 老 师。

❻ Wǒ méiyǒu shíjiān, (   ) xiànzài qù kàn diànyǐng.
我 没 有 时 间, (   ) 现 在 去 看 电 影。

❼ Wǒ (   ) dǎ ge diànhuà, (   ) yòng yíxià nǐ de diànhuà ma?
我 (   ) 打 个 电 话, (   ) 用 一 下 你 的 电 话 吗?

5. Listening comprehension 🔊 16-08

Mark true (T) or false (F) according to the short dialogues.

❶ He wants to buy a tie.   (   )
❷ The shop has the overcoat in black.   (   )
❸ She doesn't like pink.   (   )
❹ That jumper is too expensive!   (   )
❺ He wants to buy that blue tie.   (   )

6. Classroom activities

Role play:

You are in a market. You would like to buy a sweater for yourself and two ties for your friends. Talk to the shop owner, choose the right colours, and haggle for the best prices.

7. Chinese characters learning

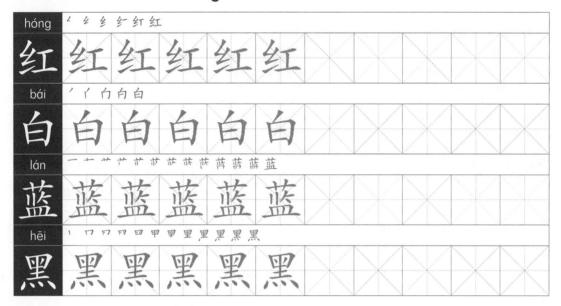

LESSON 17
SIZE & STYLE

OBJECTIVES

★ Asking about size in clothing

★ Giving opinions about clothes

RELEVANT VOCABULARY

Clothing 2 🔊 17-01		
鞋	xié	shoes
皮鞋*	píxié	leather shoes
运动鞋*	yùndòngxié	trainers
裤子	kùzi	trousers
裙子*	qúnzi	skirt
袜子*	wàzi	socks
帽子*	màozi	hat
围巾*	wéijīn	scarf
丝巾*	sījīn	silk scarf
手套	shǒutào	gloves
双	shuāng	(measure word for shoes, socks)
套*	tào	set of (measure word)

Sizes and Shapes 🔊 17-02

号	hào	size
大	dà	large
中	zhōng	medium, middle
小	xiǎo	small, little
特大号*	tèdà hào	extra large
长	cháng	long
短	duǎn	short
肥*	féi	fat, loose-fitting (clothes)
瘦*	shòu	thin, tight (clothes)

🔊 17-03

穿	chuān	to wear, to put on
戴*	dài	to wear, to put on accessories
种	zhǒng	type
正	zhèng	just
合适	héshì	fit, suitable
样子	yàngzi	style
漂亮	piàoliang	pretty, beautiful
还	hái	still
最	zuì	most
看来	kànlái	it seems, it looks as if
真	zhēn	really, truly
难	nán	difficult

KEY SENTENCES 🔊 17-04

1. Wǒ xiǎng kànkan nà shuāng xié, xíng ma?	我想看看那双鞋，行吗？	Can I have a look at that pair of shoes, please?
2. Nín chuān duō dà hào de?	您穿多大号的？	What size do you wear?
3. Zhè zhǒng shàngyī yǒu zǐsè de ma?	这种上衣有紫色的吗？	Do you have this top in purple?
4. Zài Yīngguó wǒ chuān shí'èr hào de.	在英国我穿12号的。	In England I wear size 12.
5. Wǒ xǐhuan zhè zhǒng yàngzi.	我喜欢这种样子。	I like this style.
6. Bú dà bù xiǎo, zhèng héshì.	不大不小，正合适。	It's neither too big nor too small. It fits perfectly!
7. Bù xíng, háishì duǎn.	不行，还是短。	No, (they're) still too short.
8. Zhè shì zuì dà hào.	这是最大号。	This is the largest size.

SITUATIONAL DIALOGUES

❶ (In a shoe shop) 🔊 17-05

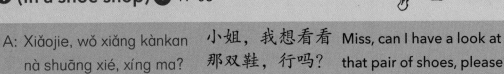

A: Xiǎojie, wǒ xiǎng kànkan nà shuāng xié, xíng ma?	小姐，我想看看那双鞋，行吗？	Miss, can I have a look at that pair of shoes, please?

B: Nǎ shuāng?	哪双？	Which ones?
A: Nà shuāng zōngsè de.	那双棕色的。	Those brown ones.
B: Nín chuān duō dà hào de?	您穿多大号的？	What size do you wear?
A: Sìshí'èr hào de.	42号的。	Size 42.
B: Shìshi zhè shuāng ba.	试试这双吧。	Try this pair.
A: Tài dà le, yǒu méiyǒu xiǎo yìdiǎnr de?	太大了，有没有小一点儿的？	They're too big. Do you have these in a smaller size?
B: Duìbuqǐ, méiyǒu.	对不起，没有。	Sorry, we don't.

❷ (In a clothes shop) 🔊 17-06

A: Xiǎojie, zhè zhǒng shàngyī yǒu zǐsè de ma?	小姐，这种上衣有紫色的吗？	Miss, do you have this top in purple?
B: Yǒu, nín chuān duō dà hào de?	有，您穿多大号的？	Yes, we do. What size do you wear?
A: Bù zhīdào. Zài Yīngguó wǒ chuān shí'èr hào de.	不知道。在英国我穿12号的。	I don't know, but in England I wear size 12.
B: Wǒmen zhèr zhǐyǒu dàhào, zhōnghào hé xiǎohào.	我们这儿只有大号、中号和小号。	We only have large, medium and small sizes.
A: Hǎo, wǒ kàn yi kàn.	好，我看一看。	Ok, I'll have a look at them.
B: Nín shìshi zhè jiàn zhōnghào de ba. Zěnmeyàng?	您试试这件中号的吧。怎么样？	Try this medium-sized one on. How is it?
A: Hǎo, bú dà bù xiǎo, zhèng héshì. Wǒ yě xǐhuan zhè zhǒng yàngzi.	好，不大不小，正合适。我也喜欢这种样子。	Good, it's neither too big nor too small. It fits perfectly! I like the style as well.
B: Nín chuān zhēn piàoliang!	您穿真漂亮！	It looks very good on you.

❸ (In a department store) 🔊 17-07

A: Zhè tiáo kùzi yǒudiǎnr duǎn, yǒu cháng yìdiǎnr de ma?	这条裤子有点儿短，有长一点儿的吗？	These trousers are a little bit short. Do you have longer ones?
B: Yǒu, nín shìshi zhè tiáo.	有，您试试这条。	Yes, we do. Please try these on.
A: Bù xíng, háishì duǎn.	不行，还是短。	No, they're still too short.
B: Duìbuqǐ, zhè shì zuì dà hào.	对不起，这是最大号的。	Sorry, these are the longest ones (largest size).
A: Kànlái, wǒ zài Zhōngguó mǎi yīfu zhēn nán a!	看来，我在中国买衣服真难啊！	Wow, it seems that buying clothes for myself in China is very difficult!

LANGUAGE POINTS

1. 'Yìdiǎnr 一点儿' and 'yǒudiǎnr 有点儿'

'Yìdiǎnr 一点儿' means 'a little' or 'a bit' and can be used to modify nouns. 'Yǒudiǎnr 有点儿' means 'somewhat' or 'a little bit'. It is also used in adverbial phrases to modify adjectives. 'Yǒudiǎnr 有点儿' normally expresses negative meanings. For example:

Wǒ huì shuō yìdiǎnr Hànyǔ.	我会说一点儿汉语。	I can speak a little Chinese.
Wǒ jīntiān yǒudiǎnr lèi.	我今天有点儿累。	I am a little bit tired today.

2. 'Bù 不' + adj. A + 'bù 不' + adj. B

It means 'not too... not too...'. The adjective A and adjective B are normally opposite. For example:

bù cháng bù duǎn	不长不短	not too long, not too short
bú dà bù xiǎo	不大不小	not too big, not too small

3. 'Zuì 最 + adj.'

It means 'the most'. For example:

zuì dà	最大	the largest
zuì hǎo	最好	the best
zuì cháng	最长	the longest

EXERCISES

1. Fill in the blanks with suitable nouns

yì běn   一 本 _____

liǎng ge   两 个 _____

sān zhāng   三 张 _____

sì kuài   四 块 _____

wǔ tiáo   五 条 _____

liù jiàn   六 件 _____

qī zhī   七 支 _____

bā liàng   八 辆 _____

jiǔ bēi   九 杯 _____

shí píng   十 瓶 _____

sān ge   三 个 _____

sì běn   四 本 _____

2. Say the following words and sentences in Chinese

❶ Clothing size: small; medium; large; extra Large

❷ Shoes size: 4; 5; 7; 8; 38; 40; 42

❸ What size shoes do you wear?

❹ What size clothing do you wear?

3. Say the following words in Chinese

❶ the best   ❷ the biggest   ❸ the smallest

❹ the longest   ❺ the least   ❻ the most beautiful

4. Translate the following into Chinese

❶ Could you tell me where I can find a shoe store?

❷ You certainly can't change money in the shop.

❸ Can I try on this pair of shoes for a minute?

5. Translate the following into English

❶ Zhè jiàn yīfu hěn piàoliang, nǐ mǎi yí jiàn ba!
这 件 衣服 很 漂 亮，你 买 一 件 吧！

❷ Yánsè zěnmeyàng? Wǒ kàn hěn piàoliang.
颜 色 怎 么 样？ 我 看 很 漂 亮。

❸ Wǒ chuān zhōnghào de, zhè shì xiǎohào de.
我 穿 中 号 的，这 是 小 号 的。

❹ Nà tiáo qúnzi de yánsè, yàngzi wǒ dōu xǐhuan.
那 条 裙子 的 颜色、样子 我 都 喜欢。

❺ Zhè tiáo kùzi tài cháng le, yǒu méiyǒu duǎn diǎnr de?
这 条 裤子 太 长 了，有 没 有 短 点儿 的？

❻ Nǐ xǐhuan shénme yánsè de yīfu?
你 喜欢 什么 颜色 的 衣服？

❼ Nà tào xīfú wǒ kàn búcuò, nǐ shìshi zěnmeyàng?
那 套 西服 我 看 不错，你 试试 怎么 样？

6. Listening comprehension 🔊 17-08

Choose the correct answers according to the short dialogues.

❶ a. 40	b. 42	c. 44
❷ a. large	b. medium	c. small
❸ a. too big	b. too small	c. neither too big, nor small
❹ a. too long	b. too short	c. neither too long, nor short
❺ a. brown	b. purple	c. black

7. Classroom activities

Role play:

You are in a market shopping for a pair of trousers and shoes. You are not sure about the size. Ask for help and try them on. Discuss the prices with the owner.

8. Chinese characters learning

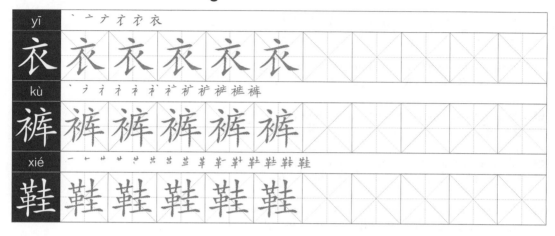

LESSON 18
SUMMARY OF LESSONS 13-17

OBJECTIVES

★ Practicing the vocabulary and grammars from lessons 13-17

★ Cultural insights: shopping in China

KEY PATTERNS

Patterns	Sentences
A gěi 给 B + verb + object	Wǒ gěi wǒ jiějie dǎ diànhuà. 我给我姐姐打电话。
Ràng 让 + someone + verb	Ràng wǒ xiǎngxiang. 让我想想。
Statement, + xíng bu xíng 行不行？	Yòng xìnyòngkǎ, xíng bu xíng？用信用卡，行不行？
Item + duōshao qián 多少钱？	Yì běn cídiǎn duōshao qián？一本词典多少钱？
Item + zěnme mài 怎么卖？	Píngguǒ zěnme mài？苹果怎么卖？
Subject + néng 能/huì 会/kěyǐ 可以 + verb + object	Nǐ míngtiān néng lái ma？你明天能来吗？ Tā huì shuō Hànyǔ. 他会说汉语。 Wǒ kěyǐ kànkan ma？我可以看看吗？
Zuì 最 + adj.	Zhè běn shū zuì hǎo. 这本书最好。
Bù 不 + adj. A + bù 不 + adj. B	bú dà bù xiǎo 不大不小

Frequently Used Measure Words ❶

▶ gè 个: a general measure word

yí ge rén	一个人
liǎng ge xuésheng	两个学生
sān ge píngguǒ	三个苹果

▶ wèi 位： for people (polite)

yí wèi xiānsheng	一位先生
liǎng wèi nǚshì	两位女士
sān wèi lǎoshī	三位老师

▶ běn 本： for books etc.

yì běn shū	一本书
liǎng běn cídiǎn	两本词典
sān běn zázhì	三本杂志

▶ zhāng 张： for flat items

yì zhāng bàozhǐ	一张报纸
liǎng zhāng piào	两张票
sān zhāng dìtú	三张地图

▶ zhī 支： for pens etc.

yì zhī bǐ	一支笔
liǎng zhī qiānbǐ	两支铅笔
sān zhī yān	三支烟

▶ zhī 只： for animals and poultry

yì zhī kǎoyā	一只烤鸭
liǎng zhī māo	两只猫
sān zhī gǒu	三只狗

▶ tiáo 条： for narrow long items

yì tiáo kùzi	一条裤子
liǎng tiáo qúnzi	两条裙子
sān tiáo yú	三条鱼

▶ jiàn 件：for clothes (top) etc.

yí jiàn shàngyī	一件上衣
liǎng jiàn chènshān	两件衬衫
sān jiàn shì	三件事

RELEVANT VOCABULARY

🔊 18-01		
最好	zuìhǎo	best, It's better...
先	xiān	first
然后	ránhòu	then, after
就	jiù	already, as early as
书法	shūfǎ	calligraphy
幅	fú	(measure word for painting)
字画	zìhuà	Chinese painting
字	zì	Chinese characters
画	huà	painting, drawing
春天	chūntiān	spring
又……又……	yòu...yòu...	both...and...
虽然……但是……	suīrán...dànshì...	although...but...
质量	zhìliàng	quality

STORY TIME

1. Listen to the following story and retell it in Chinese 🔊 18-02

Mǎi dōngxi
买东西

Wǒ yǒu yí ge péngyou jiào Mǎxiū,　tā shì
我 有一个 朋 友 叫 马 修，他 是

Yīngguórén,　xiànzài zhù zài Běijīng,　zài Yīngguó
英 国人，现 在 住 在 北 京，在 英 国

dàshǐguǎn gōngzuò. Xīngqīsān,　tā gěi　wǒ dǎ
大 使 馆 工 作。星 期三，他 给 我 打

diànhuà,　shōu xià ge yuè shì Shèngdàn Jié,　tā
电 话，说 下 个 月 是 圣 诞 节，他

yào huí Yīngguó,　xiǎng mǎi xiē　lǐwù,　ràng wǒ
要 回 英 国，想 买 些 礼 物，让 我

gēn tā　yìqǐ　qù shāngdiàn.
跟 他 一起 去 商 店。

Xīngqīliù,　wǒ hé Mǎxiū yìqǐ　qù mǎi dōngxi.　Tā wèn wǒ zài Zhōngguó néng bu néng
星 期六，我 和 马 修 一起 去 买 东 西。他 问 我 在 中 国 能 不 能

yòng xìnyòngkǎ,　wǒ shuō zài dà shāngdiàn kěyǐ,　xiǎo shāngdiàn bù xíng, nǐ zuìhǎo yòng
用 信 用 卡，我 说 在 大 商 店 可以，小 商 店 不 行，你 最 好 用

xiànjīn.
现 金。

Wǒmen xiān qù yínháng huàn qián,　ránhòu qù mǎi dōngxi.　Wǒmen zhǐ　qùle yì jiā
我 们 先 去 银 行 换 钱，然 后 去 买 东 西。我 们 只 去 了 一 家

shāngdiàn,　Mǎxiū jiù mǎile hěn duō dōngxi:　sān tiáo zhēnsī lǐngdài,　lán de, huáng de hé
商 店，马 修 就 买 了 很 多 东 西：三 条 真 丝 领 带，蓝 的、黄 的 和

zǐ de;　liǎng jiàn chènshān,　yí jiàn bái de,　yí jiàn lǜ de;　tā hái gěi tā tàitai mǎile yí
紫 的；两 件 衬 衫，一 件 白 的，一 件 绿 的；他 还 给 他 太 太 买 了 一

jiàn hóng máoyī.
件 红 毛衣。

Mǎxiū de mèimei xǐhuan Zhōngguó shūfǎ,　suǒyǐ tā hái mǎile yì fú Zhōngguó zìhuà.
马 修 的 妹 妹 喜 欢 中 国 书法，所 以 他 还 买 了 一 幅 中 国 字 画，

zhǐ yǒu yí　ge zì:　"chūn",　yīnwèi tā mèimei de shēngrì shì zài chūntiān.　Zhèxiē dōngxi
只 有 一 个 字："春"，因 为 他 妹 妹 的 生 日 是 在 春 天。这 些 东 西

bú guì yě bù piányi,　yígòng yì qiān duō kuài qián.　Mǎxiū shuō:　"jǐ nián yǐqián,　wǒ zài
不 贵 也 不 便 宜，一 共 一 千 多 块 钱。马 修 说："几 年 以 前，我 在

Zhōngguó mǎi de dōngxi yòu piàoliang yòu piányi,　xiànzài suīrán guì duō le,　dànshì zhìliàng
中 国 买 的 东西 又 漂 亮 又 便宜，现在虽然贵多了，但是质量

yě hǎo duō le!"
也好 多了！"

2. Read the story again and then answer the following questions

❶ Who is Mathew? Where does he work?

❷ Why does Mathew want to buy some gifts?

❸ Where did they go on Saturday?

❹ What gifts did Mathew buy? Can you list them?

❺ How much money did Mathew spend on the gifts?

❻ What gift did Mathew buy for his wife?

❼ What gift did Mathew buy for his younger sister? Why?

❽ Why have the prices in China risen?

CULTURAL INSIGHTS

Shopping in China

When you are shopping in China there are a wide variety of places to go.

In the recent past, foreign visitors were frequently directed towards 'friendship stores' that provided luxury goods to foreign visitors. Silk, gold or silver jewellery, jade, embroidered tablecloths, paintings and pottery were all available. All were usually very good quality but the shops were expensive and there was no bargaining. Hotels designated to receive foreign visitors had similar shops.

Although such outlets are still available, the last couple of decades have seen modern shopping centres springing up all over China where foreign visitors can find well known international stores among numerous smart local shops and similar good quality items can be bought at more competitive prices.

In many of these shops, particularly the larger ones, there are plenty of sales assistants willing to help but the payment system can be confusing to foreigners. Instead of paying for goods at the counter in the normal way, the assistant will issue a docket for your purchase which you take to a central cash kiosk to pay. The docket will then be stamped and you return to collect your purchase from the shop assistant.

Local markets and market stalls are also widely available but the goods are sometimes of more dubious quality and shoppers are expected to bargain with the stallholder. However, if you are travelling around China it is well worth looking at the local products, particularly in the smaller towns. Not only will be products often be cheaper than in the larger stores but, especially in areas where ethnic minorities live, products will be offered that are locally produced and difficult to find anywhere else in China. The items of greatest interest to a foreign visitor might be craft objects or specially embroidered garments although local foods can also be well worth trying.

CHINESE CHARACTERS LEARNING

xìn	ノ イ イ´ 亻宀 亻宀 信 信 信				
信	信	信	信	信	信
yòng	ノ 几 月 月 用				
用	用	用	用	用	
kǎ	丨 卜 上 卡 卡				
卡	卡	卡	卡	卡	卡

FOOD
& RESTAURANTS

OBJECTIVES

★ Ordering dishes

★ Asking for bills

★ Giving comments about dishes

RELEVANT VOCABULARY

Food 🔊 19-01		
素菜	sùcài	vegetable dish
豆腐	dòufu	bean curd, tofu
菠菜	bōcài	spinach
鱼	yú	fish
鸡	jī	chicken
猪肉	zhūròu	pork
牛肉	niúròu	beef
海鲜	hǎixiān	seafood
虾	xiā	prawn, shrimp
青菜	qīngcài	green vegetable
汤	tāng	soup
米饭	mǐfàn	cooked rice
炒饭	chǎofàn	fried rice

白饭	báifàn	plain rice
面条*	miàntiáo	noodles
汉堡包*	hànbǎobāo	hamburger
三明治*	sānmíngzhì	sandwich

🔊 19-02

欢迎	huānyíng	to welcome
光临	guānglín	presence, to be here
加	jiā	to add in
桌子	zhuōzi	table
椅子	yǐzi	chair
把	bǎ	(measure word for chairs)
没问题	méi wèntí	no problem
问题	wèntí	problem, question
菜单	càidān	menu
服务员	fúwùyuán	waiter / waitress
点菜	diǎncài	to order dishes
菜	cài	dish, vegetable
素食者	sùshízhě	vegetarian
就	jiù	just
或者	huòzhě	or
还是	háishì	or (only used in questions)
结账	jiézhàng	to settle the bill
买单*	mǎidān	to settle the bill
马上	mǎshàng	immediately, right now
好吃	hǎochī	delicious, tasty

KEY SENTENCES 🔊 19-03

1. Méi wèntí.	没问题。	No problem.
2. Wǒmen diǎncài.	我们点菜。	We'd like to order.
3. Wǒmen dōu shì sùshízhě, bù chī ròu.	我们都是素食者，不吃肉。	We're all vegetarians. We don't eat meat.
4. Nà jiù yào dòufu huòzhě bōcài ba.	那就要豆腐或者菠菜吧。	In that case, you can have either tofu or spinach.
5. Yào yì tiáo yú, yì zhī jī hé yí ge qīngcài.	要一条鱼，一只鸡和一个青菜。	We'd like a fish, a chicken and some vegetables.
6. Yào chǎofàn háishì báifàn?	要炒饭还是白饭？	Do you want fried rice or plain rice?
7. Qǐng jiézhàng.	请结账。	May I have the bill please?
8. Wǒ mǎshàng lái.	我马上来。	I'll come to you right now.
9. Nǐmen de cài zhēn hǎochī.	你们的菜真好吃。	The food is really delicious here!

SITUATIONAL DIALOGUES

❶ (Going into a restaurant) 🔊 19-04

A: Huānyíng guānglín, jǐ wèi?	欢迎光临，几位？	Welcome, how many people?

B: Sān wèi.	三位。	Three people.
A: Qǐng zuò zhèr. Zhǐ yǒu yì zhāng xiǎo zhuōzi le. Jiā yì bǎ yǐzi, xíng ma?	请坐这儿。只有一张小桌子了，加一把椅子，行吗？	Please sit here. There is only one small table left. Is it OK to bring a chair?
B: Méi wèntí.	没问题。	No problem.
A: Zhè shì càidān.	这是菜单。	This is the menu.
B: Xièxie.	谢谢。	Thanks.

❷ (Ordering dishes) 🔊 19-05

A: Fúwùyuán, wǒmen diǎncài.	服务员，我们点菜。	Waiter, we'd like to order.
B: Hǎo, nǐmen yào shénme cài?	好，你们要什么菜？	OK. What would you like to order?
A: Wǒmen zhǐ yào sùcài.	我们只要素菜。	We'd like vegetarian dishes only.
B: Zhǐ yào sùcài?	只要素菜？	Only vegetarian food?
A: Duì, wǒmen dōu shì sùshízhě, bù chī ròu.	对，我们都是素食者，不吃肉。	Yes, we're all vegetarians. We don't eat meat.
B: Nà jiù yào dòufu huòzhě bōcài ba.	那就要豆腐或者菠菜吧。	In that case, you can have either tofu or spinach.

❸ (Discussing the menu) 🔊 19-06

A: Nǐmen hǎo, yào shénme cài?	你们好，要什么菜？	Hello, what dish would you like to order?
B: Wǒmen kànkan càidān ba.	我们看看菜单吧。	Can we look at the menu?

A: Jī, yā, yú, ròu, wǒmen dōu yǒu.	鸡、鸭、鱼、肉，我们都有。	We have chicken, duck, fish and meat.
B: Wǒmen bù chī zhūròu.	我们不吃猪肉。	We don't eat pork.
A: Wǒmen yǒu niúròu, yángròu hé jī.	我们有牛肉、羊肉和鸡。	We have beef, lamb and chicken.
B: Yǒu hǎixiān ma?	有海鲜吗？	Do you have any seafood?
A: Yǒu yú, yǒu xiā, nín yào shénme?	有鱼，有虾，您要什么？	Yes, we have fish and shrimp. What would you like?
B: Yào yì tiáo yú, yì zhī jī hé yí ge qīngcài.	要一条鱼，一只鸡和一个青菜。	We'd like a fish, a chicken and some vegetables.
A: Yào bu yào tāng?	要不要汤？	Would you like soup?
B: Bú yào. Yǒu mǐfàn ma?	不要。有米饭吗？	No. Do you have rice?
A: Yǒu. Nín yào chǎofàn háishì báifàn?	有。您要炒饭还是白饭？	Yes. Do you want fried rice or plain rice?
B: Báifàn.	白饭。	Plain rice.

❹ (Settling the bill) 🔊 19-07

A: Fúwùyuán, qǐng jiézhàng.	服务员，请结账。	Waiter, may we have the bill please?
B: Hǎo, wǒ mǎshàng lái.	好，我马上来。	OK, I'll come to you right now.
A: Nǐmen de cài zhēn hǎochī.	你们的菜真好吃。	The food is really delicious here.
B: Xièxie.	谢谢。	Thank you.

LANGUAGE POINTS

1. '(Háishì 还是' **and** '(huòzhě 或者'

Both translate into English as 'or'. 'Háishì 还是' is used in a choice type question whereas 'huòzhě 或者' is used in a statement, which means 'either...or'. For example:

A + háishì 还是 + B?

Nǐ xǐhuan chī jī háishì chī yú?	你喜欢吃鸡还是吃鱼?	Do you like to eat chicken or fish?

A + huòzhě 或者 + B.

Nǐ kěyǐ qù Běijīng huòzhě qù Shànghǎi.	你可以去北京或者去上海。	You can either go to Beijing or Shanghai.

2. '(Hǎochī 好吃'

Literally means 'good to eat' but actually means 'delicious' or 'very tasty'. The same pattern can be used in:

hǎohē	好喝	good to drink
hǎokàn	好看	nice-looking
hǎotīng	好听	pleasant to hear

EXERCISES

1. Fill in the blanks with appropriate words

❶ Nǐ shì Zhōngguórén _____ Rìběnrén?
你是 中 国人_____ 日本人?

❷ Nǐ xǐhuan hē hóngchá _____ lǜchá?
你喜欢 喝 红茶 _____ 绿茶?

❸ Wǒmen qù chī Yìdàlì fàn _____?
我们 去吃意大利饭 _____?

❹ Nǐ xǐhuan _____ xǐhuan chī Fǎguó fàn?
你喜欢 _____ 喜欢 吃法国饭?

❺ _____ yǒu Zhōngguó fànguǎn?
_____ 有 中 国饭馆?

2. Fill in the blanks with verbs and translate into English

❶ Rìběn yīnyuè hěn hǎo _____
日本 音乐 很 好 _____

❷ Zhōngguó fàn hěn hǎo _____
中 国 饭 很 好 _____

❸ zhè jiàn yīfu hěn hǎo _____
这 件 衣服 很 好 _____

❹ lǜchá hěn hǎo _____
绿茶 很 好 _____

3. Translate the following into Chinese

❶ What would you like to eat?

❷ Do you want coffee or tea?

❸ Wait a moment, please.

❹ This restaurant's dishes are delicious.

❺ May I have the bill, please?

❻ May I ask how many of you are there?

❼ This is a menu. Have a look, please.

4. Say the following sentences in English

❶ Wǒmen hē Zhōngguóchá ba.
我 们 喝 中 国茶 吧。

❷ Nǐ xǐhuan hē hóngchá háishì lǜchá?
你喜欢 喝 红 茶 还是 绿茶?

❸ Jīntiān wǒ qǐngkè, nǐ xiǎng chī shénme?
今天 我 请客, 你 想 吃 什么?

❹ Zhèr yǒu hànbǎobāo hé sānmíngzhì, nǐ xiǎng chī shénme?
这儿有 汉 堡包 和 三 明 治, 你 想 吃 什么?

❺ Nǐ chī ròu ma? Nǐ shì bu shì sùshízhě?
你 吃 肉 吗? 你 是 不 是 素食者?

❻ Nǐ de nǚ péngyou shì Zhōngguórén háishì Měiguórén?
你 的 女 朋 友 是 中 国 人 还是 美 国 人?

5. Listening comprehension 🔊 19-08

Choose the correct answers according to the short dialogues.

❶ a. vegetables	b. meat	c. seafood
❷ a. prawn only	b. fish only	c. fish and prawn
❸ a. fried rice	b. plain rice	c. fried egg rice
❹ a. beef	b. lamb	c. pork
❺ a. chicken	b. duck	c. chicken and duck

6. Classroom activities

Role play:

Four of you are in a Chinese restaurant. Only you can speak Chinese. Please order the dishes and drinks, and then settle the bill.

7. Chinese characters learning

jī	フ ヌ ヌ' 刄 刄 鸡 鸡							
鸡	鸡	鸡	鸡	鸡	鸡			
yā	丨 冂 冂 日 甲 甲' 甲勹 甲勹 鸭 鸭							
鸭	鸭	鸭	鸭	鸭	鸭			
yú	ノ ク ク �615 �615 角 鱼 鱼							
鱼	鱼	鱼	鱼	鱼	鱼			
ròu	丨 冂 内 内 肉 肉							
肉	肉	肉	肉	肉	肉			

CAFÉS, PUBS & DRINKS

OBJECTIVES

★ Ordering drinks

★ Discussing drinks

★ Talking about past experiences

RELEVANT VOCABULARY

Drinks 🔊 20-01		
酒	jiǔ	all kinds of alcohol drinks
啤酒	píjiǔ	beer
白酒*	báijiǔ	a Chinese sprite
葡萄酒*	pútaojiǔ	wine
名酒	míngjiǔ	well-known liquor
矿泉水*	kuàngquánshuǐ	mineral water
果汁	guǒzhī	fruit juice
橘子汁*	júzizhī	orange juice
咖啡	kāfēi	coffee
茶	chá	tea
绿茶	lùchá	green tea
红茶*	hóngchá	black tea
花茶*	huāchá	jasmine tea

乌龙茶*	wūlóngchá	wulong tea
菊花茶*	júhuāchá	chrysanthemum tea
牛奶	niúnǎi	milk
可乐	kělè	Coke

◀) 20-02

有名	yǒumíng	famous
过	guò	have ever done (verbal suffix)
味道	wèidào	taste
辣	là	spicy (or strong for alcoholic drinks)
极	jí	extremely
冰	bīng	ice
杯	bēi	a cup of, a glass of (measure word)
杯子*	bēizi	cup, glass
瓶	píng	a bottle of (measure word)
瓶子*	píngzi	bottle

Proper Nouns ◀) 20-03

青岛	Qīngdǎo	Qingdao (city name)
青岛啤酒	Qīngdǎo píjiǔ	Tsingtao beer
茅台	Máotái	Maotai (a kind of baijiu)

KEY SENTENCES 🔊 20-04

1. Qīngdǎo píjiǔ hěn yǒumíng, shì ma?	青岛啤酒很有名，是吗？	Tsingtao beer is very famous, isn't it?
2. Nǐ hēguo Qīngdǎo píjiǔ ma?	你喝过青岛啤酒吗？	Have you ever drunk Tsingtao beer?
3. Hǎohē ma?	好喝吗？	Does it taste nice?
4. Hǎohē jíle.	好喝极了。	Yes, it's extremely good.
5. Nǐ hē méi hēguo Máotái?	你喝没喝过茅台？	Have you ever tried (drunk) Maotai before?
6. Wèidào zěnmeyàng?	味道怎么样？	What does it taste like?
7. Nǐmen hē diǎnr shénme?	你们喝点儿什么？	What would you like to drink?
8. Kāfēi jiā niúnǎi hé táng ma?	咖啡加牛奶和糖吗？	Would you like milk and sugar with your coffee?

SITUATIONAL DIALOGUES

❶ (In a pub) 🔊 20-05

A: Qīngdǎo píjiǔ hěn yǒumíng, shì ma?	青岛啤酒很有名，是吗？	Tsingtao beer is very famous, isn't it?
B: Shì a, hěn yǒumíng.	是啊，很有名。	Yes, it's very famous.
A: Nǐ hēguo Qīngdǎo píjiǔ ma?	你喝过青岛啤酒吗？	Have you ever drunk Tsingtao beer?

B:	Hēguo.	喝过。	Yes, I've drunk some (before).
A:	Hǎohē ma?	好喝吗？	Does it taste nice?
B:	Hǎohē jíle.	好喝极了。	Yes, it's extremely good.

❷ (In a restaurant) ◉ 20-06

A:	Nǐ hē méi hēguo Máotái?	你喝没喝过茅台？	Have you ever tried Maotai before?
B:	Méi hēguo. Shénme shì Máotái?	没喝过。什么是茅台？	No. What's Maotai?
A:	Máotái shì Zhōngguó míngjiǔ.	茅台是中国名酒。	Maotai is a famous brand of Chinese liquor.
B:	Nǐ hēguo ma?	你喝过吗？	Have you ever drunk it before?
A:	Wǒ hēguo.	我喝过。	Yes, I have.
B:	Wèidào zěnmeyàng?	味道怎么样？	What does it taste like?
A:	Bù hǎohē, là jíle.	不好喝，辣极了。	It's not that good. It's too strong.

❸ (In a café) ◉ 20-07

| A: | Nǐmen hē diǎnr shénme? | 你们喝点儿什么？ | What would you like to drink? |

B: Lái liǎng bēi kāfēi, yì bēi lǜchá, yì píng bīng kělè hé yì bēi guǒzhī.	来两杯咖啡，一杯绿茶，一瓶冰可乐和一杯果汁。	Two coffees, a cup of green tea, a bottle of iced Coke and a glass of fruit juice please.
A: Kāfēi jiā niúnǎi hé táng ma?	咖啡加牛奶和糖吗？	Would you like milk and sugar with your coffee?
B: Bù jiā, xièxie.	不加，谢谢。	No, thank you.

LANGUAGE POINTS

1. 'Verb + guò 过'

This indicates that something happened in the indefinite past. The emphasis is on the past experience as opposed to when it happened. Expressions denoting definite past (e.g. yesterday, last year) are usually not used together with 'guò 过'. 'Verb + guò 过' is similar to the English 'have ever been...' or 'have ever done...'. The negative is:

méi (yǒu) 没（有）+ verb + guò 过……

Nǐ qùguo Zhōngguó ma?	你去过中国吗？	Have you ever been to China?
Qùguo.	去过。	Yes, I have.
Wǒ méi qùguo (Zhōngguó).	我没去过(中国)。	I have never been to China.

2. 'Adj. + jíle 极了'

It means 'extremely'. For example:

máng jíle	忙极了	extremely busy
hǎo jíle	好极了	great, excellent
dà jíle	大极了	huge, enormous

EXERCISES

1. Answer the following questions

❶ Nǐ hēguo Qīngdǎo píjiǔ ma?
你 喝过 青 岛 啤酒 吗？

❷ Nǐ qùguo Běijīng ma?
你 去过 北 京 吗？

❸ Máotái shì shénme?
茅 台 是 什 么？

❹ Lǜchá hǎohē bu hǎohē?
绿茶 好喝不 好喝？

❺ Nǐ cháng qù jiǔbā ma?
你 常 去 酒吧 吗？

2. First change the following sentences into yes / no questions and then change them into negative sentences

❶ Wǒ kànguo Yīngguó diànyǐng.
我 看过 英 国 电 影。

❷ Wǒ mèimei xuéguo Déyǔ.
我 妹 妹 学 过 德 语。

❸ Wǒ bàba qùguo Xiānggǎng.
我 爸爸 去过 香 港。

❹ Wǒ de Zhōngguó péngyou láiguo wǒ jiā.
我 的 中 国 朋 友 来过 我 家。

❺ Tāmen chīguo Fǎguó fàn.
他们 吃过 法国 饭。

❻ Tā tīngguo Rìběn yīnyuè.
她 听 过 日本 音乐。

3. Fill in the blanks with measure words

❶ sān _____ shū
三 _____ 书

❷ liù _____ péngyou
六 _____ 朋 友

❸ yì _____ kùzi
一 _____ 裤子

❹ jiǔ _____ táng
九 _____ 糖

❺ wǔ _____ shūdiàn
五 _____ 书 店

❻ shí _____ rén
十 _____ 人

❼ sì _____ chá
四 _____ 茶

❽ liǎng _____ píjiǔ
两 _____ 啤酒

❾ yì _____ dìtú
一 _____ 地图

❿ sān _____ yú
三 _____ 鱼

⓫ liǎng _____ qìchē
两 _____ 汽车

⓬ qī _____ kělè
七 _____ 可乐

⓭ liǎng _____ bǐ
两 _____ 笔

⓮ sān _____ niúnǎi
三 _____ 牛奶

⓯ bā _____ dàyī
八 _____ 大衣

4. Fill in the blanks with appropriate words

❶ Běijīng kǎoyā hěn _____.
北京 烤鸭 很 _____。

❷ Nín xiǎng hē _____ shénme?
您 想 喝_____ 什 么？

❸ Tā méi qù _____ Yīngguō.
他 没 去_____ 英 国。

❹ Kāfēi _____ táng ma?
咖啡 _____ 糖 吗？

❺ Qīngdǎo píjiǔ hǎohē _____ le.

青 岛 啤酒 好喝 _____ 了。

5. Translate the following into Chinese

❶ Beijing roast duck is very famous.

❷ Have you been to Hong Kong?

❸ What do you think of Tsingtao beer?

❹ I have read that Chinese book. It is quite good.

❺ This dish is extremely spicy.

❻ Does the red wine taste good?

6. Listening comprehension 🔊 20-08

Mark true (T) or false (F) according to the short dialogues.

❶ Tsingtao beer doesn't taste very good.   (   )

❷ He has tried Chinese Maotai before.   (   )

❸ He would like a bottle of coke.   (   )

❹ This beer tastes nice.   (   )

❺ He doesn't want cream with his coffee.   (   )

7. Classroom activities

Role play:

You are in a Starbucks café with your Chinese friend. Tell him/her what you would like to drink then discuss with him/her the various Chinese and western drinks that you have tried before.

8. Chinese characters learning

pí	丿 冂 冂 冂' 冂⁺ 吖 叻 啤 啤 啤						
啤	啤	啤	啤	啤	啤		
jiǔ	丶 丶 氵 汀 汀 沂 沔 酒 酒 酒						
酒	酒	酒	酒	酒	酒		
nǎi	乚 夊 女 奶 奶						
奶	奶	奶	奶	奶	奶		
chá	一 十 艹 芐 芖 茇 茶 茶						
茶	茶	茶	茶	茶	茶		

LESSON 21
INTERNET
& COMMUNICATION

OBJECTIVES

★ Asking for information in a hotel

★ Asking about internet services

★ Talking about past events

RELEVANT VOCABULARY

Internet 🔊 21-01		
无线网	wúxiàn wǎng	Wi-Fi
登录名	dēnglùmíng	username
密码	mìmǎ	password
发	fā	to send
电子邮件	diànzǐ yóujiàn	e-mail
查	chá	to check
电脑	diànnǎo	computer
宽带	kuāndài	broadband
下载*	xiàzài	to download

🔊 21-02		
里	lǐ	inside
护照	hùzhào	passport

楼	lóu	floor, building
餐厅	cāntīng	canteen
游泳池	yóuyǒngchí	swimming pool
聊天	liáotiān	to chat
刚才	gāngcái	just now
参观	cānguān	to visit
博物院／博物馆	bówùyuàn / bówùguǎn	museum
剧院	jùyuàn	theatre
歌舞	gēwǔ	singing and dancing performance

Proper Nouns 🔊 21-03

故宫	Gùgōng	the Forbidden City, the Palace Museum
天安门	Tiān'ānmén	Tian'anmen
前门*	Qiánmén	Qianmen

KEY SENTENCES 🔊 21-04

1. Xiǎojie, fàndiàn lǐ yǒu wúxiàn wǎng ma?	小姐，饭店里有无线网吗？	Miss, is there Wi-Fi in the hotel?
2. Yóuyǒngchí zài jǐ lóu?	游泳池在几楼？	Which floor is the swimming pool on?
3. Gāngcái nǐ qù nǎr le?	刚才你去哪儿了？	Where have you been just now?
4. Wǒ hé péngyou zài wǎngshang liáotiān le.	我和朋友在网上聊天了。	I was chatting with my friends online.

5.	Dāngrán le.	当然了。	Of course.
6.	Wǒ zěnme bù zhīdào?	我怎么不知道？	How come I didn't know?
7.	Nǐ shì shénme shíhou qù de?	你是什么时候去的？	When did you go?
8.	Xiàwǔ wǒ qù cānguān Gùgōng Bówùyuàn le.	下午我去参观故宫博物院了。	I went to visit the Palace Museum in the afternoon.

SITUATIONAL DIALOGUES

❶ (At the hotel reception desk) 🔊 21-05

A:	Xiǎojie, fàndiàn lǐ yǒu wúxiàn wǎng ma?	小姐，饭店里有无线网吗？	Miss, is there Wi-Fi in the hotel?
B:	Yǒu, dēnglùmíng shì nǐ de fángjiān hào, mìmǎ shì nǐ de hùzhào hào.	有，登录名是你的房间号，密码是你的护照号。	Yes, the username is your room number and the password is your passport number.
A:	Xièxie. Qǐngwèn, zǎofàn jǐ diǎn kāishǐ?	谢谢。请问,早饭几点开始？	Thank you. May I ask, what time does breakfast start?
B:	Zǎoshang liù diǎn bàn. Zài yī lóu cāntīng.	早上六点半。在一楼餐厅。	6:30 am. It's in the canteen on the first floor.
A:	Yóuyǒngchí zài jǐ lóu?	游泳池在几楼？	Which floor is the swimming pool on?
B:	Zài bā lóu.	在八楼。	The 8th floor.

❷ (In the hotel lobby) 🔊 21-06

A: Gāngcái nǐ qù nǎr le?	刚才你去哪儿了？	Where have you been just now?
B: Wǒ zài fángjiān lǐ fā diànzǐ yóujiàn, hái hé péngyou zài wǎngshang liáotiān le.	我在房间里发电子邮件，还和朋友在网上聊天了。	I was sending e-mails in my room. I was also chatting with my friends online.
A: Ó, zhèr yǒu wúxiàn wǎng?	噢，这儿有无线网？	Oh, is there Wi-Fi here?
B: Dāngrán le.	当然了。	Of course.
A: Wǒ zěnme bù zhīdào?	我怎么不知道？	How come I didn't know?
B: Nǐ xiànzài bú shì zhīdào le ma?	你现在不是知道了吗？	You know now, don't you?
A: Nà wǒ néng yòng nǐ de diànnǎo chá yíxià wǒ de diǎnzǐ yóujiàn ma?	那我能用你的电脑查一下我的电子邮件吗？	In that case, can I use your computer to check my e-mails?
B: Méi wèntí.	没问题。	No problem.

❸ (Chatting online) 🔊 21-07

A: Jīntiān nǐ zuò shénme le?	今天你做什么了？	What did you do today?

B: Wǒ qù Tiān'ānmén le.	我去天安门了。	I went to Tian'anmen Square.
A: Nǐ shì shénme shíhou qù de?	你是什么时候去的？	When did you go?
B: Wǒ shì shàngwǔ qù de.	我是上午去的。	I went there in the morning.
A: Xiàwǔ ne?	下午呢？	What about in the afternoon?
B: Xiàwǔ wǒ qù cānguān Gùgōng Bówùyuàn le.	下午我去参观故宫博物院了。	I went to visit the Palace Museum in the afternoon.
A: Wǎnshang ne?	晚上呢？	What about in the evening?
B: Péngyou lái kàn wǒ, wǒmen yìqǐ qù jùyuàn kàn Zhōngguó gēwǔ le.	朋友来看我，我们一起去剧院看中国歌舞了。	My friends came to see me. We went to a theatre to watch Chinese singing and dancing together.

LANGUAGE POINTS

1. Particle 'le 了'

There are many uses for the particle 'le 了'. In this lesson it indicates that an event happened in the past (especially when a time related phrase or word such as 'yesterday' is used). 'Méi 没' is used in a negative sentence and 'le 了' is omitted. For example:

Zuótiān wǒ qù kàn péngyou le.	昨天我去看朋友了。	I went to see my friends yesterday.
Zuótiān wǒ méi qù kàn péngyou.	昨天我没去看朋友。	I didn't go to see my friends yesterday.

2. 'Verb + guò 过' and 'Verb + le 了'

The distinction between past experience 'guò 过' and completed action 'le 了' can be seen from the following examples:

Tā qùle Zhōngguó.	她去了中国。	She has gone to China. (She is in China now.)
Tā qùguo Zhōngguó.	她去过中国。	She has been to China before. (She is not in China now.)

3. 'Shì...de 是……的' construction

When an event or action took place in the past, the 'shì...de 是……的' construction is used to highlight the circumstances of the event or action. It is usually used when the interest is in time, location, method and manner. The pattern is:

Subject + shì 是 + circumstance + verb + de 的

Nǐ shì zài nǎr mǎi de?	你是在哪儿买的？	Where did you buy it?
Ni shì zěnme lái de?	你是怎么来的？	How did you come?

EXERCISES

1. Match the Chinese with the English

❶ diànshì
电视

❷ diànnǎo
电脑

❸ diànhuà
电话

❹ diànzǐ yóujiàn
电子邮件

❺ chuánzhēn
传真

a. telephone

c. fax

d. e-mail

e. television

f. computer

2. Translate the following into Chinese

❶ check e-mail
❷ send a fax
❸ go on the internet
❹ write a letter
❺ post a letter
❻ make a phone call
❼ of course
❽ no problem
❾ excellent

3. Say the following sentences in Chinese

❶ How can I help you?
❷ Where have you been?
❸ I went to the shopping centre yesterday.
❹ I've had my breakfast already.
❺ I went to a Chinese restaurant with my friends last night.

4. Change the following sentences into negatives

❶ Zuótiān wǎnshang wǒ kàn diànshì le.
昨天晚上我看电视了。

❷ Xīngqīliù wǎnshang wǒ qù kàn péngyou le.
星期六晚上我去看朋友了。

❸ Yínháng guānmén le.
银 行 关 门 了。

❹ Tā qù shāngdiàn mǎi dōngxi le.
他 去 商 店 买 东 西 了。

❺ Wǒ chī wǔfàn le.
我 吃 午 饭 了。

5. Rewrite the following sentences using the (shì...de 是……的) construction

❶ Nǐ zài nǎr chūshēng?
你 在 哪 儿 出 生?

❷ Tā cóng Lúndūn lái.
他 从 伦 敦 来。

❸ Tā kāichē qù Bālí.
她 开 车 去 巴 黎。

❹ Wǒ jiǔ diǎn dào dàshǐguǎn.
我 九 点 到 大 使 馆。

6. Listening comprehension ◉ 21-08

Choose the correct answers according to the short dialogues.

❶ a. shop	b. bank	c. hospital
❷ a. check e-mail	b. send e-mail	c. make a phone call
❸ a. café	b. restaurant	c. pub
❹ a. the 1st floor	b. the 2nd floor	c. the 3rd floor
❺ a. send fax	b. send e-mail	c. surf the internet

7. Classroom activities

Talk about what you did last weekend with your classmates and find out what they did.

8. Chinese characters learning

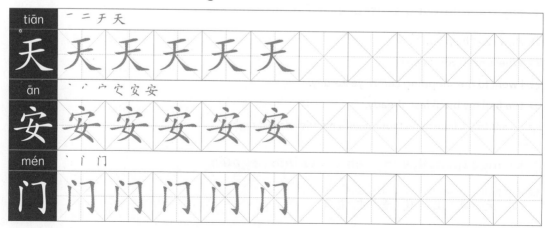

tiān 天	一 二 于 天
	天 天 天 天 天

ān 安	丶 丷 宀 宀 安 安
	安 安 安 安 安

mén 门	丶 门 门
	门 门 门 门 门

LESSON 22
TRAVEL
& TRANSPORT

OBJECTIVES

★ Talking about travel methods

★ Asking about how to get to a place

RELEVANT VOCABULARY

Transportation 🔊 22-01		
地铁	dìtiě	underground, tube
车	chē	vehicle
火车	huǒchē	train
公共汽车	gōnggòng qìchē	public bus
飞机	fēijī	airplane
船	chuán	boat, ship
出租车*	chūzūchē	taxi
长途汽车*	chángtú qìchē	coach
摩托车*	mótuōchē	motorbike
自行车	zìxíngchē	bicycle
走路	zǒulù	to walk, to go on foot
开车	kāichē	to drive (a car)
坐	zuò	to sit, by
骑	qí	to ride

走	zǒu	to walk, to leave, to go
打的*	dǎdī	to call a taxi

Places 🔊 22-02

站	zhàn	station, stop
地铁站	dìtiě zhàn	subway station
火车站	huǒchē zhàn	train station
汽车站*	qìchē zhàn	bus stop
加油站*	jiāyóu zhàn	petrol station
飞机场*	fēijī chǎng	airport
停车场*	tíngchē chǎng	car park

🔊 22-03

离	lí	from (in giving distances)
远	yuǎn	far
近	jìn	near, close
附近	fùjìn	nearby
超市	chāoshì	supermarket
那么	nàme	in that case, then
经常	jīngcháng	often
舒服	shūfu	comfortable

Proper Noun 🔊 22-04

爱丁堡	Àidīngbǎo	Edinburgh

KEY SENTENCES 🔊 22-05

1. Qǐngwèn, cóng zhèr zěnme qù Tiān'ānmén Guǎngchǎng?	请问，从这儿怎么去天安门广场？	Excuse me, how do I get to Tian'anmen Square from here?
2. Nǐ kěyǐ zuò dìtiě qù, yě kěyǐ zuò gōnggòng qìchē qù.	你可以坐地铁去，也可以坐公共汽车去。	You can either take the tube or the bus.
3. Zuò jǐ zhàn?	坐几站？	How many stops?
4. Nǐ jiā lí dìtiě zhàn yuǎn bu yuǎn?	你家离地铁站远不远？	Is the subway station far away from your home?
5. Wǒ qí zìxíngchē qù huǒchē zhàn.	我骑自行车去火车站。	I ride a bicycle to the train station.
6. Nǐ jiā fùjìn yǒu chāoshì ma?	你家附近有超市吗？	Are there any supermarkets near your home?
7. Zuò huǒchē háishì zuò chuán?	坐火车还是坐船？	By train or by boat?
8. Wǒ kāichē qù.	我开车去。	I'm going to drive there.

SITUATIONAL DIALOGUES

❶ (In the language centre) 🔊 22-06

A: Nǐ měi tiān zěnme qù shàngbān?	你每天怎么去上班？	How do you get to work every day?
B: Wǒ zuò dìtiě qù shàngbān.	我坐地铁去上班。	I take the underground to work.

A: Nǐ àirén ne? Tā zěnme qù? 你爱人呢？他怎么去？What about your partner?

B: Tā zuò gōnggòng qìchē qù. 他坐公共汽车去。 He goes by bus.

❷ (On a street in Beijing) 🔊 22-07

A: Qǐngwèn, cóng zhèr zěnme qù Tiān'ānmén Guǎngchǎng?	请问，从这儿怎么去天安门广场？	Excuse me, how do I get to Tian'anmen Square from here?
B: Nǐ kěyǐ zuò dìtiě qù, yě kěyǐ zuò gōnggòng qìchē qù.	你可以坐地铁去，也可以坐公共汽车去。	You can either take the tube or the bus.
A: Zuò jǐ zhàn?	坐几站？	How many stops?
B: Zuò dìtiě zhǐ yǒu sān zhàn.	坐地铁只有三站。	It's only three stops by tube.

❸ (At a friend's home) 🔊 22-08

A: Nǐ jiā lí dìtiě zhàn yuǎn bu yuǎn?	你家离地铁站远不远？	Is the subway station far away from your home?
B: Bú tài yuǎn, wǒ qí zìxíngchē qù dìtiě zhàn, hěn kuài.	不太远，我骑自行车去地铁站，很快。	Not very far. I can ride a bicycle to the subway station and arrive soon.

| A: Nǐ jiā fùjìn yǒu chāoshì ma? | 你家附近有超市吗？ | Are there any supermarkets near your home? |
| B: Yǒu, hěn jìn. Wǒ zǒulù qù chāoshì. | 有，很近。我走路去超市。 | Yes, I can walk to the supermarket. |

❹ (In the office) 🔊 22-09

A: Zhōumò nǐ qù nǎr?	周末你去哪儿？	Where are you going at the weekend?
B: Qù Bālí.	去巴黎。	I'm going to Paris.
A: Zěnme qù? Zuò huǒchē háishì zuò chuán?	怎么去？坐火车还是坐船？	How will you get there? By train or by boat?
B: Zuò huǒchē. Nǐ ne? Qù nǎr?	坐火车。你呢？去哪儿？	By train. What about you? Where are you going?
A: Wǒ qù Àidīngbǎo.	我去爱丁堡。	I'm going to Edinburgh.
B: Nǐ kāi chē qù háishì zuò huǒchē qù?	你开车去还是坐火车去？	Will you drive or go by train?
A: Wǒ kāi chē qù.	我开车去。	I'm going to drive there.

❺ (At a party) 🔊 22-10

A: Nǐ cháng qù Zhōngguó ma?	你常去中国吗？	Do you go to China often?
B: Cháng qù.	常去。	Yes, I go often.
A: Nàme, nǐ shì bu shì jīngcháng zuò fēijī?	那么，你是不是经常坐飞机？	In that case, do you often go by plane?
B: Shì a, dànshì wǒ bù xǐhuan zuò fēijī, hěn bù shūfu.	是啊，但是我不喜欢坐飞机，很不舒服。	Yes, but I don't like going by plane. It's very uncomfortable.

LANGUAGE POINTS

1. Transport

'Zuò 坐' is used when you are a passenger on any form of transport whereas 'qí 骑' means 'to ride (bicycles, horses etc.). 'Kāi 开' means 'to operate' and is used to express driving a car, flying an airplane etc. The pattern is:

Subject + zuò坐 + transport + verb

qí 骑

kāi 开

Tā zuò huǒchē qù shàngbān.	他坐火车去上班。	He goes to work by train.
Tā kāi chē qù chāoshì.	他开车去超市。	He drives to the supermarket.
Wǒ qí zìxíngchē qù huǒchē zhàn.	我骑自行车去火车站	I ride a bicycle to the train station.

2. 'Lí 离'

In framing statements about distance from a given point, the key word is 'lí 离'. The pattern is:

A + lí 离 + B + distance. For example:

Nǐ jiā lí chāoshì yuǎn ma?	你家离超市远吗?	Is it far from your home to the supermarket?
Wǒ jiā lí dìtiě zhàn hěn jìn.	我家离地铁站很近。	My home is very close to the tube station.

EXERCISES

1. Answer the following questions

❶ Nǐ gōngzuò ma? Nǐ měi tiān zěnme qù shàngbān?
你工作吗? 你每天怎么去上班?

❷ Nǐ shì bu shì xuésheng? Nǐ měi tiān zěnme qù shàngxué?
你是不是学生? 你每天怎么去上学?

❸ Nǐ jiā fùjìn yǒu dìtiě zhàn ma?
你家附近有地铁站吗?

❹ Nǐ jiā lí huǒchē zhàn yuǎn bu yuǎn?
你家离火车站远不远?

❺ Nǐ zěnme qù chāoshì?
你怎么去超市?

❻ Zhè ge zhōumò nǐ zuò shénme?
这个周末你做什么?

2. Translate the following into Chinese

❶ call a taxi   ❷ take a bus   ❸ drive a car   ❹ on foot

❺ ride a bike   ❻ by airplane   ❼ ride a horse   ❽ by boat

3. Translate the following into Chinese

❶ Beijing is very far from Guangzhou.

❷ Is there an underground system in Nanjing?

❸ How do you go to Guangzhou from Hong Kong?

❹ Many Chinese go to work by bicycle.

❺ My friend won't stay in a hotel. He will stay in my house.

❻ I often travel to Paris by Euro-star.

4. Fill in the blanks with appropriate words

❶ Dìtiě zhàn zài _____?

地铁 站 在 _____?

❷ Nǐ _____ qù Xiānggǎng? Shì zuò fēijī _____ zuò chuán?

你 _____ 去 香 港? 是 坐 飞机 _____ 坐 船?

❸ _____ Běijīng _____ Shànghǎi zuò huǒchē hěn kuài.

_____ 北京 _____ 上 海 坐 火 车 很 快。

❹ Gùgōng _____ wǒmen de fàndiàn hěn jìn.

故 宫 _____ 我 们 的 饭店 很 近。

❺ Míngtiān shì nǐ tàitai de shēngrì, nǐmen qù _____ chīfàn?

明 天 是 你 太太 的 生 日,你 们 去 _____ 吃饭?

❻ Qí zìxíngchē qù xuéxiào yuǎn _____ yuǎn?

骑 自 行 车 去 学 校 远 _____ 远?

❼ Hángzhōu _____ Shànghǎi bù yuǎn.

杭 州 _____ 上 海 不 远。

5. Listening comprehension 🔊 22-11

Choose the correct answers according to the short dialogues.

❶ a. ride a bicycle	b. by bus	c. by underground
❷ a. very far	b. very close	c. not too far
❸ a. drive a car	b. go on foot	c. by bus

❹ a. by boat   b. by train   c. by car

❺ a. by airplane   b. by train   c. by boat

6. Classroom activities

Role play:

Your Chinese friends have come to visit your country. Organise a three-day trip with them including one day around your home town.

7. Chinese characters learning

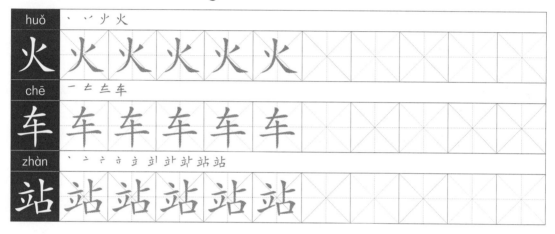

LESSON 23
PLACES & DIRECTIONS

OBJECTIVES

★ Asking and describing locations

★ Finding out and giving directions

★ Talking about length of time

RELEVANT VOCABULARY

Directions and Locations 23-01		
东*	dōng	east
西	xī	west
南*	nán	south
北	běi	north
西北	xīběi	northwest
前	qián	ahead, front, forward
后*	hòu	behind, back
左	zuǒ	left
右	yòu	right
上*	shàng	up, above
下*	xià	down, under
里*	lǐ	inside
外*	wài	outside

边	biān	side
旁边*	pángbiān	next to, beside
对面*	duìmiàn	opposite
中间*	zhōngjiān	middle, between

多长时间	duōcháng shíjiān	how long
小时	xiǎoshí	hour
分钟	fēnzhōng	minute (duration)
出	chū	out
向	xiàng	towards
拐	guǎi	to turn
一直	yìzhí	straight
往	wǎng	towards
到	dào	to reach, to arrive
停	tíng	to stop
大概	dàgài	approximate, about
上车	shàng chē	to get on (a vehicle)
下车*	xià chē	to get off (a vehicle)
十字路口	shízì lùkǒu	crossroads
路口	lùkǒu	junction, crossing

KEY SENTENCES 🔊 23-03

1. Chángchéng zài nǎr?	长城在哪儿？	Where is the Great Wall?
2. Chángchéng zài Běijīng de xīběi biān.	长城在北京的西北边。	The Great Wall is in the northwest of Beijing.
3. Kāi chē yào duōcháng shíjiān?	开车要多长时间？	How long would it take to drive there?
4. Kāi chē yào liǎng ge duō xiǎoshí.	开车要两个多小时。	More than 2 hours by car.
5. Zěnme zǒu?	怎么走？	How do we get there (on foot)?
6. Xiàng yòu guǎi, yìzhí wǎng qián zǒu.	向右拐，一直往前走。	Turn right and (it's) straight ahead.
7. Nín rènshi lù ma?	您认识路吗？	Do you know the way there?
8. Dào le, jiù tíng zhèr ba.	到了，就停这儿吧。	We've arrived, just stop here.

SITUATIONAL DIALOGUES

❶ (In a travel agency) 🔊 23-04

A: Chángchéng zài nǎr?	长城在哪儿？	Where is the Great Wall?
B: Zài Běijīng de xīběi biān.	在北京的西北边。	It is in the northwest of Beijing.
A: Lí zhèr yuǎn bu yuǎn?	离这儿远不远？	Is it far from here?
B: Bú tài jìn.	不太近。	It's not very close.

SITUATIONAL DIALOGUES

167

A: Kāi chē yào duōcháng shíjiān?	开车要多长时间？	How long would it take to drive there?
B: Yào liǎng ge duō xiǎoshí.	要两个多小时。	More than 2 hours.

❷ (At the hotel reception desk) 🔊 23-05

A: Xiǎojie, wǒmen xiǎng qù Gùgōng, yòng zuò chē ma?	小姐，我们想去故宫，用坐车吗？	Miss, we'd like to go to the Imperial Palace. Do we have to go by car?
B: Bú yòng, lí zhèr bù yuǎn.	不用，离这儿不远。	No, it's not far from here.
A: Zěnme zǒu?	怎么走？	How do we get there (on foot)?
B: Chū mén xiàng yòu guǎi, yìzhí wǎng qián zǒu.	出门向右拐，一直往前走。	Go out, turn right and (it's) straight ahead.
A: Yào zǒu duōcháng shíjiān?	要走多长时间？	How long does it take to walk there?
B: Dàgài èrshí fēnzhōng.	大概二十分钟。	Around 20 minutes.

❸ (Calling a taxi) 🔊 23-06

A: Nín qù nǎr?	您去哪儿？	Where are you going?
B: Chángchéng Fàndiàn.	长城饭店。	Great Wall Hotel.
A: Hǎo, shàng chē ba. Nín rènshi lù ma?	好，上车吧。您认识路吗？	OK, please get in. Do you know the way there?
B: Rènshi, jiù zài Guānghuá Lù fùjìn.	认识，就在光华路附近。	Yes, I do. It's near Guanghua Road.
A: Hǎo.	好。	OK.

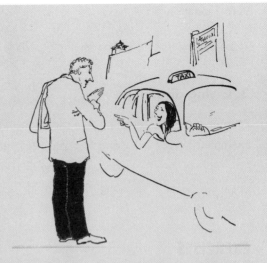

B: Dào shízì lùkǒu xiàng zuǒ guǎi, yìzhí kāi.	到十字路口向左拐，一直开。	When you get to the crossroads, turn left then carry on going straight ahead.
A: Méi wèntí.	没问题。	No problem.
B: Dào le, jiù tíng zhèr ba.	到了，就停这儿吧。	We've arrived, just stop here.

LANGUAGE POINTS

1. Describe location

a. A + zài 在 + B (de 的) + location

Chángchéng zài Běijīng (de) xīběi biān.	长城在北京（的）西北边。	The Great wall is in the northwest of Beijing.

b. A + zài 在 + B + hé 和 + C (de 的) + zhōngjiān 中间

Tiān'ānmén zài Gùgōng hé Qiánmén (de) zhōngjiān.	天安门在故宫和前门（的）中间。	Tian'anmen is between the Imperial Palace and Qianmen.

2. Duration of time

If it is a positive statement, the time word (duration) will come after the verb in the sentence. The pattern is:

Verb + duration

| Zuò huǒchē yào duōcháng shíjiān? | 坐火车要多长时间? | How long will it take by train? |

3. Giving directions

Pattern: wǎng 往 or xiàng 向 + direction + verb

Example: xiàng 向   zuǒ 左   guǎi 拐 (turn)

                     xiàng 向   dōng 东   kāi 开 (drive)

                     xiàng 向   qián 前   zǒu 走 (walk)

EXERCISES

1. Fill in the blanks with the correct word in brackets

❶ Bàngōngshì lǐ _____ hěn duō rén. （zài, shì, yǒu）
办公室里_____很多人。（在，是，有）

❷ Shāngdiàn hé yínháng zhōngjiān _____ xuéxiào. （zài, shì, yǒu）
商店和银行中间_____学校。（在，是，有）

❸ Yínháng _____ gòuwù zhōngxīn dōngbiān. （yǒu, shì, zài）
银行_____购物中心东边。（有，是，在）

❹ Kāfēitīng _____ jiǔbā xībiān. （yǒu, shì, zài）
咖啡厅_____酒吧西边。（有，是，在）

2. Say the following words in Chinese

❶ on the left   ❷ turn right   ❸ in the middle

❹ front   ❺ behind   ❻ east

❼ west   ❽ south   ❾ north

3. Translate the following into English

❶ Qǐngwèn, huǒchē zhàn zài qiánbiān ma?
请问，火车站在前边吗?

❷ Qù Běijīng Fàndiàn zěnme zǒu?
去北京饭店怎么走?

❸ Yìzhí wǎng qián zǒu, xiàng zuǒ guǎi.
一直往前走，向左拐。

❹ Cóng Lúndūn dào Àidīngbǎo zuò huǒchē yào duōcháng shíjiān?
从伦敦到爱丁堡坐火车要多长时间?

❺ Zhèr lí dàshǐguǎn yuǎn bu yuǎn? Zǒulù yào duōcháng shíjiān?
这儿离大使馆 远不远？ 走路要多长 时间？

4. Translate the following into Chinese

❶ Could you tell me how to get to the train station?

❷ The supermarket is not far from here, it is just ahead.

❸ The bookshop is in front of the bank.

❹ The café is behind the shopping centre.

❺ There is a very big supermarket near my home.

5. Listening comprehension 🔊 23-07

Choose the correct answers according to the short dialogues.

❶ a. east	b. centre	c. west
❷ a. east	b. west	c. northwest
❸ a. left	b. right	c. south
❹ a. 3 hours	b. 4 hours	c. 5 hours
❺ a. 9 hours	b. 10 hours	c. 11 hours

6. Classroom activities

Role play:

You would like to invite your Chinese friend to your home. Give him/her directions how to get there.

7. Chinese characters learning

dōng	一 七 车 东 东				
东	东	东	东	东	东
xī	一 ㄱ 亓 西 西				
西	西	西	西	西	西
nán	一 十 忄 宁 内 内 南 南				
南	南	南	南	南	南
běi	丨 ㅓ ㅓ 北 北				
北	北	北	北	北	北

LESSON 24
SUMMARY OF LESSONS 19-23

OBJECTIVES

★ Practicing the vocabulary and grammars from lessons 19-23

★ Cultural insights: Chinese food and drinks

KEY PATTERNS

Patterns	Sentences
A háishì 还是 B?	Nǐ hē chá háishì hē kāfēi? 你喝茶还是喝咖啡？
A huòzhě 或者 B	Nǐ kěyǐ qù Běijīng huòzhě qù Shànghǎi. 你可以去北京或者去上海。
Subject + (méi 没) verb + guo 过 + object	Tā (méi) qùguo Zhōngguó. 他（没）去过中国。
Adjective + jíle 极了	Wǒ máng jíle. 我忙极了。
Subject + verb + le 了 + object	Wǒ hēle liǎng bēi chá. 我喝了两杯茶。
Subject + verb + object + le 了	Tā qù Zhōngguó le. 他去中国了。
Subject + méi 没 + verb + (object)	Tā méi qù Zhōngguó. 他没去中国。
Subject + shì 是 + circumstance + verb + de 的	Nǐ shì zài nǎr mǎi de? 你是在哪儿买的？
Subject + zuò 坐 + transport + verb qí 骑 kāi 开	Tā zuò huǒchē qù shàngbān. 他坐火车去上班。
A lí 离 B + distance	Wǒ jiā lí dìtiě zhàn hěn jìn. 我家离地铁站很近。
A zài 在 B (de 的) + location	Shāngdiàn zài huǒchē zhàn de zuǒbiān. 商店在火车站的左边。
A zài 在 B hé 和 C (de 的) zhōngjiān 中间	Yínháng zài shūdiàn hé fànguǎn de zhōngjiān. 银行在书店和饭馆的中间。

wǎng 往 or xiàng 向 + direction + verb	xiàng zuǒ guǎi 向左拐
Verb + duration of time	Kāi chē yào liǎng ge xiǎoshí. 开车要两个小时。

Frequently Used Measure Words ❷

▶ bēi 杯：a cup of, a glass of

yì bēi chá	一杯茶
liǎng bēi kāfēi	两杯咖啡
sān bēi píjiǔ	三杯啤酒

▶ píng 瓶：a bottle of

yì píng niúnǎi	一瓶牛奶
liǎng píng kělè	两瓶可乐
sān píng shuǐ	三瓶水

▶ kuài 块：a piece of, a lump of

yí kuài qiǎokèlì	一块巧克力
liǎng kuài bīng	两块冰
sān kuài dàngāo	三块蛋糕

▶ liàng 辆：for vehicles

yí liàng chē	一辆车
liǎng liàng gōnggòng qìchē	两辆公共汽车
sān liàng zìxíngchē	三辆自行车

▶ wǎn 碗：for bowls

yì wǎn mǐfàn	一碗米饭
yì wǎn jītāng	一碗鸡汤
yì wǎn miàntiáo	一碗面条

RELEVANT VOCABULARY

🔊 24-01		
完	wán	finish, end
容易	róngyì	easy
市中心	shì zhōngxīn	city centre, downtown
公园	gōngyuán	park
听说	tīngshuō	it is said, heard
玩儿	wánr	to have fun, to enjoy, to play
客厅	kètīng	living room, sitting room
厨房	chúfáng	kitchen
桌	zhuō	(measure word, table of [dishes])
碗	wǎn	bowl (measure word)
炸	zhá	to fry
炸薯条	zháshǔtiáo	chips
最后	zuìhòu	the last, finally
巧克力	qiǎokèlì	chocolate
蛋糕	dàngāo	cake
大家	dàjiā	everybody
满意	mǎnyì	satisfied

STORY TIME

1. Listen to the following story and retell it in Chinese 🔊 24-02

Yīngguó fàn
英国饭

Mǎiwán dōngxi,　Mǎxiū hé wǒ dōu lèi　jíle.　Wǒmen qùle　yì jiā kāfēitīng.　Tā
买完 东西，马修和我都 累极了。我们 去了一家咖啡厅。他

yàole yì bēi Yīngguó chá,   wǒ yàole yì bēi kāfēi.   Wǒ gàosu tā wǒ de nǚ péngyou xiǎng
要了一杯 英国 茶，我 要了一杯咖啡。 我 告诉他我的女 朋 友 想

chī Yīngguó fàn,   kěshì wǒ méi chīguo,   yě méi zuòguo.   Wǒ wèn tā huì bu huì zuò,   tā
吃英国饭， 可是我没吃过，也没做过。我问他会不会做，他

shuō zuò Yīngguó fàn tài róngyì le.
说 做 英国饭太容易了。

　　Xīngqītiān xiàwǔ,   Mǎxiū gēn wǒ yìqǐ qù Lìli jiā.   Lìli jiā zài shì zhōngxīn,
　　星期天 下午， 马修 跟 我一起去丽丽家。 丽丽家在市 中心，

lí qìchē zhàn hé dìtiě zhàn dōu hěn jìn.   Tā jiā de zuǒbiān shì yí ge gōngyuán, yòubiān
离汽车 站 和地铁站 都 很近。她家的左边是一个公园，右边

shì yí ge xuéxiào, tā jiā fùjìn hái yǒu hěn duō shāngdiàn hé kāfēidiàn. Wǒ hé Mǎxiū shì
是一个学校，她家附近还有很多 商 店和咖啡店。我和马修是

kāichē qù de.
开车去的。

　　Lìli de bàba māma tīngshuō wǒmen yào qù tāmen jiā dōu hěn gāoxìng, yīnwèi yǒu
　　丽丽的爸爸妈妈 听说 我们 要 去他们家都 很 高兴，因为有

Yīngguó péngyou lái tāmen jiā wánr,   hái yào gěi tāmen zuò Yīngguó fàn,   tài hǎo le!
英 国 朋 友来他们 家玩儿，还要给他们做 英 国饭，太好了!

Tāmen yǐqián dōu méi chīguo Yīngguó fàn.
他们 以前 都 没吃过英国饭。

　　Dàole Lìli   jiā, wǒmen xiān zài kètīng hē chá,   ránhòu wǒ gēn Mǎxiū yìqǐ   qù
　　到了丽丽 家我们 先在客厅喝茶，然后我跟马修一起去

chúfáng zuòfàn.   Wǒmen yòngle yí ge duō xiǎoshí,   zuòhǎole yì zhuō Yīngguó fàn. Wǒmen
厨房 做饭。我们 用了一个多 小时， 做好了一桌 英国饭! 我们

měi rén xiān lái yì wǎn tāng, ránhòu yì rén yì tiáo zháyú hé yìxiē zháshǔtiáo, zuìhòu shì
每人先来一碗 汤， 然后一人一条炸鱼和一些炸薯条， 最后是

qiǎokèlì dàngāo hé kāfēi.
巧克力蛋糕和咖啡。

　　Dàjiā dōu shuō hǎochī jíle.   Wǒ yě
　　大家都 说 好吃极了。我也

fēicháng gāoxìng, yīnwèi Lìli yì jiā rén dōu
非常 高兴，因为丽丽一家人都

hěn mǎnyì.
很 满意。

2. Read the story again and then answer the following questions

❶ Where did Mathew and the writer go after they went shopping?

❷ Why did the writer invite Mathew to Lili's home?

❸ Where is Lili's house? Is there any bus stop or train station nearby?

❹ Can you describe the area surrounding Lili's house?

❺ How did the writer and Mathew get to Lili's house?

❻ Why were Lili's parents so happy when they heard Mathew would visit them?

❼ What dishes did Mathew cook?

❽ How long did it take to cook all the dishes?

CULTURAL INSIGHTS

Chinese food and drinks

Meals are called fàn（饭）in Chinese. A typical Chinese meal consists of two parts: fàn（饭）which means meal, and cài（菜）which means dishes. Fàn（饭）is grain, or starch-based staple, such as rice, noodle or steamed bread. It comes in a bowl which is served individually. Cài（菜）refers to dishes which consists of two types - sùcài（素菜）and hūncài（荤菜）. Sùcài（素菜）are vegetable dishes and hūncài（荤菜）are dishes with meat or fish. Dishes are usually served on a separate plate which is shared by everybody.

Tāng（汤）means soup and is part of cài（菜）. It can be of many varieties and, unlike the West, tāng（汤）is served either with the meal or at the end, the latter more common in northern China.

Tea in Chinese is called chá（茶）. It is more than an everyday drink; it is a part of the culture. Visitors to someone's house will be served tea without asking. Chinese teas might be green tea, black tea (which is actually called red tea in China), jasmine tea, or wulong tea, each of which can be further divided. The classification is often based on the manner in which a particular kind of tea is produced. Green tea is unfermented, black tea is fermented, wulong tea is semi-fermented, and jasmine tea is made from a combination of black tea, green tea, wulong tea and some fragrant flowers. Although the taste for tea is of course individual, people in southern China prefer green tea, while those in northern China prefer jasmine tea. Wulong tea is the favourite in areas of Guangdong and Fujian.

Unlike English people, Chinese people drink tea using boiled water only and serve it without adding milk or sugar.

CHINESE CHARACTERS LEARNING

kā	丨 ㄇ 口 叨 叻 叻 咖 咖
咖	咖 咖 咖 咖 咖
fēi	丨 ㄇ 口 叮 叮 叮 叮 叮 唯 啡 啡
啡	啡 啡 啡 啡 啡
tīng	一 厂 斤 厅
厅	厅 厅 厅 厅 厅

LESSON 25
WEATHER & SEASONS

OBJECTIVES

★ Talking about the weather

★ Comparing the weather in different places

RELEVANT VOCABULARY

Seasons 🔊 25-01

季节*	jìjié	season
春（天／季）	chūn (tiān / jì)	spring
夏（天／季）	xià (tiān / jì)	summer
秋（天／季）	qiū (tiān / jì)	autumn
冬（天／季）	dōng (tiān / jì)	winter

Weather 🔊 25-02

天气	tiānqì	weather
气温	qìwēn	air temperature
度	dù	degree
冷	lěng	cold
热	rè	hot
干燥	gānzào	dry
暖和*	nuǎnhuo	warm

凉快*	liángkuai	cool
潮湿*	cháoshī	damp
阴天	yīntiān	cloudy
晴天*	qíngtiān	sunshine, sunny day
雨	yǔ	rain
下雨	xià yǔ	to rain
雪	xuě	snow
下雪	xià xuě	to snow
风	fēng	wind
刮风	guā fēng	to be windy
零下	língxià	below zero

🔊 25-03

比	bǐ	to compare, than (preposition)
一样	yíyàng	same
左右	zuǒyòu	(after a numeral) about, or so

Antonym Adjectives 🔊 25-04

大*	dà	big, large
小*	xiǎo	small, little
多*	duō	many, much, more
少*	shǎo	less, little, few
高*	gāo	tall, high
矮*	ǎi	short (in height), low
长*	cháng	long, length
短*	duǎn	short (in length)

| 快* | kuài | fast, quick |
| 慢* | màn | slow |

Proper Noun 🔊 25-05

| 广州 | Guǎngzhōu | Guangzhou (a city in China) |

KEY SENTENCES 🔊 25-06

1.	Jīntiān tiānqì zěnmeyàng?	今天天气怎么样？	What's the weather like today?
2.	Jīntiān duōshao dù?	今天多少度？	What's the temperature today?
3.	Jīntiān bǐ zuótiān rè.	今天比昨天热。	Today is hotter than yesterday.
4.	Míngtiān shì yīntiān, yǒu yǔ.	明天是阴天，有雨。	It will be cloudy with rain tomorrow.
5.	Qiūtiān bù lěng bú rè.	秋天不冷不热。	The autumn is neither hot nor cold.
6.	Běijīng de dōngtiān bǐ Lúndūn de dōngtiān lěng duō le.	北京的冬天比伦敦的冬天冷多了。	Beijing is much colder than London in winter.
7.	Guǎngzhōu de dōngtiān shì bu shì gēn Lúndūn de yíyàng?	广州的冬天是不是跟伦敦的一样？	Is Guangzhou's winter the same as London's?
8.	Guǎngzhōu de dōngtiān méiyǒu Lúndūn de dōngtiān lěng.	广州的冬天没有伦敦的冬天冷。	Guangzhou's winter is not as cold as London's.

SITUATIONAL DIALOGUES

❶ (At home) 🔊 25-07

A: Jīntiān tiānqì zěnmeyàng?	今天天气怎么样？	What's the weather like today?
B: Hěn rè.	很热。	It's very hot.
A: Jīntiān duōshao dù?	今天多少度？	What's the temperature today?
B: Sānshísān dù.	三十三度。	33 degrees Celsius.
A: Jīntiān rè háishì zuótiān rè?	今天热还是昨天热？	Is it hot today or yesterday?
B: Jīntiān bǐ zuótiān rè.	今天比昨天热。	Yes, today is hotter than yesterday.
A: Míngtiān me?	明天呢？	What about tomorrow?
B: Míngtiān shì yīntiān, yǒu yǔ.	明天是阴天，有雨。	It will be cloudy with rain tomorrow.
A: Shì dà yǔ háishì xiǎo yǔ?	是大雨还是小雨？	Will the rain be heavy or not?
B: Shì xiǎo yǔ.	是小雨。	No, it will just be drizzling.

❷ (At a friend's home) 🔊 25-08

A: Běijīng de tiānqì zěnmeyàng?	北京的天气怎么样？	What is Beijing's weather like?
B: Xiàtiān hěn rè, dōngtiān hěn lěng.	夏天很热，冬天很冷。	In summer it is very hot and in winter very cold.
A: Chūntiān hé qiūtiān ne?	春天和秋天呢？	What about in spring and autumn?

B: Chūntiān hěn gānzào, qiūtiān zuì hǎo.	春天很干燥，秋天最好。	The spring is very dry but the autumn is the best time.
A: Wèishénme?	为什么？	Why?
B: Qiūtiān bù lěng bú rè.	秋天不冷不热。	The autumn is neither hot nor cold.
A: Běijīng dōngtiān cháng xià xuě ma?	北京冬天常下雪吗？	Does it often snow in Beijing in winter?
B: Yǒushí xià xuě.	有时下雪。	It does sometimes.
A: Guā fēng ma?	刮风吗？	Is it windy?
B: Chángcháng guā dà fēng.	常常刮大风。	There are often strong winds.
A: Běijīng de dōngtiān shì bu shì bǐ Lúndūn de dōngtiān lěng?	北京的冬天是不是比伦敦的冬天冷？	Is London's winter colder than Beijing's?
B: Běijīng de dōngtiān bǐ Lúndūn de dōngtiān lěng duō le.	北京的冬天比伦敦的冬天冷多了。	Beijing is much colder than London in winter.
A: Zhēnde?	真的？	Really?
B: Shì a. Yǒushíhou qìwēn zài língxià shí dù zuǒyòu.	是啊，有时候气温在零下10度左右。	Yes, sometimes the temperature is about 10 degrees below zero.

❸ (In the park) 🔊 25-09

| A: Guǎngzhōu xiàtiān rè bu rè? | 广州夏天热不热？ | Is it hot in Guangzhou in summer? |
| B: Guǎngzhōu xiàntiān bǐ Běijīng rè. | 广州夏天比北京热。 | Guangzhou is hotter than Beijing in summer. |

SITUATIONAL DIALOGUES

A: Qìwēn duōshao dù?	气温多少度？	What is the usual temperature?
B: Qìwēn chángcháng sānshíqī, bā dù.	气温常常三十七、八度。	It is often 37 or 38 degrees Celsius.
A: Dōngtiān ne?	冬天呢？	How about in winter?
B: Dōngtiān bú tài lěng, kěshì cháng xià yǔ.	冬天不太冷，可是常下雨。	It is not too cold in winter but it often rains.
A: Guǎngzhōu de dōngtiān shì bu shì gēn Lúndūn de yíyàng?	广州的冬天是不是跟伦敦的一样？	Is Guangzhou's winter the same as London's?
B: Bù yíyàng. Guǎngzhōu de dōngtiān méiyǒu Lúndūn de dōngtiān lěng.	不一样。广州的冬天没有伦敦的冬天冷。	No. Guangzhou's winter is not as cold as London's.

LANGUAGE POINTS

1. Comparison using 'bǐ 比'

The pattern is:

A + bǐ 比 + B + adj.

Jīntiān bǐ zuótiān lěng.	今天比昨天冷。	Today is colder than yesterday.

Words marking degrees of comparison 'yìdiǎnr 一点儿', 'de duō 得多' and 'duō le 多了' follow the adjective. The pattern is:

A + bǐ 比 + B + adj. + degree

Jīntiān bǐ zuótiān lěng yìdiǎnr.	今天比昨天冷一点儿。	Today is a little colder than yesterday.
Jīntiān bǐ zuótiān lěng de duō.	今天比昨天冷得多。	Today is much colder than yesterday.
Jīntiān bǐ zuótiān lěng duō le.	今天比昨天冷多了。	Today is much colder than yesterday.

2. Negative comparison using 'méiyǒu 没有'

The pattern is:

A + méiyǒu 没有 + B + adj.

Jīntiān méiyǒu zuótiān lěng.	今天没有昨天冷。

3. 'Yíyàng 一样'

The pattern is:

A + gēn 跟 + B + (bù 不) yíyàng 一样

Zhè běn shū gēn nà běn (bù) yíyàng.	这本书跟那本（不）一样。	This book is (not) the same as that one.

EXERCISES

1. Fill in the blanks with the appropriate words or phrases

❶ Dǎ diànhuà _____ xiě xìn kuài. (bǐ, gēn)
  打 电 话 _____ 写 信 快。（比，跟）

❷ Tā de cídiǎn gēn _____ yíyàng. (cídiǎn, wǒ de cídiǎn)
  他 的 词 典 跟 _____ 一样。（词典，我的词典）

❸ Zhè ge fàndiàn _____ nà ge fàndiàn guì. (bǐ, gēn)
  这 个 饭 店 _____ 那 个 饭 店 贵。（比，跟）

❹ Jīntiān hé _____ yíyàng_____. (zuótiān, rè; míngtiān, xià xuě)
  今 天 和 _____ 一 样 _____。（昨天，热；明天，下雪）

❺ Zhè zhāng dìtú _____ nà zhāng dìtú _____. (bǐ, dà; gēn, dà)
  这 张 地 图 _____ 那 张 地 图 _____。（比，大；跟，大）

❻ Zhè běn shū hé _____ bù yíyàng. (shū, nà běn shū)
  这 本 书 和 _____ 不 一样。（书，那本书）

2. Translate the following sentences into English

❶ Zhè běn shū bǐ nà běn shū guì de duō.
这 本 书 比 那 本 书 贵 得 多。

❷ Jīntiān shì yīntiān, hěn lěng, fēng hěn dà.
今 天 是 阴 天，很 冷，风 很 大。

❸ Yīngguórén xiàtiān xǐhuan zuò shénme?
英 国 人 夏 天 喜 欢 做 什 么?

❹ Qùnián dōngtiān bù lěng, xiàtiān bú rè.
去 年 冬 天 不 冷，夏 天 不 热。

❺ Wǒ bù xǐhuan Běijīng de chūntiān, fēng tài dà.
我 不 喜 欢 北 京 的 春 天，风 太 大。

❻ Zuótiān de yǔ dà háishì jīntiān de yǔ dà?
昨 天 的 雨 大 还 是 今 天 的 雨 大?

❼ Wǒ gēge bǐ wǒ gāo duō le.
我 哥 哥 比 我 高 多 了。

3. Make negative comparisions using the information in the following sentences

❶ Fēijī kuài. Huǒchē bú kuài.
飞 机 快。火 车 不 快。

❷ Wǒ gēge gāo. Wǒ dìdi bù gāo.
我 哥 哥 高。我 弟 弟 不 高。

❸ Wǒ bàba máng. Wǒ māma bù máng.
我 爸 爸 忙。我 妈 妈 不 忙。

❹ Jīntiān de xuě dà. Zuótiān de xuě bú dà.
今 天 的 雪 大。昨 天 的 雪 不 大。

❺ Běijīng dōngtiān lěng. Guǎngzhōu dōngtiān bù lěng.
北 京 冬 天 冷。广 州 冬 天 不 冷。

❻ Zhè běn shū wǔshí kuài. Nà běn shū sānshí kuài.
这 本 书 50 块。那 本 书 30 块。

❼ Jīntiān èrshíbā dù. Zuótiān èrshísān dù.
今 天 28 度。昨 天 23 度。

4. Translate the following into Chinese

❶ What is the weather like in London in winter?

❷ Does it often rain in summer in Beijing?

❸ It's going to be a sunny day tomorrow.

❹ Is there snow in Guangzhou?

❺ In spring it is very windy in Beijing.

❻ What was the temperature yesterday?

❼ Today the temperature is 21 degrees.

❽ There has been a lot of snow in France this year.

❾ The weather in Guangzhou is best in spring.

❿ How heavy was the rain yesterday?

5. Listening comprehension 🔊 25-10

Choose the correct answers according to the short dialogues.

❶ a. not too cold	b. not too hot	c. neither hot nor cold
❷ a. 21 degrees	b. 22 degrees	c. 23 degrees
❸ a. colder	b. hotter	c. the same
❹ a. snow	b. windy	c. rain
❺ a. drizzling	b. heavy rain	c. won't be rain

6. Classroom activities

Describe and compare two countries' weather conditions with your classmate.

7. Chinese characters learning

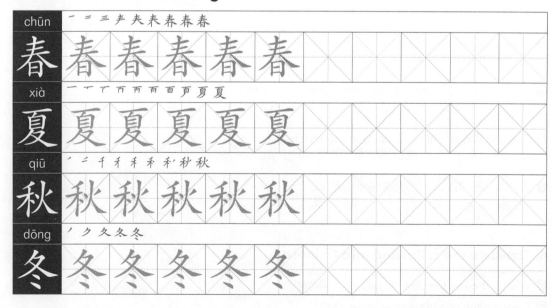

LESSON 26
ACTIVITIES & PROGRESSION

OBJECTIVES

★ Talking about ongoing actions

★ Describing progression

RELEVANT VOCABULARY

● 26-01		
进	jìn	to enter, to come in
在	zài	(continuous particle)
正在	zhèngzài	in process of
公寓	gōngyù	apartment
……的时候	...de shíhou	when, while
……以前*	...yǐqián	before, ago
……以后*	...yǐhòu	after
好像	hǎoxiàng	to seem, to be like
小说	xiǎoshuō	novel
（看）懂	(kàn) dǒng	to understand
（看）见	(kàn) jiàn	to meet
一边……一边……	yìbiān...yìbiān...	at the same time
跟……打招呼	gēn...dǎ zhāohu	say hello to somebody

Proper Nouns 🔊 26-02

| 国贸中心 | Guómào zhōngxīn | (a shopping centre name) |
| 星巴克 | Xīngbākè | Starbucks |

KEY SENTENCES 🔊 26-03

1.	Tā zài zuò shénme?	他在做什么？	What is he doing?
2.	Tā zài yòng wēixìn liáotiān ne.	他在用微信聊天呢。	He is chatting on WeChat.
3.	Wǒ qù de shíhou, Lín Nán zhèngzài dǎ diànhuà.	我去的时候，林南正在打电话。	When I got there, Lin Nan was on the phone.
4.	Wǒ tīng bu dǒng.	我听不懂。	I couldn't understand what I heard.
5.	Tā kàn de dǒng ma?	他看得懂吗？	Can he understand what he is reading?
6.	Tā kànjiàn nǐ le ma?	他看见你了吗？	Did he see you?
7.	Tā méi kànjiàn wǒ.	他没看见我。	He didn't see me.
8.	Tā zhèng gēn yí ge péngyou yìbiān hē kāfēi yìbiān liáotiān.	他正跟一个朋友一边喝咖啡，一边聊天。	He was drinking coffee and chatting with a friend.

SITUATIONAL DIALOGUES

❶ (At Wang Dan's home) ▶ 26-04

A: Wáng Dān zài jiā ma?	王丹在家吗？	Is Wang Dan at home?
B: Zài, qǐng jìn ba.	在，请进吧。	Yes, he is. Please come in.
A: Tā zài zuò shénme?	他在做什么？	What is he doing?
B: Tā zài yòng wēixìn liáotiān ne.	他在用微信聊天呢。	He is chatting on WeChat.
A: Gēn shéi liáotiān?	跟谁聊天？	Who is he chatting with?
B: Gēn tā de dàxué tóngxué.	跟他的大学同学。	He is chatting with his university classmate.
A: Liáo shénme ne?	聊什么呢？	What are they chatting about?
B: Tāmen shuō Fǎyǔ. Wǒ tīng bu dǒng.	他们说法语。我听不懂。	They are speaking French. I can't understand.

❷ (At Zhang Yan's flat) ▶ 26-05

A: Zhāng Yàn, zuótiān wànshang nǐ qù nàr le?	张燕，昨天晚上你去哪儿了？	Zhang Yan, where did you go last night?
B: Wǒ qù Lín Nán hé Xiǎo Bái de gōngyù le.	我去林南和小白的公寓了。	I went to Lin Nan and Xiao Bai's apartment.

A: Tāmen dōu zài ma?	他们都在吗?	Were they both in?
B: Zài. Wǒ qù de shíhou, Lín Nán zhèngzài dǎ diànhuà, Xiǎo Bái zhèngzài kàn shū.	在。我去的时候，林南正在打电话，小白正在看书。	Yes, when I got there, Lin Nan was on the phone, Xiao Bai was reading.
A: Xiǎo Bái zài kàn shénme shū?	小白在看什么书?	What kind of book was Xiao Bai reading?
B: Hǎoxiàng shì yì běn Yīngwén xiǎoshuō.	好像是一本英文小说。	It looked like an English novel.
A: Zhēnde? Tā kàn de dǒng ma?	真的? 他看得懂吗?	Really? Can he understand what he is reading?
B: Dāngrán kàn de dǒng. Nǐ bù zhīdào, tā xuéguo Yīngwén, hái zài Lúndūn zhùguo sān nián ne!	当然看得懂。你不知道，他学过英文，还在伦敦住过三年呢!	Of course. Don't you know he learned English before, and lived in London for 3 years!

❸ (On the way to library) 🔊 26-06

A: Zuótiān wǒ zài Guómào zhōngxīn kànjiàn Mǎxiū le.	昨天我在国贸中心看见马修了。	I saw Mathew at the Guomao centre yesterday.
B: Tā zài nàli zuò shénme?	他在那里做什么?	What was he doing there?
A: Tā zài Xīngbākè kāfēitīng lǐ.	他在星巴克咖啡厅里。	He was in a Starbucks Café.
B: Tā kànjiàn nǐ le ma?	他看见你了吗?	Did he see you?

A: Méiyǒu, tā zhèng gēn yí ge péngyou yìbiān hē kāfēi, yìbiān liáotiān ne, méi kànjiàn wǒ.	没有，他正跟一个朋友一边喝咖啡，一边聊天呢，没看见我。	No, he was drinking coffee and chatting with a friend. He didn't see me.
B: Nǐ gēn tā dǎ zhāohu le ma?	你跟他打招呼了吗？	Did you say hello to him?
A: Dāngrán, wǒ mǎiwán kāfēi jiù qù gēn tā dǎ zhāohu le. Ránhòu wǒmen yìqǐ liáotiān, hē kāfēi.	当然，我买完咖啡就去跟他打招呼了。然后我们一起聊天，喝咖啡。	Yes, I said hello to him after I bought coffee. Then we chatted and drank coffee together.

LANGUAGE POINTS

1. Progression

To indicate action in progress, zhèng 正, zài 在 or zhèngzài 正在 is used before a verb. The pattern is:

Subject + (zhèng) zài (正) 在 + verb (ne 呢)

Tā zhèng kàn diànshì (ne).	他正看电视（呢）。	He is watching TV right now.
Tā zài kàn diànshì (ne).	他在看电视（呢）。	He is watching TV right now.
Tā zhèngzài kàn diànshì.	他正在看电视。	He is watching TV right now.

2. The verb complement

In Chinese, a verb or an adjective is frequently followed by an element providing further detail or explanation. This is called the complement.

❶ Resultative Complement

The Resultative Complement shows the direct result of the action initiated by the verb. It's usually a verb immediately followed by another verb or an adjective. The pattern is:

Verb + complement (verb / adjective)

tīngdǒng	听懂	to listen and understand
kànwán	看完	to read and finish
zuòhǎo	做好	to do properly
xiěcuò	写错	to write incorrectly
kàndào	看到	to catch sight of

'Méi 没' is used for the negative sentences. For example:

Wǒ zuò le, kěshì méi zuòwán.	我做了，可是没做完。	I did it, but didn't finish it.

Note：zuòwán 做完 (finish doing): the complement 'wán 完' (finish) shows the result of verb 'zuò 做'. The negative is 'méi zuòwán 没做完'.

Wo kàn le, kěshì méi kàn dǒng.	我看了，可是没看懂。	I have read it, but I don't understand it.

Note: kàndǒng 看懂 (understand what you read): the complement 'dǒng 懂' (understand) shows the result of verb 'kàn 看'. The negative is 'méi kàndǒng 没看懂'.

❷ Potential Complement

The Potential Complement shows the potential result of the action initiated by the verb. The pattern is:

Positive: Verb + de 得 + complement (verb / adjective)

Negative: Verb + bù 不 + complement (verb / adjective)

tīng de dǒng / tīng bu dǒng	听得懂 / 听不懂	to listen and (not) able to understand
kàn de wán / kàn bu wán	看得完 / 看不完	to read and (not) able to finish
zuò de hǎo / zuò bu hǎo	做得好 / 做不好	to be (not) able to do it properly
kàn de dào / kàn bu dào	看得到 / 看不到	to be (not) able to catch sight of
Zhè běn shū tài róngyì le, wǒ dāngrán kàn de dǒng.	这本书太容易了，我当然看得懂。	This book is too easy. Of course I can understand.
Zhè běn shū tài nán le, wǒ kàn bu dǒng.	这本书太难了，我看不懂。	This book is too difficult. I can't understand.

EXERCISES

1. Answer the following questions

❶ Chén xiānsheng zài jiā ma?
陈 先 生 在 家 吗?

❷ Nǐ zhèngzài máng shénme ne?
你 正 在 忙 什 么 呢?

❸ Tā zài gàn shénme ne?
她 在 干 什 么 呢?

❹ Tā zài gēn shéi liáotiān?
她 在 跟 谁 聊 天?

❺ Nǐ xiànzài yǒu shíjiān ma?
你 现 在 有 时 间 吗?

2. Translate the following into English

❶ Jīnnián xiàtiān wǒ mèimei xué huì yóuyǒng le.
今 年 夏 天 我 妹 妹 学 会 游 泳 了。

❷ Nǐ néng tīngjiàn wǒ shuōhuà ma?
你 能 听 见 我 说 话 吗?

❸ Cóng zhèr néng kànjiàn huǒchē zhàn, liǎng fēnzhōng jiù néng zǒudào.
从 这 儿 能 看 见 火 车 站, 两 分 钟 就 能 走 到。

❹ Zuótiān wǒ qù tā jiā, méi jiàndào tā bàba, zhǐ jiàndào tā māma le.
昨 天 我 去 他 家, 没 见 到 他 爸 爸, 只 见 到 他 妈 妈 了。

❺ Wǒmen chīwán wǎnfàn qù kàn diànyǐng ba.
我 们 吃 完 晚 饭 去 看 电 影 吧。

❻ Wǒ shàng dàxué de shíhou xǐhuan dǎ bǎnqiú.
我 上 大 学 的 时 候 喜 欢 打 板 球。

❼ Wǒ xiǎo de shíhou, xuéguo tán gāngqín.
我 小 的 时 候 学 过 弹 钢 琴。

❽ Gāngcái wǒ gēn tā dǎ zhāohu, tā méi tīngjiàn.
刚 才 我 跟 他 打 招 呼, 他 没 听 见。

❾ Tāmen yìbiān liáotiān, yìbiān hē píjiǔ.
他 们 一 边 聊 天, 一 边 喝 啤 酒。

❿ Wǒ xǐhuan yìbiān kànshū, yìbiān tīng yīnyuè.
我 喜 欢 一 边 看 书, 一 边 听 音 乐。

3. Fill in the blanks with the words given

A. huì	B. hǎo	C. dào	D. dǒng	E. wán
会	好	到	懂	完

❶ Zhè běn shū wǒ kàn (　　　) le, gěi nǐ ba.
这 本 书 我 看 (　　　) 了，给 你 吧。

❷ Wǒ xué (　　　) kāichē le.
我 学 (　　　) 开车 了。

❸ Nà běn shū wǒ méi mǎi (　　　).
那 本 书 我 没 买 (　　　)。

❹ Māma zuò (　　　) wǎnfàn le.
妈妈 做 (　　　) 晚饭 了。

❺ Wǒ néng kàn (　　　) Zhōngwén bàozhǐ le.
我 能 看 (　　　) 中 文 报纸 了。

4. Choose the correct word to complete the sentences

❶ Wǒ zài liǎnshū shàng _____ nǐ de míngzi.
我 在 脸书 上 _____ 你 的 名字。

　　bù zhǎo dào　　　　zhǎo bu dào　　　　zhǎo le dào
　a. 不 找 到　　　b. 找 不 到　　　c. 找 了 到

❷ Wǒmen zài wǎng shàng _____ huǒchē piào ma?
我 们 在 网 上 _____ 火车 票 吗？

　　dìng de dào　　　　bù dìng dào　　　　dìng le dào
　a. 订 得 到　　　b. 不 订 到　　　c. 订 了 到

❸ Nǐ diǎnle zhème duō cài, wǒmen _____ ma?
你 点 了 这么 多 菜，我们 _____ 吗？

　　chī wán le　　　　bù chī wán　　　　chī de wán
　a. 吃 完 了　　　b. 不 吃 完　　　c. 吃 得 完

❹ Zhè liàng gōnggòng qìchē rén tài duō, kàn yàngzi wǒmen _____ le.
这 辆 公 共 汽车 人 太 多，看 样子 我们 _____ 了。

　　bù shàng qù　　　　shàng bu qù　　　　bù qù shàng
　a. 不 上 去　　　b. 上 不 去　　　c. 不 去 上

❺ Zhè běn Yīngyǔ shū tài nán le, nǐ _____ ma?
这 本 英语 书 太 难 了，你 _____ 吗？

　　kàn de dǒng　　　　bù kàn dǒng　　　　méi kàn dǒng
　a. 看 得 懂　　　b. 不 看 懂　　　c. 没 看 懂

5. Listening comprehension 🔊 26-07

Choose the correct answers according to the short dialogues.

❶ a. watch TV	b. read book	c. watch film
❷ a. send e-mail	b. check e-mail	c. chat on the internet
❸ a. drinking	b. cooking	c. eating
❹ a. train station	b. supermarket	c. shopping
❺ a. friend's home	b. shop	c. on the train

6. Chinese characters learning

kàn	一 二 三 チ 禾 看 看 看 看
看	看 看 看 看 看
dǒng	丶 丶 忄 忄 忄 忄 忄 忄 忄 忄 忄 懂 懂 懂
懂	懂 懂 懂 懂 懂
xiǎo	亅 小 小
小	小 小 小 小 小
shuō	丶 讠 讠 讠 讠 说 说 说 说
说	说 说 说 说 说

LESSON 27
INTENTIONS & PLANS

OBJECTIVES

★ Talking about future activities

★ Talking about imminent actions

★ Making travel plans

RELEVANT VOCABULARY

Holiday 🔊 27-01		
订	dìng	to book
票	piào	ticket
直飞	zhífēi	direct flight
旅游	lǚyóu	to travel
放假	fàngjià	to have a holiday or vacation
签证	qiānzhèng	visa

Verb-complement Construction 🔊 27-02		
订好	dìnghǎo	to have made reservation
卖完	màiwán	to be sold out
换成	huànchéng	to change into

🔊 27-03

已经	yǐjīng	already
把	bǎ	(grammar particle)
借	jiè	to borrow, to lend
将	jiāng	will, be about to
打算	dǎsuàn	to plan
计划	jìhuà	plan, to plan
多久	duō jiǔ	how long
最近	zuìjìn	recently, lately
办	bàn	to deal with, to manage, to tackle
需要	xūyào	to need, to require
帮	bāng	to help
帮忙	bāngmáng	to give a hand, to do a favour
还	huán	to return

Proper Nouns 🔊 27-04

| 英航 | Yīngháng | British Airways |
| 国航 | Guóháng | Air China |

KEY SENTENCES 🔊 27-05

| 1. | Wǒ hěn kuài jiù yào qù Běijīng le. | 我很快就要去北京了。 | I'm going to Beijing very soon. |

2. Fēijī piào yǐjīng dìnghǎo le.	飞机票已经订好了。	I have already booked the ticket.
3. Zhífēi de piào dōu màiwán le.	直飞的票都卖完了。	Direct tickets have all been sold out.
4. Qǐng bǎ Zhōngguó dìtú jiè wǒ yòng yíxià, hǎo ma?	请把中国地图借我用一下，好吗？	Can I borrow the map of China, please?
5. Xià ge yuè wǒ yào qù Běijīng hé Shànghǎi lǚyóu.	下个月我要去北京和上海旅游。	I'm going on holiday to Beijing and Shanghai next month.
6. Nǐ dǎsuàn zài Zhōngguó zhù duō jiǔ?	你打算在中国住多久？	How long do you intend to stay in China?
7. Wǒ yǒu hěn duō shì yào bàn.	我有很多事要办。	I have a lot of things to do.
8. Wǒ xiǎng bǎ Yīngbàng huànchéng Rénmínbì.	我想把英镑换成人民币。	I want to change some sterling into RMB.

SITUATIONAL DIALOGUES

❶ (At dinner) 🔊 27-06

A: Wǒ hěn kuài jiù yào qù Běijīng le.	我很快就要去北京了。	I'm going to Beijing very soon.
B: Shì ma? Shénme shíhou qù?	是吗？什么时候去？	Really? When?
A: Xià ge yuè.	下个月。	Next month.
B: Fēijī piào dìnghǎole ma?	飞机票订好了吗？	Have you booked a ticket yet?

A:	Yǐjīng dìnghǎo le.	已经订好了。	Yes, I have.
B:	Shì Yīngháng zhífēi Běijīng de ma?	是英航直飞北京的吗？	Is it British Airways direct to Beijing?
A:	Bú shì, zhífēi de piào dōu màiwán le.	不是，直飞的票都卖完了。	No, direct tickets have all been sold out.

❷ (In the library) 🔊 27-07

A:	Qǐng bǎ Zhōngguó dìtú jiè wǒ yòng yíxià, hǎo ma?	请把中国地图借我用一下，好吗？	Can I borrow the map of China, please?
B:	Kěyǐ, nǐ yào qù Zhōngguó ma?	可以，你要去中国吗？	OK, are you going to China?
A:	Shì a, xià ge yuè wǒ yào qù Běijīng hé Shànghǎi lǚyóu.	是啊，下个月我要去北京和上海旅游。	Yes. I'm going on holiday to Beijing and Shanghai next month.
B:	Nǐ dǎsuàn zài Zhōngguó zhù duō jiǔ?	你打算在中国住多久？	How long do you intend to stay in China?
A:	Wǒ jìhuà zhù sān ge xīngqī.	我计划住三个星期。	I'm planning to stay for 3 weeks.
B:	Zhēn búcuò a!	真不错啊！	That's great!

❸ (At a party) 🔊 27-08

A:	Peter, nǐ hǎo! Zuìjìn zěnmeyàng?	皮特，你好！最近怎么样？	Hello, Peter! How are you?
B:	Zuìjìn wǒ máng jíle.	最近我忙极了。	I've been extremely busy recently.
A:	Xuéxiào kuài fàngjià le, nǐ hái máng shénme?	学校快放假了，你还忙什么？	School holidays will start soon. Why are you still busy?

B: Wǒ mǎshàng yào qù Zhōngguó le, yǒu hěn duō shì yào bàn.

我马上要去中国了，有很多事要办。

I'm going to China very soon. I have a lot of things to do.

A: Zhēnde? Nǐ yǒu shénme shì yào bàn a?

真的？你有什么事要办啊？

Really? What kind of things need to be done?

B: Wǒ yào qù dàshǐguǎn bàn qiānzhèng, qù yínháng bǎ Yīngbàng huànchéng Rénmínbì, hái yào dìng fēijī piào.

我要去大使馆办签证，去银行把英镑换成人民币，还要订飞机票。

I need to get a visa from the embassy, to change some sterling into RMB, and I also need to book the airplane tickets.

A: Nǐ xūyào bāngmáng ma?

你需要帮忙吗？

Do you need any help?

B: Nǐ néng bāng wǒ bǎ zhè běn shū huán gěi túshūguǎn ma?

你能帮我把这本书还给图书馆吗？

Can you return this book to the library for me please?

A: Méi wèntí.

没问题。

No problem.

B: Tài xièxie nǐ le!

太谢谢你了！

Thank you very much!

LANGUAGE POINTS

1. 'Yào...le 要……了'

It is to indicate imminent action. 'Kuài...le 快……了' is similar meaning. For example:

| Huǒchē yào dào le. | 火车要到了。 | The train is coming soon. |
| Tā kuài qù Zhōngguó le. | 他快去中国了。 | He is going to China soon. |

2. 'Yào 要'

In addition to the meaning of 'to want' or 'to need', 'yào 要' can also be used in front of verbs to indicate that something, often a planned action, is happening in the near future. It is similar to 'jiāng 将' which is more formal. For example:

| Wǒ yào qù Běijīng xué Hànyǔ. | 我要去北京学汉语。 | I will go to Beijing to learn Chinese. |

3. 'Bǎ 把' sentence

This is unique to the Chinese language and has the effect of shifting the object of the verb in the sentence to a pre-verbal position. In general, when we want to emphasise how something (object) is changed or influenced by the action (verb) and the result of the change and the influence, we use 'bǎ 把' sentence. It is most often used with action verbs. The pattern is:

(S) + bǎ 把 + O. definite + V + other elements

For example:

Qǐng bǎ mén guānshang.	请把门关上。	Please shut the door properly.
Tā bǎ jiǔ hēwán le.	他把酒喝完了。	He has drunk all the wine.
Wǒ xiǎng bǎ Yīngbàng huànchéng Rénmínbì.	我想把英镑换成人民币。	I would like to change some sterling into RMB.

EXERCISES

1. Answer the following questions

❶ Nǐ dǎsuàn shénme shíhou qù Běijīng?
你打算什么时候去北京?

❷ Nǐ qù Shànghǎi zuò shénme?
你去上海做什么?

❸ Nǐ dǎsuàn zài Xiānggǎng zhù duō jiǔ?
你打算在香港住多久?

❹ Nǐ xiǎng qù Zhōngguó shénme dìfang?
你想去中国什么地方?

❺ Nǐ xiǎng qù Guǎngzhōu kànkan ma?
你想去广州看看吗?

2. Fill in the blanks with the words or phrases given

A. dǎsuàn	B. qǐng gěi wǒ	C. xiǎng	D. yào	E. ràng
打 算	请 给 我	想	要	让

❶ (　　　　) yì bēi chá.
　 (　　　　) 一 杯 茶。

❷ Míngnián sān yuè wǒ (　　　) qù Běijīng.
　 明 年 三 月 我 (　　　) 去 北 京。

❸ Tā (　　　) qù Běijīng xué Hànyǔ, dànshì tā fùmǔ bù tóngyì.
　 他 (　　　) 去 北 京 学 汉 语, 但 是 他 父 母 不 同 意。

❹ Tā (　　　) wǒ bāng tā mǎi yì zhāng piào.
　 他 (　　　) 我 帮 他 买 一 张 票。

❺ Kàn, tiān (　　　) xià yǔ le.
　 看, 天 (　　　) 下 雨 了。

3. Link the phrases and translate into English

❶ zhè tiáo qúnzi　　　　　　　　　a. hǎohē jíle
　 这 条 裙子　　　　　　　　　　　 好 喝 极 了

❷ zhè zhāng dìtú　　　　　　　　　 b. tài rè le
　 这 张 地图　　　　　　　　　　　 太 热 了

❸ jīntiān tiānqì　　　　　　　　　　c. piàoliang jíle
　 今 天 天 气　　　　　　　　　　　 漂 亮 极 了

❹ Shànghǎi de rén　　　　　　　　 d. tài dà le
　 上 海 的 人　　　　　　　　　　　 太 大 了

❺ zhè bēi kāfēi　　　　　　　　　　 e. duō jíle
　 这 杯 咖啡　　　　　　　　　　　 多 极 了

4. Use the 'bǎ 把' structure to rewrite the following sentences

❶ Qǐng hēwán zhè bēi kāfēi.
　 请 喝 完 这 杯 咖啡。

❷ Wǒ xiěcuòle zhè ge zì.
　 我 写 错 了 这 个 字。

❸ Zhè ge wèntí lǎoshī shuō qīngchǔ le.
　 这 个 问题老师 说 清 楚 了。

❹ Nà běn shū wǒ huán gěi túshūguǎn le.
　 那 本 书 我 还 给 图书 馆 了。

❺ Dìdi bù xiǎoxīn dǎsuìle huāpíng.
　 弟弟 不 小 心 打 碎 了 花 瓶。

5. Translate the following into Chinese

❶ I heard that your mother is coming to London.

❷ When do you want to go to Beijing?

❸ How long will you stay in China?

❹ I would like to visit the Forbidden City.

❺ I am going to go to the Great Wall tomorrow.

❻ I plan to go to London next year for the Wimbledon Championship.

❼ Where will you stay in Shanghai?

❽ I will go to New York next month.

6. Listening comprehension 🔊 27-09

Circle the correct answers according to the short dialogues.

❶ a. next spring	b. this summer	c. this autumn
❷ a. Beijing	b. Shanghai	c. Guangzhou
❸ a. two weeks	b. two months	c. three weeks
❹ a. visit friend	b. take a tour	c. learn Chinese
❺ a. Saturday morning	b. Saturday afternoon	c. Sunday morning

7. Chinese characters learning

dìng	`丶 讠 订 订`							
订	订	订	订	订	订			
fēi	`乙 飞 飞`							
飞	飞	飞	飞	飞	飞			
jī	`一 十 才 木 机 机`							
机	机	机	机	机	机			
piào	`一 ㇀ 戸 币 两 西 覀 覀 票 票 票`							
票	票	票	票	票	票			

LESSON 28
HEALTH & BODY

OBJECTIVES

★ Talking about health issues

★ Seeing a doctor

★ Asking about how to take a medicine

RELEVANT VOCABULARY

The Parts of the Human Body ◑ 28-01		
身体*	shēntǐ	body
头	tóu	head
头发*	tóufa	hair
脸*	liǎn	face
牙*	yá	tooth
胃*	wèi	stomach
肚子*	dùzi	abdomen, stomach, belly
嗓子	sǎngzi	throat
手	shǒu	hand
脚*	jiǎo	foot
腿*	tuǐ	leg
肩*	jiān	shoulder

腰*	yāo	lower back, waist
后背*	hòubèi	back (of the body)
胳膊	gēbo	arm
眼睛*	yǎnjing	eye

Sickness 🔊 28-02

疼	téng	ache, pain, hurt
头疼	tóu téng	headache
牙疼	yá téng	toothache
咳嗽	késou	to cough
发烧	fāshāo	to have a fever / temperature
感冒	gǎnmào	to have a cold
病	bìng	sick, ill
看病	kàn bìng	to see a doctor
药	yào	medicine
西药*	xīyào	Western medicine
中药	zhōngyào	Chinese medicine

🔊 28-03

次	cì	times
片	piàn	tablet, pill
后	hòu	after, behind
被	bèi	(passive grammar particle)
撞	zhuàng	to hit, to run into, to meet by accident
受伤	shòushāng	be injured, be wounded

摔破	shuāipò	to injure (break into pieces) in a fall
严重	yánzhòng	serious, critical
摔坏	shuāihuài	to drop and break
修	xiū	to repair, to mend
倒霉	dǎoméi	to have bad luck, be out of luck

KEY SENTENCES 🔊 28-04

1. Nǐ zěnme le?	你怎么了？	What's the matter?
2. Wǒ bú tài shūfu.	我不太舒服。	I am feeling unwell.
3. Wǒ tóu téng, késou, sǎngzi yě téng.	我头疼，咳嗽，嗓子也疼。	I've got a headache, cough and sore throat.
4. Zhè yào zěnme chī?	这药怎么吃？	How should I take this medicine?
5. Yì tiān sān cì, yí cì liǎng piàn.	一天三次，一次两片。	2 tablets 3 times a day.
6. Zuótiān wǒ bèi zìxíngchē zhuàng le.	昨天我被自行车撞了。	I was hit by a bike yesterday.
7. (Wèntí) yánzhòng ma?	（问题）严重吗？	Is it serious?
8. Wǒ de shǒujī bèi shuāihuài le.	我的手机被摔坏了。	My mobile phone dropped and got broken.

SITUATIONAL DIALOGUES

❶ (At the doctor's) 🔊 28-05

A: Nǐ zěnme le?	你怎么了？	What's the matter?
B: Wǒ bú tài shūfu.	我不太舒服。	I am feeling unwell.
A: Nǐ nǎr bù shūfu?	你哪儿不舒服？	What's troubling you?
B: Wǒ tóu téng, késou, sǎngzi yě téng.	我头疼，咳嗽，嗓子也疼。	I've got a headache, cough and sore throat.
A: Fāshāo ma?	发烧吗？	Do you have a temperature?
B: Zuówǎn yǒu yìdiǎnr.	昨晚有一点儿。	Last night it was a little high.
A: Duōshao dù?	多少度？	What was the temperature?
B: Sānshíqī dù bā.	三十七度八。	37.8 Degrees Celsius.
A: Nǐ kěnéng gǎnmào le.	你可能感冒了。	You probably have a cold.
B: Nín néng gěi wǒ diǎnr zhōngyào ma?	您能给我点儿中药吗？	Can you give me some Chinese herbal medicine?
A: Kěyǐ.	可以。	Yes, of course.

❷ (At the pharmacy) 🔊 28-06

A: Qǐngwèn, zhè yào zěnme chī?	请问，这药怎么吃？	Excuse me, how should I take this medicine?

B: Yì tiān sān cì, yí cì liǎng piàn.	一天三次，一次两片。	2 tablets 3 times a day.
A: Shì fàn qián chī háishì fàn hòu chī?	是饭前吃还是饭后吃？	Do I take them before or after meals?
B: Fàn qián chī.	饭前吃。	Before meals.

❸ (In the office) 🔊 28-07

A: Nǐ de shǒu zěnme le?	你的手怎么了？	What's wrong with your hand?
B: Zuótiān wǒ bèi zìxíngchē zhuàng le.	昨天我被自行车撞了。	I was hit by a bike yesterday.
A: Nǐ shòushāngle ma?	你受伤了吗？	Were you injured?
B: Shì a. Gēbo hé shǒu dōu shuāipò le.	是啊。胳膊和手都摔破了。	Yes. My arm and hand both got injured.
A: (Wèntí) yánzhòng ma? Qù méi qù yīyuàn?	（问题）严重吗？去没去医院？	Is it serious? Did you go to a hospital?
B: Qù le, yīshēng shuō wèntí bú dà. Kěshì wǒ de shǒujī bèi shuāihuài le.	去了，医生说问题不大。可是我的手机被摔坏了。	Yes, the doctor said it was not serious but my mobile phone dropped and got broken.
A: Rén méi shuāihuài jiù hǎo, shǒujī huàile kěyǐ xiū ma.	人没摔坏就好，手机坏了可以修嘛。	That's fine, as long as you weren't hurt. The mobile phone can be repaired.
B: Zhēn dǎoméi!	真倒霉！	Really bad luck!

LANGUAGE POINTS

1. '*Wǒ tóu téng* 我头疼'

It means 'I have a headache'. Notice that in describing an illness, the verb 'to have' is left out. Never say '*wǒ yǒu tóu téng* 我有头疼'.

2. '*Zěnme le* 怎么了'

It means 'what's the matter' or 'what's wrong'.

3. '*Bèi* 被' **sentence**

'*Bèi* 被' is used in a passive sentence to introduce either the doer of the action or the action itself if the doer is not mentioned. The subject of a passive sentence is the receiver of the action; the '*bèi* 被' structure is usually used to relate a realized fact and is often used in negative sentences. The pattern is:

S (receiver) + *bèi* 被 + O (doer) + V + other element

For example:

| Tā bèi zìxíngchē zhuàng le. | 他被自行车撞了。 | He was knocked over by a bike. |
| Wǒ de hùzhào bèi tōu le. | 我的护照被偷了。 | My passport was stolen. |

In spoken Chinese the preposition '*bèi* 被' can be replaced by '*jiào* 叫' or '*ràng* 让'.

EXERCISES

1. Use lines to join the matching phrases together

❶ xià yǔ le
下 雨 了

    a. yǒudiǎnr guì
有 点 儿 贵

❷ qù yīyuàn
去 医 院

    b. yǒudiǎnr tóu téng
有 点 儿 头 疼

❸ gǎnmào le
感 冒 了

    c. yǒudiǎnr lěng
有 点 儿 冷

❹ zhè ge yào
这 个 药

    d. kàn bìng
看 病

2. Match the Chinese with the English

❶ gǎnmào
感冒

a. doctor

❷ tóu téng
头 疼

b. have a toothache

❸ wèi téng
胃 疼

c. Western medicine

❹ yá téng
牙 疼

d. hospital

❺ késou
咳嗽

e. have a cold

❻ fāshāo
发烧

f. Chinese medicine

❼ zhōngyào
中 药

g. cough

❽ xīyào
西药

h. have a stomachache

❾ yīyuàn
医 院

i. have a headache

❿ yīshēng
医 生

j. have a temperature

3. Translate the following into Chinese

❶ have a meal **❷** eat a chocolate **❸** take medicine
❹ go to hospital **❺** see a doctor **❻** feel unwell

4. Translate the following into English

❶ Nǐ zěnme le? Nǎr bù shūfu?
你 怎 么 了？哪儿不 舒服？

❷ Tā jīntiān gǎnmào le,   bù néng lái shàngbān.
他 今 天 感 冒 了，不 能 来 上 班。

❸ Tā tóu téng, sǎngzi téng, fāshāo sānshíbā dù wǔ.
他 头 疼，嗓子疼，发 烧 38 度 5。

❹ Wǒ jīntiān shàngwǔ qù yīyuàn kàn bìng le.
我 今天　上　午去医院　看　病 了。

❺ Nǐ xiǎng chī zhōngyào háishì xīyào?
你 想　吃　中　药 还是西药?

❻ Zhè ge yào měi tiān chī jǐ cì? Zěnme chī?
这 个 药 每 天 吃几次? 怎么 吃?

5. Translate the following into Chinese

❶ I have got a slight headache.

❷ You should go to the hospital.

❸ I am very healthy. I have got no illness.

❹ I am not feeling very well today.

❺ Lao Wang, how is your health?

❻ His health has not been very good recently.

❼ I don't like to take medicine. I would like to take more rest.

6. Change the following sentences into the passive construction with "bèi 被"

Example:

Xiǎo māo bǎ yú chī le.　→　Yú bèi xiǎo māo chī le.
　小　猫 把鱼 吃 了。 → 鱼被 小　猫 吃 了。

❶ Tā bǎ wǒ de jiǔ hēwán le.
他把我 的 酒喝完 了。

❷ Wǒ dìdi bǎ wǒ de chē kāizǒu le.
我弟弟把我 的 车 开走了。

❸ Xiǎotōu bǎ wǒ de diànnǎo tōuzǒu le.
　小　偷把我的 电 脑 偷 走了。

❹ Wǒ mèimei bǎ wǒ de dàngāo dōu chīwán le.
我 妹 妹把我的 蛋 糕 都 吃 完了。

❺ Wǒ bǎ Hànyǔ cídiǎn jiè gěi Xiǎo Bái le.
我把汉语词典借给 小　白了。

7. Listening comprehension 📢 28-08

Choose the correct answers according to the short dialogues.

❶ a. have a cold	b. have a fever	c. stomachache
❷ a. stomachache	b. headache	c. sore throat

❸ a. 37.8	b. 38.2	c. 38.5
❹ a. three times a day after meals	b. twice a day in the morning & evening	c. three times a day before meals
❺ a. one	b. two	c. three

8. Chinese characters learning

tóu	`丶 丷 二 头 头`				
头	头	头	头	头	头
téng	`丶 亠 广 广 广 疒 疒 疼 疼 疼`				
疼	疼	疼	疼	疼	疼
gǎn	`一 厂 厂 厂 厂 咸 咸 咸 咸 感 感 感`				
感	感	感	感	感	感
mào	`丨 冂 冂 冃 冃 冒 冒 冒 冒`				
冒	冒	冒	冒	冒	冒

LESSON 29
COMPLIMENTS & WISHES

OBJECTIVES

★ Describing movements and actions

★ Making comments

★ Blessing and praise

RELEVANT VOCABULARY

🔊 29-01		
得	de	(complement marker)
流利	liúlì	fluent
写	xiě	to write
汉字	Hànzì	Chinese character
这么	zhème	such, so, like this
办法	bànfǎ	way, means, method
练	liàn	to practice
过	guò	to pass, to go through, to celebrate
祝	zhù	to wish
快乐	kuàilè	happy
干杯	gānbēi	cheers

Sport and Entertainment 🔊 29-02

打球	dǎqiú	to play ball
走*	zǒu	to walk
走路*	zǒulù	go on foot
跑*	pǎo	to run
跑步*	pǎobù	jogging
跳*	tiào	to jump
跳高*	tiàogāo	high jump
跳远*	tiàoyuǎn	long jump
跳水*	tiàoshuǐ	diving
跳舞*	tiàowǔ	to dance, dancing
唱歌*	chànggē	to sing (a song)
游泳*	yóuyǒng	to swim, swimming

KEY SENTENCES 🔊 29-03

1.	Tīngshuō nǐ wǎngqiú dǎ de búcuò a.	听说你网球打得不错啊。	I've heard that you play tennis very well.
2.	Nǎli nǎli.	哪里哪里。	Not at all, you're too kind!
3.	Nǐ de Hànyǔ shuō de zhēn liúlì!	你的汉语说得真流利！	You speak Chinese very fluently!
4.	Nǐ zěnme xiě de zhème hǎo?	你怎么写得这么好？	How do you write so well?

5. Zhǐyǒu yí ge bànfǎ, jiù shì shì duō xiě, duō liàn!	只有一个办法，就是多写、多练！	There is only one way which is to write more and to practice more!
6. Zhù nǐ xīnnián kuàilè!	祝你新年快乐！	I wish you a Happy New Year!
7. Zhù nǐ shēngrì kuàilè!	祝你生日快乐！	I wish you a happy birthday!
8. Gānbēi!	干杯！	Cheers!

SITUATIONAL DIALOGUES

❶ (At a bus stop) 🔊 29-04

A: Tīngshuō nǐ wǎngqiú dǎ de búcuò a.	听说你网球打得不错啊。	I've heard that you play tennis very well.
B: Nǎli nǎli.	哪里哪里。	Not really, you're too kind!
A: Xīngqītiān wǒmen yìqǐ qù dǎ wǎngqiú ba!	星期天我们一起去打网球吧！	Shall we play tennis on Sunday?
B: Hǎo a.	好啊。	OK.

❷ (At a party) 🔊 29-05

A: Nǐ de Hànyǔ shuō de zhēn liúlì!	你的汉语说得真流利！	You speak Chinese very fluently!
B: Nǎli nǎli.	哪里哪里。	Not at all, you're too kind!
A: Shéi shì nǐ de lǎoshī?	谁是你的老师？	Who is your teacher?
B: Wáng lǎoshī, tā shì Běijīng rén.	王老师，她是北京人。	Miss Wang. She is from Beijing.

SITUATIONAL DIALOGUES

❸ (In the class) 🔊 29-06

A:	Nǐ de Hànzì xiě de zhēn piàoliang!	你的汉字写得真漂亮!	You write Chinese characters very beautifully!
B:	Shì ma? Xièxie.	是吗? 谢谢。	Really? Thank you!
A:	Nǐ zěnme xiě de zhème hǎo?	你怎么写得这么好?	How do you write so well?
B:	Zhǐyǒu yí ge bànfǎ, jiù shì duō xiě, duō liàn!	只有一个办法，就是多写、多练!	There is only one way which is to write more and to practice more!

❹ (At a New Year's reception) 🔊 29-07

A:	Shíjiān guò de zhēn kuài, xīnnián dào le.	时间过得真快，新年到了。	The time has passed very quickly. The New Year is here!
B:	Zhù nǐ xīnnián kuàilè!	祝你新年快乐!	I wish you a Happy New Year!
A:	Zhù dàjiā xīnnián hǎo!	祝大家新年好!	Happy New Year, everyone!

❺ (At a birthday party) 🔊 29-08

A:	Jīntiān shì nǐ de shēngrì, zhù nǐ shēngrì kuàilè!	今天是你的生日，祝你生日快乐!	Today is your birthday. I wish you a happy birthday!
B:	Gānbēi!	干杯!	Cheers!
All:	Gānbēi!	干杯!	Cheers!

LANGUAGE POINTS

1. The particle 'de 得'

It is used to link a verb with an adverb to describe the degree of an action. This is a different 'de 的' from 'wǒ de 我的' (my / mine). Note that 'de 得' must follow the verb directly but, where there is an object, it has to be before the verb. The pattern is:

S + (O) + Verb + 得 + (Adv.) + Adj.

For example:

Nǐ (Hànyǔ) shuō de zhēn hǎo.	你（汉语）说得真好。	You speak Chinese really well.
Tā pǎo de hěn kuài.	他跑得很快。	He runs very fast.

2. 'Nǎli nǎli 哪里哪里'

A variant form of 'nǎr 哪儿' is 'nǎlǐ 哪里'. Traditionally 'nǎlǐ 哪里' is used as a polite self-deprecating response to praise or flattery, as if to say 'not really'. With increasing Western influence more and more people just say 'xièxie 谢谢' in response to a compliment.

EXERCISES

1. Use lines to join the matching phrases together with 'de 得'

❶ Hànyǔ shuō
汉语 说

❷ wǎnfàn chī
晚饭 吃

❸ pǎo
跑

❹ wǎngqiú dǎ
网球 打

❺ shēngrì guò
生日 过

❻ shíjiān guò
时间 过

❼ Hànzì xiě
汉字 写

❽ shuì
睡

a. hěn shūfu
很 舒服

b. zhēn kuài
真 快

c. hěn liúlì
很 流利

d. hěn màn
很 慢

e. hěn yúkuài
很 愉快

f. hěn hǎo
很 好

g. zhēn piàoliang
真 漂亮

h. hěn kuài
很 快

2. Translate the following into English

① Nǐ de Yīngyǔ shuō de tài hǎo le.
你的 英语 说 得太好了。

③ Tā de Fǎyǔ shuō de hěn liúlì.
他的 法语 说 得 很流利。

② Nǎli nǎli.
哪里哪里。

④ Tā chī de hěn màn.
他吃 得 很 慢。

⑤ Tā pǎo de hěn kuài.
他跑 得 很 快。

⑦ Wǒ de Hànyǔ shuō de bú tài hǎo.
我 的 汉语 说 得不太 好。

⑥ Shíjiān guò de tài kuài le.
时间 过 得太快 了。

⑧ Tā de Hànzi xiě de hěn piàoliang.
他的 汉字 写得很 漂 亮。

3. Translate the following into Chinese, using (de 得)

① The student read slowly.

② The child ate a lot.

③ The man jumped really high.

④ Lucy can speak Mandarin very fluently.

⑤ I got up very early this morning.

⑥ The teacher teaches well.

⑦ He runs very fast.

⑧ It's raining heavily.

⑨ The little girl was beautifully dressed.

4. Say the following sentences in Chinese

① Happy New Year! **②** Happy Christmas! **③** Happy birthday to you!

④ Have a nice weekend! **⑤** I wish you good luck!

5. Classroom activities

Practise with your classmates using the pattern: verb + de 得 + adjective.

(Examples: 写得不好，说得太快，玩得很愉快)

6. Chinese characters learning

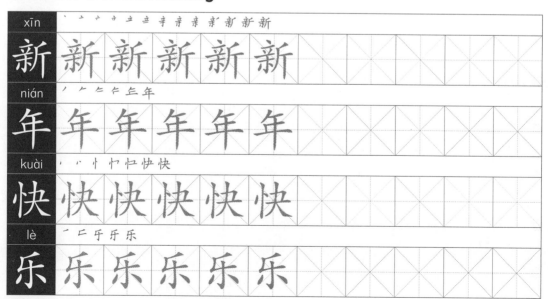

xīn	、 ⸀ ㇏ ㇏ 立 立 辛 亲 亲 亲 新 新 新				
新	新	新	新	新	新
nián	ノ ⸀ ㇒ ㇋ 仁 年				
年	年	年	年	年	年
kuài	、 丶 忄 忄 忙 快 快				
快	快	快	快	快	快
lè	㇒ 二 午 牙 乐				
乐	乐	乐	乐	乐	乐

LESSON 30
SUMMARY
LESSONS 25-29

OBJECTIVES

★ Practicing the vocabulary and grammars from lessons 25-29

★ Cultural insights: travel in China

KEY PATTERNS

Patterns	Sentences
A bǐ 比 B + adj.	Jīntiān bǐ zuótiān lěng. 今天比昨天冷。
A méiyǒu 没有 B + adj.	Zuótiān méiyǒu jīntiān lěng. 昨天没有今天冷。
A bǐ 比 B + adj. + degree	Jīntiān bǐ zuótiān lěng yìdiǎnr. 今天比昨天冷一点儿。 Jīntiān bǐ zuótiān lěng de duō. 今天比昨天冷得多。
A gēn 跟 B (bù 不) + yíyàng 一样	Zhè běn shū gēn nà běn yíyàng. 这本书跟那本一样。
A gēn 跟 B + yíyàng 一样 + adj.	Wǒ gēn wǒ dìdi yíyàng gāo. 我跟我弟弟一样高。
Subject + (zhèng 正) zài 在 + verb + (ne 呢)	Tā zhèngzài kàn shū ne. 他正在看书呢。 Tā zài dǎ diànhuà. 他在打电话。
Resultative Complement: verb + complement (verb / adjective)	Nǐ kànjiàn Lǐ lǎoshī le ma? 你看见李老师了吗?
Potential Complement: verb + de 得 / bu 不 + complement (verb / adjective)	Wǒ kàn de / bu dǒng. 我看得 / 不懂。
(S) + kuài 快 / yào 要 + V. + le 了	Tiān yào xià yǔ le. 天要下雨了。 Huǒchē kuài dào le. 火车快到了。
(S) + bǎ 把 + O. definite + V. + other elements	Qǐng bǎ mén guānshang. 请把门关上。 Tā bǎ jiǔ hēwán le. 他把酒喝完了。
S (receiver) + bèi 被 + O (doer) + V + other element	Wǒ de shǒujī bèi dìdi shuāihuài le. 我的手机被弟弟摔坏了。
Subject + (O) + verb + de 得 + (adv.) + adj.	Nǐ Hànyǔ shuō de zhēn hǎo. 你汉语说得真好。

RELEVANT VOCABULARY

🔊 30-01		
美	měi	beautiful, pretty
旅途	lǔtú	journey, trip
愉快	yúkuài	happy, joyful
新春	Xīnchūn	Chinese New Year
开心	kāixīn	have a good time, enjoy
顺利	shùnlì	smooth
事业	shìyè	career
成功	chénggōng	successful
幸福	xìngfú	happiness
健康	jiànkāng	healthy

STORY TIME

Listen to the following story and retell it in Chinese 🔊 30-02

Qù Xiānggǎng lǚyóu
去 香 港 旅游

Chūntiān yào dào le,　tiānqì nuǎnhuo le.　Wǒ xǐhuan Běijīng de chūntiān,　suīrán yǒu
春 天 要 到 了, 天 气 暖 和 了。我 喜欢 北京 的 春天, 虽然 有

shíhou guā fēng,　yǒudiǎnr gānzào,　kěshì tiāntiān dōu shì qíngtiān,　hěn shǎo xià yǔ.　Běijīng
时候 刮 风, 有点儿 干燥, 可是 天天 都 是 晴天, 很 少 下 雨。北京

de xiàtiān fēicháng rè,　qìwēn hěn gāo,　sānshí duō dù,　yǒushí xià dà yǔ,　hěn bù shūfu.
的 夏天 非常 热, 气温 很 高, 三十 多 度, 有时 下 大雨, 很 不 舒服。

Běijīng de qiūtiān zuì měi,　bù lěng bú rè.　Běijīng de dōngtiān hěn lěng,　yǒushí xià xuě,
北京 的 秋天 最 美, 不 冷 不 热。北京 的 冬天 很 冷, 有时 下 雪,

dànshì hěn piàoliang.
但是 很 漂亮。

Wǒ hé　Lìli　jìhuà jīnnián sān yuè qù Xiānggǎng lǚyóu,　wǒmen dǎsuàn zài　nàli　zhù
我 和 丽丽 计划 今年 三 月 去 香 港 旅游, 我们 打算 在 那里 住

wǔ tiān.　Wǒmen dōu méi qùguo Xiānggǎng,　dànshì tīngshuō Xiānggǎng de chūntiān tiānqì
五天。我们 都 没去过 香 港，但是 听说 香 港 的春天天气

hěn hǎo,　bǐ Běijīng rè de duō; Xiānggǎng de hǎixiān yě hěn yǒumíng,　bǐ Běijīng de hǎo chī
很 好，比 北京 热得多；香 港 的海鲜也很 有名，比 北京 的好吃

de duō.　　Lìli　hé wǒ dōu xǐhuan rè de dìfang,　yě dōu xǐhuan chī hǎixiān.
得多。丽丽和我都喜欢 热的地方，也都喜欢吃 海鲜。

　　Qù Xiānggǎng lǚyóu yǐqián,　wǒ hé　Lìli　dōu hěn máng,　wǒmen yào dìng　fēijī piào,
去 香 港旅游以前，我和丽丽 都 很 忙，我们 要 订飞机票、

dìng fàndiàn,　hái yào bǎ Rénmínbì huànchéng Gǎngbì.　Qù bàn qiānzhèng de shíhou,
订 饭店，还要把人民币换 成 港币。去办 签 证 的时候，

wǒmen jiàndaole　yí ge duō nián méi jiàn de lǎo tóngxué,　tā yě yào　qù Xiānggǎng lǚyóu.
我们 见到了一个多 年 没见的老 同学，他也要 去 香 港旅游。

Bànwán qiānzhèng yǐhòu,　wǒmen yìqǐ　qùle yì jiā kāfēitīng,　yìbiān liáotiān,　yìbiān hē
办完 签 证 以后，我们 一起 去了一家咖啡厅，一边 聊天，一边 喝

kāfēi,　dàjiā liáo de hěn gāoxìng. Zuìhòu,
咖啡，大家聊 得很 高兴。最后，

wǒ de péngyou zhù wǒ hé　Lìli　lǚtú　yúkuài,
我的 朋 友祝我和丽丽旅途愉快，

zài Xiānggǎng wánr　de kāixīn.　Wǒmen yě zhù
在 香 港 玩儿得开心。我们 也祝

tā yílù　shùnfēng,　wánr　de yúkuài.
他一路 顺 风，玩儿得愉快。

GREETING PHRASES 🔊 30-03

Zhù nǐ Xīnnián kuàilè.	祝你新年快乐。	Happy New Year.
Zhù nǐ Xīnchūn yúkuài.	祝你新春愉快。	Happy Chinese New Year.
Zhù nǐ shēngrì kuàilè.	祝你生日快乐。	Happy birthday.
Zhù nǐ gōngzuò shùnlì.	祝你工作顺利。	I wish you success in your work.
Zhù nǐ shìyè chénggōng.	祝你事业成功。	I wish you success in your career.
Zhù nǐ xìngfú kuàilè.	祝你幸福快乐。	I wish you happiness.
Zhù nǐ lǚtú yúkuài.	祝你旅途愉快。	I wish you a pleasant journey.
Zhù nǐ yílù shùnfēng.	祝你一路顺风。	I wish you a smooth journey.
Zhù nǐ shēntǐ jiànkāng.	祝你身体健康。	I wish you good health.

CULTURAL INSIGHTS

Travel in China

When Katie Melua sang that there were nine million bicycles in Beijing, that probably was a fact. For decades bicycles have been the primary means of personal transport, not just in Beijing but throughout China, simply because they were cheap and readily available.

Over the past decade, however, China has seen a phenomenal growth in the number of cars on the road as an increasing number of people have become wealthy enough to afford them. Indeed, there might well be as many cars on China's roads now as there were bicycles a few years ago.

Many families in China might now own both forms of transport to get around but visitors to China will find it difficult to hire a car because foreign travellers need a special licence to drive. Bicycles might be more freely available but they too are subject to special rules and regulations about how and where they can be ridden. For most tourists, taxis and public transport are a more practical option and a more relaxed way to see the country.

Which option you choose depends on where you are going. China is a vast country and if you are travelling from one region to another, it's probably best to fly and even that could take a long time. For example a direct flight from Beijing to Hong Kong takes about three hours, from Harbin in the north to Haikou in the south will take closer to six hours!

For those with a little more time on their hands, it would be worth considering China's new High Speed Railway or the 'bullet trains' as they are called. The network is still being developed but it currently connects all the major cities using trains that travel at incredible speeds up to around 200mph. They are comfortably modern, smooth and quiet and almost as fast as air travel.

Traditional railways, of course, cover the rest of the country and allow tourists to travel from one city to another and enjoy the views at a more relaxed pace.

Within the cities there are urban railway systems connecting all areas, some of which are underground. Beijing and Shanghai in particular have modern, comprehensive subway systems that are almost as big as those found in London or New York. Above ground, buses are a cheap alternative and have bus conductors who can help you find the right stop provided, of course, you can speak Chinese. Buses are a good way to get around but can get very crowded at rush hours.

For the less adventurous, there are plenty of taxis and taxi drivers willing to take you to places of interest. Taxis are relatively inexpensive when compared to somewhere like London, but the system of ordering a taxi has become very high-tech recently which can be a bit off-putting if you don't understand it or don't have the right application on your smart phone. To those who have the right equipment and know-how a taxi driver can be ordered within minutes, can be tracked on-screen so that you know how long you will need to wait and will arrive already paid and fully aware who you are and where you are going!

If that all sounds too much, there are still low tech pedal powered rickshaws which can be hired very cheaply and will only take cash. They will be restricted to travelling only a few streets and can be fun but, personally, I prefer to walk.

CHINESE CHARACTERS LEARNING

lǚ	、 一 亍 方 方 方 旅 旅 旅 旅								
旅	旅	旅	旅	旅	旅				
tú	ノ 人 ム 合 合 余 余 涂 涂 途								
途	途	途	途	途	途				
yú	、 ´ 忄 忄 忙 忙 恰 恰 愉 愉 愉								
愉	愉	愉	愉	愉	愉				
kuài	、 ´ 忄 忙 忙 快 快								
快	快	快	快	快	快				

INDEX I
LISTENING SCRIPTS

Lesson 1

▶ **Circle the correct answers according to the phrases you have heard.** 🔊 01-09

❶ 你好　　❷ 你好吗?　　❸ 你怎么样?　　❹ 我很好

❺ 不错　　❻ 马马虎虎　　❼ 再见　　❽ 明天见

Lesson 2

▶ **Mark true (T) or false (F) according to the short dialogues.** 🔊 02-09

❶ 男：您贵姓?　　　　　　　❷ 男：你叫什么?
　 女：我姓梁。　　　　　　　　女：我叫林晓红。

❸ 女：他是谁?　　　　　　　❹ 女：我姓赵，您呢?
　 男：他是王峰。　　　　　　　男：我姓张。

❺ 男：他姓什么?
　 女：他姓刘，叫刘浩然。

Lesson 3

▶ **Mark true (T) or false (F) according to the short dialogues.** 🔊 03-10

❶ 男：请问您是哪国人?　　　❷ 男：您说法语吗?
　 女：我是奥地利人。　　　　　女：不，我说德语。

❸ 男：马修是英国人吗?　　　❹ 女：我是法国人，你呢?
　 女：他是英国人。　　　　　　男：我也是法国人。

❺ 女：你从哪儿来?
　 男：我从慕尼黑来。

Lesson 4

▶ **Choose the correct answers according to the short dialogues.** 🔊 04-10

❶ 男：今天几号?　　　　　　❷ 男：明天星期几?
　 女：今天四号。　　　　　　　女：明天星期天。

　 男：*What is the date today?*　　男：*What day is tomorrow?*

❸ 男：现在是几月？

　　女：现在是九月。

　　男：*What month is it now?*

❺ 男：昨天是你的生日吗？

　　女：不是，我的生日是明天。

　　男：*When is her birthday?*

❹ 男：你的生日是几月几号？

　　女：我的生日是五月二号。

　　男：*When is her birthday?*

Lesson 5

▶ **Choose the correct answers according to the short dialogues.** 🔊 05-08

❶ 女：请问，现在几点？

　　男：现在十点十分。

❸ 女：你几点吃早饭？

　　男：差十分八点。

❺ 女：商店几点开门？

　　男：早上九点。

❷ 女：你每天早上几点起床？

　　男：七点一刻。

❹ 女：你几点吃晚饭？

　　男：六点半。

Lesson 7

▶ **Choose the correct answers according to the short dialogues.** 🔊 07-10

❶ 男：你住哪儿？

　　女：我住北京饭店。

❸ 男：你的电话是多少？

　　女：02078031649。

❺ 男：美国大使馆在哪儿？

　　女：在安家楼路55号。

❷ 男：你的房间是多少号？

　　女：1425。

❹ 男：你的手机号是多少？

　　女：07981462315。

Lesson 8

▶ **Choose the correct answers according to the short dialogues.** 🔊 08-08

❶ 男：你家有几口人？

　　女：我家有五口人。

　　男：*How many people are there in her family?*

❸ 男：你弟弟多大？

　　女：他今年十六岁。

　　男：*How old is her younger brother?*

❺ 男：你儿子几岁？

　　女：八岁。

　　男：*How old is her son?*

❷ 男：你有哥哥吗？

　　女：没有，我有弟弟。

　　男：*Does she have younger brothers?*

❹ 男：你妈妈多大年纪？

　　女：她五十七岁。

　　男：*How old is her mother?*

Lesson 9

▶ **Mark true (T) or false (F) according to the short dialogues.** 🔊 09-09

❶ 女：你在哪儿工作？
　　男：我在银行工作。我是会计。

❷ 男：你在哪儿工作？
　　女：我医院工作。

❸ 男：你是医生吗？
　　女：不是，我是护士。

❹ 女：你是不是老师？
　　男：我不是老师，是律师。

❺ 女：我在公司工作，你呢？
　　男：我不工作。

Lesson 10

▶ **Mark true (T) or false (F) according to the short dialogues.** 🔊 10-09

❶ 男：你喜欢看哪国电影？
　　女：我喜欢看美国电影。

❷ 男：你会做意大利饭吗？
　　女：不会。我会做法国饭。

❸ 男：周末你喜欢做什么？
　　女：我喜欢去商店买东西。

❹ 女：你喜欢吃中国饭吗？
　　男：很喜欢。

❺ 女：你会不会做中国饭？
　　男：会一点儿。

Lesson 11

▶ **Mark true (T) or false (F) according to the short dialogues.** 🔊 11-07

❶ 男：周末我们去看电影好吗？
　　女：对不起，我没时间。

❷ 男：明天晚上我们去吃中国饭吧？
　　女：太好了，几点？

❸ 女：你现在有时间吗？
　　男：有，你有事吗？

❹ 男：星期六我请你吃北京烤鸭吧？
　　女：我不喜欢吃烤鸭。

❺ 女：今晚我们去酒吧喝酒好吗？
　　男：好啊，七点怎么样？

Lesson 13

▶ **Mark true (T) or false (F) according to the short dialogues.** 🔊 13-08

❶ 男：请问张先生在吗？
　　女：对不起，他不在。

　　男：我是英国大使馆的艾德华。

❸ 女：张先生不在，要留言吗？
　　男：谢谢，请他给我回电话。

❹ 男：喂，是长城饭店吗？
　　女：是啊，您找谁？

❺ 男：1102房间的赵之杰。
　　女：好，请等一下。

❷ 女：您是哪位？

Lesson 14

► **Choose the correct answers according to the phrases you have heard.**

🔊 14-07

❶ 一百块　　　❷ 一百二十块　　　❸ 五毛　　　❹ 六十九块四

❺ 七块八　　　❻ 二十九块九　　　❼ 五分　　　❽ 三十三块九毛九

Lesson 15

► **Choose the correct answers according to the short dialogues.** 🔊 15-10

❶ 女：你去哪儿？
　　男：我去书店。
　　女：*Where is he going?*

❷ 女：您买什么？
　　男：我想买中国地图。
　　女：*What does he want to buy?*

❸ 男：多少钱一张？
　　女：八块五。
　　男：*How much is it?*

❹ 男：你们收美元吗？
　　女：不收，我们只收人民币。
　　男：*What kind of currency does the shop accept?*

❺ 男：这本词典多少钱？
　　女：二十二块九毛五。
　　男：*How much is the dictionary?*

Lesson 16

► **Mark true (T) or false (F) according to the short dialogues.** 🔊 16-08

❶ 女：您买什么？
　　男：我想买一条领带。

❷ 男：这种大衣有黑色的吗？
　　女：没有，有蓝的和灰的。

❸ 男：你喜欢这件红毛衣吗？
　　女：不喜欢，我喜欢粉的。

❹ 男：这件毛衣很漂亮，买一件吧。
　　女：不要，太贵了！

❺ 女：这条蓝领带不错，要一条吧。
　　男：我想要那条绿的。

Lesson 17

► **Choose the correct answers according to the short dialogues.** 🔊 17-08

❶ 女：您穿多大号的鞋？
　　男：我穿42号的。
　　女：*What size of shoes does he wear?*

❷ 男：您穿多大号的衣服？
　　女：我穿中号的。
　　男：*What size clothing does she wear?*

❸ 女：这双鞋合适吗？
　　男：不大不小，正合适。
　　女：*Do the shoes fit him?*

❹ 女：这条裤子合适吗？
　　男：不行，太短了。
　　女：*Do the trousers fit him?*

❺ 男：你喜欢什么颜色的上衣？
　　女：我喜欢紫色的。
　　男：*What kind of colour does she like?*

Lesson 19

▶ **Choose the correct answers according to the short dialogues.** 🔊 19-08

❶ 女：你们要什么菜？
　　男：我们只要素菜，不要肉。
　　女：*What kind of dishes do they want?*

❷ 女：我们有海鲜，要吗？
　　男：只要鱼，不要虾。
　　女：*What kind of seafood do they want?*

❸ 女：你们要炒饭还是白饭？
　　男：要炒饭。
　　女：*What kind of rice do they want?*

❹ 男：你喜欢吃牛肉还是羊肉？
　　女：我喜欢吃猪肉。
　　男：*What kind of meat dose she like to eat?*

❺ 男：我们要鸡还是要鸭？
　　女：鸡和鸭我们都要。
　　男：*Do they want chicken or duck?*

Lesson 20

▶ **Mark true (T) or false (F) according to the short dialogues.** 🔊 20-08

❶ 女：青岛啤酒好喝吗？
　　男：好喝极了。

❷ 女：你喝过中国的茅台吗？
　　男：没喝过。

❸ 女：您想喝点儿什么？
　　男：一瓶可乐。

❹ 女：这个啤酒的味道怎么样？
　　男：不好喝。

❺ 女：冰咖啡要加奶油吗？
　　男：谢谢，不加。

Lesson 21

▶ **Choose the correct answers according to the short dialogues.** 🔊 21-08

❶ 女：刚才你去哪儿了？
　　男：我去银行了。
　　女：*Where has he been?*

❷ 女：你去商务中心做什么？
　　男：我去查电子邮件。
　　女：*What did he do in the Business Centre?*

❸ 女：昨天晚上你去哪儿了？
　　男：我去酒吧了。
　　女：*Where did he go last night?*

❹ 男：请问，卫生间在哪儿？
　　女：在二楼。
　　男：*Where is the toilet?*

❺ 女：先生，您有事吗？
　　男：我想发传真。
　　女：*What did he want?*

Lesson 22

▶ **Choose the correct answers according to the short dialogues.** 🔊 22-11

❶ 男：你每天怎么去上班？
女：我坐地铁去上班。

❷ 男：你家离火车站远不远？
女：不太远。

❸ 男：你怎么去超市买东西？
女：我开车去。

❹ 女：周末你怎么去巴黎？
男：我坐火车去。

❺ 女：你怎么去上海？
男：我坐飞机去。

Lesson 23

▶ **Choose the correct answers according to the short dialogues.** 🔊 23-07

❶ 男：北京饭店在哪儿？
女：在北京的中心。

❷ 男：故宫在哪儿？
女：在北京饭店的西北边。

❸ 男：银行是不是在书店前边？
女：不是，银行在书店左边。

❹ 男：从伦敦到曼城开车要多长时间？
女：大概三个小时。

❺ 男：从伦敦到北京坐飞机要多长时间？
女：大概十个小时。

Lesson 25

▶ **Choose the correct answers according to the short dialogues.** 🔊 25-09

❶ 男：今天天气怎么样？
女：今天天气不太冷。

❷ 男：昨天气温是多少度？
女：昨天气温是21度。

❸ 男：今天热还是昨天热？
女：今天比昨天热。

❹ 男：广州冬天天气怎么样？
女：常常下雨。

❺ 男：明天有雨吗？
女：大概有小雨。

Lesson 26

▶ **Choose the correct answers according to the short dialogues.** 🔊 26-07

❶ 男：陈刚在干什么呢？
女：他正在看电视。

❷ 男：张燕在做什么呢？
女：她正在上网聊天。

❸ 男：王丹，你在忙什么？
女：我正忙着做饭呢。

❹ 男：林南在家吗？
女：不在，她去买东西了。

❺ 女：喂，皮特你现在在哪儿？
男：我在朋友家。

Lesson 27

▶ **Circle the correct answers according to the short dialogues.** 🔊 27-09

❶ 男：你打算什么时候去中国？　　❷ 男：你想去中国什么地方？
　　女：今年秋天。　　　　　　　　　女：广州。

❸ 男：你计划在上海住多久？　　　❹ 男：爱玛为什么去北京？
　　女：两个星期。　　　　　　　　　女：她去旅游。

❺ 男：你打算什么时候去购物中心？
　　女：星期六下午。

Lesson 28

▶ **Choose the correct answers according to the short dialogues.** 🔊 28-08

❶ 女：你怎么了？　　　　　　　　❷ 女：你哪儿不舒服？
　　男：我感冒了。　　　　　　　　　男：我头疼。

❸ 女：小林发烧多少度？　　　　　❹ 男：这个药怎么吃？
　　男：38度5。　　　　　　　　　　女：一天三次，饭后吃。

❺ 男：这个药一次吃几片？
　　女：一次吃两片。

INDEX II
KEY TO THE EXERCISES

The Sounds of Chinese-*Pinyin*

3.

nǐ hǎo 你好	fàndiàn 饭店
fùjìn 附近	yǒumíng 有名
yīshēng 医生	lǎoshī 老师
Hànyǔ 汉语	míngtiān 明天

jī 鸡	qù 去	xī 西
jiā 家	qī 七	xiā 虾
jiào 叫	qián 钱	xiǎng 想
jiē 街	qǐng 请	xiǎo 小
jīntiān 今天	qiūtiān 秋天	xiānsheng 先生
jīnglǐ 经理	qúnzi 裙子	xìngmíng 姓名

zǎo 早	cài 菜	sān 三
zài 在	cì 次	sì 四
zǒu 走	cóng 从	suì 岁
zǐsè 紫色	cídiǎn 辞典	suīrán 虽然

zhǎo 找	zhè 这	Zhōngguó 中国
chá 茶	chē 车	chī 吃
shì 是	shū 书	shénme 什么
rén 人	rì 日	rènshi 认识

Lesson 1

1. ❶ c **❷** d **❸** b **❹** b **❺** a

2. ❶ A：你好！Peter。

B：你好！Emma。

A：你好吗？

B：我很好。谢谢你。你呢？

A：我也很好。谢谢！

❷ A：Penny，你好吗？

B：马马虎虎，你呢？

A：我也马马虎虎。

❸ A：Jessica，你怎么样？

B：不错。你呢？

A：我也不错。

❹ A：David，你忙吗？

B：不太忙。你呢？

A：我很忙。

❺ A：Lucy，你累吗？

B：我很累。你呢？

A：我也很累。

3. ❶ 你好 **❷** 再见 **❸** 谢谢

❹ 好 **❺** 很好 **❻** 不错

❼ 马马虎虎 **❽** 不太忙

❾ 很累 **❿** 谢谢你

4. ❶ b **❷** a **❸** c **❹** a **❺** b

❻ c **❼** b **❽** a

Lesson 2

2. ❶ 我姓Jones。

❷ 我叫Helen。

❸ 我朋友叫Lisa。

❹ 王小姐是我朋友。

❺ 李先生也是我朋友。

❻ 很高兴认识你。

❼ 你叫什么名字？

❽ 请问，她是张小姐吗？

❾ 您贵姓？

❿ 这是什么？

3. ❶—d **❷**—j **❸**—i **❹**—g

❺—h **❻**—b **❼**—c **❽**—e

❾—a **❿**—f

4. ❶ F **❷** T **❸** F **❹** F **❺** T

Lesson 3

1. ❶ 中国 英国 美国 法国 俄罗斯

德国 加拿大 日本 意大利

丹麦 荷兰 西班牙

❷ 中国人 英国人 法国人 德国人

加拿大人 意大利人 日本人

丹麦人

❸ 汉语 英语 法语 意大利语

德语 日语 阿拉伯语 西班牙语

俄语 印度尼西亚语

2. ❶—f **❷**—h **❸**—e **❹**—b

❺—a **❻**—i **❼**—j **❽**—d

❾—c **❿**—g

3. ❶ B **❷** I **❸** D **❹** C **❺** J

❻ A **❼** G **❽** F **❾** H **❿** E

4. ❶ 你是中国人吗？

❷ 我不是中国人。我是日本人。

❸ 你说日语吗？

❹ 他是不是从巴黎来？

❺ 你是哪国人？

❻ Lucy不是英国人。她是加拿大人。

❼ 他太太说德语。

❽ Matthew从哪儿来？

❾ Anna不说意大利语，她说西班牙语。

❿ 我们都说汉语。

5. ❶ F **❷** T **❸** T **❹** F **❺** F

Lesson 4

1. ❶ 今天星期几？

❷ 昨天是几月几号？

❸ 今年春节是几月几号星期几？

❹ 他的生日是几月几号？

❺ 明天是几月几号星期几?

2. ❶ 今天是十月十一号。

❷ 明天是星期三。

❸ 昨天是我的生日。

❹ 我妈妈的生日是一九六四年十二月二十号。

❺ 我爸爸的生日是一九六七年一月十七号。

❻ Bobby的生日是一九八七年四月二十三号。

❼ 圣诞节是十二月二十五号。

❽ 新年是一月一号。

❾ 今年春节是一月二十九号。

❿ 丽丽下个月去上海。

3. ❶ —f ❷ —l ❸ —h ❹ —k

❺ —d ❻ —i ❼ —a ❽ —j

❾ —e ❿ —g ⓫ —b ⓬ —c

4. ❶ b ❷ a ❸ b ❹ c ❺ c

Lesson 5

1. ❶ 六点,八点二十(分),差五分两点,三点半

❷ 十二点三十五(分),十一点十分,两点二十(分),差一刻十点

❸ 五点一刻,十点五分,五点半,差一刻五点

❹ 六点八分,差五分四点,七点四十五(分),两点半

❺ 四点五分,十二点十分,九点一刻,两点三十五(分)

2. ❶ 差五分十二点

❷ 差十分八点

❸ 差五分八点

❹ 七点三十五(分)

❺ 差一刻十一点

❻ 六点二十五(分)

❼ 十一点三十五(分)

❽ 八点半

❾ 九点

❿ 七点五分

⓫ 十二点二十五(分)

⓬ 十一点半

⓭ 四点三十五(分)

⓮ 八点五分

⓯ 差十分九点

⓰ 四点五分

4. ❶ 每天 ❷ 每月 ❸ 每星期

❹ 每年 ❺ 每人 ❻ 每晚

5. ❶ 1978年6月19号星期一上午

❷ 1958年8月30号星期六下午

❸ 1986年12月8号星期一晚上

❹ 2012年2月14号星期二下午

❺ 3月30号星期三早上8点

6. ❶ a ❷ b ❸ c ❹ b ❺ b

Lesson 7

1. ❶ 在 ❷ 北京饭店 ❸ 哪儿

❹ 在 ❺ 哪儿

2. ❶ 你家在哪儿? or你家在什么地方?

❷ 英语学校在哪儿? or英语学校在什么地方?

❸ 你的电话是多少?

❹ 你的手机号是多少?

❺ 你住在哪儿? or你住在什么地方?

3. ❶ May I ask, where is the Bank of China?

❷ Where are you going now?

❸ My wife is not at home. She is in the office now.

❹ My father and mother are living in Shanghai.

❺ We are going to a Chinese restaurant to have a meal.

❻ He is going to the shop to do some shopping on Saturday.

7 Excuse me, where is Starbucks?

8 I go to Chinese school every Wednesday.

9 Teacher Gao's home is not in Beijing.

10 This is my e-mail address.

4. 1 我妈妈不在家。

2 我的汉语老师住在伦敦。

3 你住哪儿?

4 请问，厕所在哪儿?

5 你的手机号是多少?

6 你的电话是多少?

7 请问您的电子信箱是什么?

8 陈先生在他的办公室。

9 你的房间号码是多少?

10 你家在哪儿? or你家在什么地方?

5. 1 a　**2** b　**3** a　**4** c　**5** b

Lesson 8

1. 1 你是不是英国人?

2 他有没有孩子?

3 王丹在不在家?

4 这是不是你的书?

5 你们学不学汉语?

6 你的汉语老师是不是中国人?

7 她是不是你姐姐?

8 你的家在不在伦敦?

2. 1 他哥哥多大?

2 你女儿几岁?

3 您父亲多大年纪?

3. 1—j　**2**—l　**3**—d　**4**—k

5—i　**6**—e　**7**—f　**8**—g

9—b　**10**—a　**11**—c　**12**—h

4. 1 我家有四口人，我太太、我儿子、
我女儿和我。

2 你有几个孩子?

3 你儿子几岁?

4 你有女朋友吗? 她叫什么?

5 她是不是你太太?

6 你有几个哥哥?

7 你弟弟多大?

8 你妈妈多大年纪?

9 你妹妹有男朋友吗?

10 我儿子叫Patrick，我女儿叫Grace。

5. 1 b　**2** a　**3** c　**4** b　**5** c

Lesson 9

1. 1—g　**2**—h　**3**—b　**4**—j

5—a　**6**—i　**7**—e　**8**—c

9—d　**10**—f

2. 1 hospital

2 school

3 company

4 primary school

5 secondary school

6 university

7 factory

8 shop

9 bank

3. 1 这是我弟弟，不是我哥哥。

2 你父亲做什么（工作）?

3 你母亲在哪儿工作?

4 我父亲是律师，我母亲是医生。

5 我哥哥是工程师，他在德国公司
工作。

6 我弟弟是学生，他在大学学习。

7 我姐姐是老师，她在中学工作。

8 我妹妹是会计，她在银行工作。

9 我父亲和母亲年纪都很大，他们都
退休了。

10 我父亲退休了，我母亲也退休了。

4. 1 T　**2** F　**3** F　**4** T　**5** T

Lesson 10

1. 1 B　**2** A　**3** D　**4** E　**5** F　**6** C

2. 1 I often go to the library on Sundays.

2 My wife likes shopping, but she doesn't
like cooking.

❸ What do you like to do at weekends?

❹ Can you speak French?

❺ Do you like to watch Chinese films?

❻ I can speak a little bit of Spanish.

❼ At weekends, sometimes I like swimming, sometimes I like dancing.

❽ I really want to go to Beijing next year.

3. ❶ 你喜欢法国电影吗？

❷ 我不喜欢法国电影。

❸ 你喜欢什么电影？

❹ 我很喜欢中国电影。

❺ 我喜欢打篮球和网球，也喜欢游泳。

❻ 我喜欢游泳，不喜欢网球。

❼ 我不喜欢踢足球，但是我喜欢看足球。

❽ 你想喝点儿什么？

❾ 你想去哪儿？

❿ 我想明年四月去上海。

4. ❶ T　❷ F　❸ F　❹ T　❺ F

Lesson 11

2. 看电视　吃／做饭　喝啤酒　去商店
买东西　开会　有时间　说汉语
是英国人　见朋友

3. ❶ 我什么时间能见你？

❷ 你什么时候有空？

❸ 明天你有事吗？

❹ 这个新电影怎么样？—太好了！

❺ 我们七点在酒吧见吧？

❻ 今天我请你，你想吃什么？

❼ 陈先生请我们下星期天去他家。

❽ 周末你有空吗？or周末你做什么？

❾ 这个星期我很忙，没有时间。

❿ 星期三可以，我不忙。

4. ❶ F　❷ T　❸ F　❹ T　❺ T

Lesson 13

2. ❶ 打电话　❷ 留言　❸ 回电话

❹ 等一下　❺ 转告　❻ 占线

3. ❶ 谁　❷ 哪　❸ 在　❹ 是

❺ 要　要

4. ❶ 我是Maria。

❷ 您是哪位？

❸ 对不起，你打错了。

❹ 你要留言吗？

❺ 你有手机吗？

❻ 你的手机号是多少？

5. ❶ A：喂，是中国大使馆吗？

　　B：是啊，你找谁？

　　A：请问王先生在吗？

　　B：对不起，他不在。

❷ A：你好，是东方饭店。

　　B：请转1464。

　　A：请等一下。

　　B：谢谢。

　　A：对不起，占线。

6. ❶ T　❷ F　❸ F　❹ T　❺ F

Lesson 14

2. ❶ I don't have US dollars. I have Euros.

❷ One US dollar can be exchanged for 6.35RMB.

❸ I go to the Bank of China to exchange money.

❹ I would like to work in Shanghai.

❺ You are going to Beijing next year, aren't you?

❻ We are going to Chinatown to have a Chinese meal tomorrow.

3. ❶ 人民币　❷ 美元　❸ 日元

❹ 英镑　❺ 卢布　❻ 欧元

4. ❶ 我去银行。

❷ 我想换美元。

❸ 一英镑换多少人民币？

❹ 一英镑换9块1（九块一）人民币。

❺ 您想换多少？

❻ 我想换500美元。

5. ❶ b ❷ a ❸ c ❹ c ❺ a ❻ b
   ❼ b ❽ b

Lesson 15

1. ❶ 本 ❷ 本 ❸ 本 ❹ 张 ❺ 个
   ❻ 个 ❼ 位 ❽ 张 ❾ 个 ❿ 本

2. ❶ 多少 ❷ 收 ❸ 有 ❹ 行
   ❺ 什么

3. ❶ 去书店买书。
   ❷ 去鱼店买鱼。
   ❸ 去面包店买面包。
   ❹ 去肉店买羊肉。
   ❺ 去鞋店买鞋。
   ❻ 去服装店买衣服。
   ❼ 去百货公司买茶杯。
   ❽ 去超市买牛奶。
   ❾ 去菜店买菜。
   ❿ 去购物中心买东西。

4. ❶ I don't have cash. I have only got cheques.
   ❷ There are a lot of English books in that bookstore.
   ❸ I like to go to the shopping centre to do shopping.
   ❹ Many small shops don't accept credit cards.
   ❺ How much is this map?

5. ❶ 这本词典多少钱?
   ❷ 对不起,我们只收现金,不收支票。
   ❸ 请问,鞋店在哪儿?
   ❹ 北京超市多吗?
   ❺ 我想星期天去购物中心。

6. ❶ c ❷ b ❸ a ❹ c ❺ b

Lesson 16

1. ❶ —d ❷ —f ❸ —g ❹ —h
   ❺ —b ❻ —c ❼ —e ❽ —a

2. ❶ 两个英国人 ❷ 三本汉语书
   ❸ 十二个月 ❹ 一杯中国茶
   ❺ 四瓶啤酒 ❻ 五支铅笔
   ❼ 两个妹妹 ❽ 一个哥哥
   ❾ 两个孩子

3. ❶ I'd like to buy a red jumper.
   ❷ Excuse me, how much is that black overcoat?
   ❸ Is this tie made of pure silk?
   ❹ Do you have it in green?
   ❺ I want that (top) in light blue.

4. ❶ C ❷ B B ❸ A ❹ D D
   ❺ B B ❻ C ❼ B D

5. ❶ T ❷ F ❸ F ❹ T ❺ F

Lesson 17

2. ❶ 小号,中号,大号,特大号
   ❷ 4号,5号,7号,8号,38号,40号,42号
   ❸ 你穿多大号的鞋?
   ❹ 你穿多大号的衣服?

3. ❶ 最好 ❷ 最大 ❸ 最小
   ❹ 最长 ❺ 最少 ❻ 最漂亮

4. ❶ 请问哪儿有鞋店?
   ❷ 商店里不能换钱。
   ❸ 我能试试这双鞋吗?

5. ❶ This piece of clothing is really beautiful. You should buy it.
   ❷ What do you think of this colour? I think it's very pretty.
   ❸ I wear medium, but this is small.
   ❹ I like the colour and the style of that skirt.
   ❺ These trousers are too long. Do you have any shorter ones?
   ❻ What color of the clothes do you like?
   ❼ I think those suits look pretty good. How about trying them on?

6. ❶b ❷b ❸c ❹b ❺b

Lesson 19

1. ❶还是 ❷还是 ❸怎么样
❹不 ❺哪儿

2. ❶听 ❷吃 ❸看 ❹喝

3. ❶你想吃什么？
❷你要咖啡还是要茶？
❸请等一下。
❹这个饭馆的菜很好吃。
❺请结账。
❻你们几位？
❼这是菜单，您看看吧。

4. ❶ Shall we have Chinese tea?
❷ Do you like to drink black tea or green tea?
❸ Today is my treat. What would you like to eat?
❹ There are hamburgers and sandwiches, what would you like to eat?
❺ Do you eat meat? Are you a vegetarian?
❻ Is your girlfriend Chinese or American?

5. ❶a ❷b ❸a ❹c ❺c

Lesson 20

2. ❶你看没看过英国电影？我没看过英国电影。
❷你妹妹学没学过德语？我妹妹没学过德语。
❸你爸爸去没去过香港？我爸爸没去过香港。
❹你的中国朋友来没来过你家？我的中国朋友没来过我家。
❺他们吃没吃过法国饭？我们没吃过法国饭。
❻她听没听过日本音乐？她没听过日本音乐。

3. ❶本 ❷个 ❸条 ❹块 ❺个
❻个 ❼杯 ❽瓶 ❾张 ❿条
⓫辆 ⓬瓶 ⓭支 ⓮瓶 ⓯件

4. ❶有名 ❷点儿 ❸过 ❹加
❺极

5. ❶北京烤鸭很有名。
❷你去过香港吗？
❸青岛啤酒怎么样？
❹我看过那本中文书，非常好。
❺这个菜辣极了。
❻这个红葡萄酒好喝吗？

6. ❶F ❷F ❸T ❹F ❺T

Lesson 21

1. ❶—e ❷—f ❸—a ❹—d
❺—c

2. ❶查电子邮件 ❷发传真 ❸上网
❹写信 ❺寄信 ❻打电话
❼当然 ❽没问题 ❾太好了

3. ❶您有事吗？ or您需要帮助吗？
❷你去哪儿了？
❸昨天我去购物中心了。
❹我吃早饭了。
❺昨晚我和朋友去中国饭馆了。

4. ❶昨天晚上我没看电视。
❷星期六晚上我没去看朋友。
❸银行没关门。
❹他没去商店买东西。
❺我没吃午饭。

5. ❶你是在哪儿出生的？
❷他是从伦敦来的。
❸她是开车去巴黎的。
❹我是九点到大使馆的。

6. ❶b ❷a ❸c ❹b ❺a

Lesson 22

2. ❶叫出租车 ❷坐公共汽车

❸ 开车　　❹ 走路　❺ 骑自行车

❻ 坐飞机　❼ 骑马　❽ 坐船

3. ❶ 北京离广州很远。

❷ 南京有地铁吗?

❸ 从香港到广州你怎么去?

❹ 很多中国人骑自行车上班。

❺ 我朋友不住饭店，他住在我家。

❻ 我常坐欧洲之星去巴黎。

4. ❶ 哪儿　❷ 怎么　还是　❸ 从　到

❹ 离　❺ 哪儿　❻ 不　❼ 离

5. ❶ c　❷ c　❸ a　❹ b　❺ a

Lesson 23

1. ❶ 有　❷ 是　❸ 在　❹ 在

2. ❶ 在左边　❷ 向右拐　❸ 在中间

❹ 前边　❺ 后边　❻ 东

❼ 西　❽ 南　❾ 北

3. ❶ Excuse me, is the train station right ahead?

❷ How can I get to the Beijing Hotel?

❸ Go straight ahead and turn left.

❹ How long would it take from London to Edinburgh by train?

❺ Is it far from here to the Embassy? How long would it to walk there?

4. ❶ 请问，去火车站怎么走?

❷ 超市离这儿不远，一直往前走。

❸ 书店在银行前边。

❹ 咖啡店在购物中心后边。

❺ 我家附近有一个很大的超市。

5. ❶ b　❷ c　❸ a　❹ a　❺ b

Lesson 25

1. ❶ 比　❷ 我的词典　❸ 比

❹ 昨天，热　❺ 比，大　❻ 那本书

2. ❶ This book is much more expensive than that book.

❷ Today is a cloudy day. It's very cold and very windy.

❸ What do English people like to do in summer?

❹ Last year, the winter was not cold and the summer was not hot.

❺ I don't like spring in Beijing. It's very windy.

❻ Was yesterday's rain heavier than today's?

❼ My elder brother is much taller than me.

3. ❶ 火车没有飞机快。

❷ 我弟弟没有我哥哥高。

❸ 我妈妈没有我爸爸忙。

❹ 昨天的雪没有今天的雪大。

❺ 广州冬天没有北京冬天冷。

❻ 那本书没有这本书贵。

❼ 昨天没有今天热。

4. ❶ 伦敦冬天天气怎么样?

❷ 北京夏天常下雨吗?

❸ 明天是晴天。

❹ 广州下雪吗?

❺ 北京春天风很大。

❻ 昨天气温是多少度?

❼ 今天气温是21度。

❽ 今年法国下了很多雪。

❾ 广州的春天最好。

❿ 昨天的雨大不大?

5. ❶ a　❷ a　❸ b　❹ c　❺ a

Lesson 26

2. ❶ My younger sister has learned how to swim this summer.

❷ Can you hear when I speak?

❸ You can see the train station from here. It takes 2 minutes to walk there.

❹ I went to his house yesterday. I didn't meet his dad, I only met his mum.

❺ Shall we go to watch a film after we've finished dinner?

⑥ I liked to play cricket when I was in university.

⑦ I learned to play the piano when I was little.

⑧ I said "Hello" to him just now, but he didn't hear me.

⑨ They were chatting and drinking beer at the same time.

⑩ I like reading books and listening to music at the same time.

3. **①** E **②** A **③** C **④** B **⑤** D

4. **①** b **②** a **③** c **④** b **⑤** a

5. **①** a **②** c **③** b **④** c **⑤** a

Lesson 27

2. **①** B **②** A **③** C **④** E **⑤** D

3. **①**—c **②**—d **③**—b **④**—e
⑤—a

4. **①** 请把这杯咖啡喝完。
② 我把这个字写错了。
③ 老师把这个问题说清楚了。
④ 我把那本书还给图书馆了。
⑤ 弟弟不小心把花瓶打碎了。

5. **①** 我听说你妈妈要来伦敦。
② 你想什么时候去北京?
③ 你打算在中国住多久?
④ 我想参观故宫。
⑤ 明天我去长城。
⑥ 我计划明年去伦敦看温布顿看网球赛。
⑦ 在上海你住哪儿?
⑧ 下月我要去纽约。

6. **①** c **②** c **③** a **④** b **⑤** b

Lesson 28

1. **①**—c **②**—d **③**—b **④**—a

2. **①**—e **②**—i **③**—h **④**—b

⑤—g **⑥**—j **⑦**—f **⑧**—c
⑨—d **⑩**—a

3. **①** 吃饭 **②** 吃巧克力 **③** 吃药
④ 去医院 **⑤** 看病 **⑥** 不舒服

4. **①** What's wrong with you? Are you feeling unwell?

② He has got a cold and is unable to come to work.

③ He has got a headache, sore throat and has a fever of 38.5 degrees.

④ I went to the hospital to see a doctor this morning.

⑤ Do you want to take Chinese herbal medicine or Western medicine?

⑥ How do I take this medicine? How many times should I take it per day?

5. **①** 我有点儿头疼。
② 你应该去医院。
③ 我很健康,我没病。
④ 今天我不舒服。
⑤ 老王,你身体好吗?
⑥ 他最近身体不太好。
⑦ 我不喜欢吃药,休息一下就行。

6. **①** 我的酒被他喝完了。
② 我的车被我弟弟开走了。
③ 我的电脑被小偷偷走了。
④ 我的蛋糕被我妹妹吃完了。
⑤ 汉语词典被小白借走了。

7. **①** a **②** b **③** c **④** a **⑤** b

Lesson 29

1. **①**—c/f **②**—a/f **③**—b/d/h
④—f **⑤**—e/f **⑥**—d/h
⑦—b/d/f/g/h **⑧**—a/f

2. **①** You speak English excellently!

② Not at all, you are too kind!

③ He speaks French very fluently!

④ He eats slowly.

❺ He runs very fast.

❻ The time has passed very quickly.

❼ I don't speak Mandarin very well.

❽ He writes Chinese characters very beautifully.

3. ❶ 这个学生看得很慢。

❷ 这个孩子吃得很多。

❸ 这个男人跳得很高。

❹ Lucy汉语说得很流利。

❺ 今天早上我起得很早。

❻ 这个老师教得很好。

❼ 他跑得很快。

❽ 雨下得很大。

❾ 这个小女孩穿得很漂亮。

4. ❶ 新年快乐！

❷ 圣诞快乐！

❸ 祝你生日快乐！

❹ 周末快乐！

❺ 祝你好运！

INDEX III
CHINESE-ENGLISH VOCABULARY LIST

Character	*Pinyin*	English	Lesson
A			
啊	a	(exclamatory particle)	6
爱	ài	love, to love	10
爱丁堡	Àidīngbǎo	Edinburgh	22
奥地利	Àodìlì	Austria	3
B			
八	bā	eight	4
巴黎	Bālí	Paris	3
把	bǎ	(grammar particle)	27
把	bǎ	(measure word for chairs)	19
爸爸	bàba	dad / father	8
吧	ba	(suggesting particle)	11
白	bái	white	16
白饭	báifàn	plain rice	19
百	bǎi	hundred	14
办	bàn	to deal with, to manage, to tackle	27
办法	bànfǎ	way, means, method	29
半	bàn	half	5
帮	bāng	to help	27
帮忙	bāngmáng	to give a hand, to do a favour	27
保持联系	bǎochí liánxi	to keep in touch	7
杯	bēi	a cup of, a glass of (measure word)	20
北	běi	north	23
被	bèi	(passive grammar particle)	28
本	běn	(measure word for books)	15
比	bǐ	to compare, than (preposition)	25
边	biān	side	23

便宜	piányi	cheap	15
别的	bié de	other	16
冰	bīng	ice	20
病	bìng	sick, ill	28
菠菜	bōcài	spinach	19
博客	bókè	blog	10
博物院／博物馆	bówùyuàn / bówùguǎn	museum	21
不	bù	no, not	1
不错	búcuò	not bad, pretty good	1
不客气	bú kèqi	you're welcome	5

C

菜	cài	dish, vegetable	19
菜单	càidān	menu	19
参观	cānguān	to visit	21
餐厅	cāntīng	canteen	21
茶	chá	tea	20
查	chá	to check	21
差	chà	less, to (for time)	5
常／常常	cháng / chángcháng	often	10
超市	chāoshì	supermarket	22
炒饭	chǎofàn	fried rice	19
车	chē	vehicle	22
成功	chénggōng	successful	30
出	chū	out	23
厨房	chúfáng	kitchen	24
穿	chuān	to wear, to put on	17
船	chuán	boat, ship	22
春（天／季）	chūn (tiān / jì)	spring	25
春节	Chūn Jié	Spring Festival (Chinese New Year)	4
春天	chūntiān	spring	18
词典	cídiǎn	dictionary	15
次	cì	times	28
从	cóng	from	3
从……来	cóng...lái	to come from···	3
长	cháng	long	17
长安大街	Cháng'ān Dàjiē	Chang'an Avenue	7
长城	Chángchéng	the Great Wall	7
长城饭店	Chángchéng fàndiàn	Great Wall Hotel	7

D

打	dǎ	to play (in a sport or game), to hit	10
打球	dǎqiú	to play ball	29
打算	dǎsuàn	to plan	27
打网球	dǎ wǎngqiú	to play tennis	10
大	dà	large	17
大概	dàgài	approximate, about	23
大家	dàjiā	everybody	24
大街	dàjiē	avenue	7
大使馆	dàshǐguǎn	embassy	7
大衣	dàyī	overcoat	16
但是	dànshì	but	6
蛋糕	dàngāo	cake	24
当然	dāngrán	of course	16
倒霉	dǎoméi	to have bad luck, be out of luck	28
到	dào	to reach, to arrive	23
得	de	(complement marker)	29
德国	Déguó	Germany	3
的	de	structural particle	4
登录名	dēnglùmíng	username	21
等	děng	to wait	13
地方	dìfang	place	3
地铁	dìtiě	underground, tube	22
地铁站	dìtiě zhàn	subway station	22
地图	dìtú	map	15
地址	dìzhǐ	address	7
弟弟	dìdi	younger brother	8
点	diǎn	o'clock	5
点菜	diǎncài	to order dishes	19
电话	diànhuà	telephone	7
电脑	diànnǎo	computer	21
电影	diànyǐng	film, movie	6
电子邮件	diànzǐ yóujiàn	e-mail	21
订	dìng	to book	27
订好	dìnghǎo	to have made reservation	27
东城区	Dōngchéng Qū	Dongcheng District	7
东西	dōngxi	things	10
冬（天／季）	dōng (tiān / jì)	winter	25
都	dōu	both, all	3

豆腐	dòufu	bean curd, tofu	19
读书	dú shū	to read a book	9
度	dù	degree	25
短	duǎn	short	17
对	duì	correct	3
对不起	duìbuqǐ	sorry	5
多大	duō dà	how old	8
多久	duō jiǔ	how long	27
多少	duōshao	how many, how much	7
多少钱	duōshao qián	how much is it?	15
多长时间	duōcháng shíjiān	how long	23

E

二	èr	two	4

F

发	fā	to send	21
发烧	fāshāo	to have a fever / temperature	28
法国	Fǎguó	France	3
法语	Fǎyǔ	French language	3
饭店	fàndiàn	hotel, restaurant	7
饭馆	fànguǎn	restaurant	6
房间	fángjiān	room	7
放假	fàngjià	to have a holiday or vacation	27
飞机	fēijī	airplane	22
非常	fēicháng	very, extremely	10
分	fēn	minute	5
分钟	fēnzhōng	minute (duration)	23
粉	fěn	pink	16
风	fēng	wind	25
服务员	fúwùyuán	waiter / waitress	19
父亲	fùqin	father	8
附近	fùjìn	nearby	22
幅	fú	(measure word for painting)	18

G

感冒	gǎnmào	to have a cold	28
干杯	gānbēi	cheers	29
干燥	gānzào	dry	25
刚才	gāngcái	just now	21
高兴	gāoxìng	happy, glad	2

告诉	gàosu	to tell	13
哥哥	gēge	elder brother	8
胳膊	gēbo	arm	28
歌舞	gēwǔ	singing and dancing performance	21
给	gěi	to give, for	13
跟	gēn	with, and	12
跟……打招呼	gēn...dǎ zhāohu	say hello to somebody	26
工作	gōngzuò	work, job	9
公共汽车	gōnggòng qìchē	public bus	22
公司	gōngsī	company	9
公寓	gōngyù	apartment	26
公园	gōngyuán	park	24
功夫	gōngfu	kung fu	10
故宫	Gùgōng	the Forbidden City, the Palace Museum	21
刮风	guā fēng	to be windy	25
拐	guǎi	to turn	23
关	guān	to close, to turn off	5
光华路	Guānghuá Lù	Guanghua Road (road name)	7
光临	guānglín	presence, to be here	19
广州	Guǎngzhōu	Guangzhou (a city in China)	25
贵	guì	expensive	15
贵	guì	honored, noble, expensive	2
国	guó	country, state	3
国航	Guóháng	Air China	27
国贸中心	Guómào zhōngxīn	a shopping centre name	26
果汁	guǒzhī	fruit juice	20
过	guò	have ever done (verbal suffix)	20
过	guò	to pass, to go through, to celebrate	29

H

还	hái	also, as well	12
还	hái	still	17
还	huán	to return	27
还是	háishì	or (only used in questions)	19
海鲜	hǎixiān	seafood	19
汉堡	Hànbǎo	Hamburg	3
汉字	Hànzì	Chinese character	29
行	xíng	all right, ok	15
好	hǎo	good, well	1
好吃	hǎochī	delicious, tasty	19

好像	hǎoxiàng	to seem, to be like	26
号	hào	date	4
号	hào	number	7
号	hào	size	17
合适	héshì	fit, suitable	17
和	hé	and	8
黑	hēi	black	16
很	hěn	very	1
很好	hěn hǎo	very well, very good	1
红	hóng	red	16
后	hòu	after, behind	28
护士	hùshi	nurse	9
护照	hùzhào	passport	21
画	huà	painting, drawing	18
欢迎	huānyíng	to welcome	19
换	huàn	to change, to exchange	14
换成	huànchéng	to change into	27
回	huí	to return	13
回电话	huí diànhuà	to call back	13
汇率	huìlǜ	exchange rate	14
会	huì	can, be able to	10
会	huì	meeting	11
会计	kuàijì	accountant	9
火车	huǒchē	train	22
火车站	huǒchē zhàn	train station	22
或者	huòzhě	or	19

J

鸡	jī	chicken	19
极	jí	extremely	20
几	jǐ	how many, what (date, time)	4
计划	jìhuà	plan, to plan	27
加	jiā	to add in	19
家	jiā	home, family	7
家	jiā	(measure word)	12
件	jiàn	(measure word)	16
建国门	Jiànguómén	Jianguomen (place name)	7
健康	jiànkāng	healthy	30
健身房	jiànshēnfáng	gym	10
将	jiāng	will, be about to	27

口	kǒu	(measure word for family members)	8
裤子	kùzi	trousers	17
块	kuài	yuan (informal)	14
快乐	kuàilè	happy	29
宽带	kuāndài	broadband	21

L

辣	là	spicy (or strong for alcoholic drinks)	20
来	lái	to come	3
蓝	lán	blue	16
老师	lǎoshī	teacher	9
了	le	(particle)	9
累	lèi	tired	1
冷	lěng	cold	25
离	lí	from (in giving distances)	22
里	lǐ	inside	21
礼物	lǐwù	gift, present	6
练	liàn	to practice	29
两	liǎng	two	5
聊天	liáotiān	to chat	21
零下	língxià	below zero	25
领带	lǐngdài	tie	16
流利	liúlì	fluent	29
六	liù	six	4
楼	lóu	floor, building	21
路	lù	road	7
路口	lùkǒu	junction, crossing	23
伦敦	Lúndūn	London	3
旅途	lǚtú	journey, trip	30
旅游	lǚyóu	to travel	27
律师	lùshī	lawyer	9
绿（色）	lù (sè)	green (colour)	16
绿茶	lùchá	green tea	20

M

妈妈	māma	mum / mother	8
马马虎虎	mǎmǎhūhū	so-so	1
马上	mǎshàng	immediately, right now	19
吗	ma	(question particle)	1
买	mǎi	to buy	6

卖	mài	to sell	15
卖完	màiwán	to be sold out	27
满意	mǎnyì	satisfied	24
忙	máng	busy	1
毛衣	máoyī	jumper, sweater	16
茅台	Máotái	Maotai (a kind of baijiu)	20
没关系	méi guānxi	it doesn't matter	5
没问题	méi wèntí	no problem	19
没有	méiyǒu	not have, there is not	8
每	měi	each, every	5
每天	měi tiān	every day	5
美	měi	beautiful, pretty	30
美国	Měiguó	USA	3
美元	Měiyuán	US dollar	14
妹妹	mèimei	younger sister	8
门	mén	door	5
米饭	mǐfàn	cooked rice	19
秘书	mìshū	secretary	9
密码	mìmǎ	password	21
名酒	míngjiǔ	well-known liquor	20
名片	míngpiàn	business card	7
名字	míngzi	name	2
明年	míngnián	next year	4
明天	míngtiān	tomorrow	4
母亲	mǔqin	mother	8

N

哪	nǎ / něi	which	3
哪儿	nǎr	where	3
那	nà / nèi	that	2
那么	nàme	in that case, then	22
难	nán	difficult	17
呢	ne	(particle for following up question)	1
能	néng	may, can, to have the permission to	16
你	nǐ	you	1
你好	nǐ hǎo	hello	1
年	nián	year	4
年纪	niánjì	age	8
您贵姓	nín guìxìng	What's your surname? (polite)	2
牛奶	niúnǎi	milk	20

牛肉	niúròu	beef	19
纽约	Niǔyuē	New York	3
女儿	nǚ' ér	daughter	8

O

| 哦 | ò | oh | 9 |
| 欧元 | Ōuyuán | Euro | 14 |

P

跑步	pǎobù	to run	10
朋友	péngyou	friend	2
啤酒	píjiǔ	beer	20
片	piàn	tablet, pill	28
漂亮	piàoliang	pretty, beautiful	17
票	piào	ticket	27
苹果	píngguò	apple	15
瓶	píng	a bottle of (measure word)	20
普通话	Pǔtōnghuà	Modern standard Chinese	6

Q

七	qī	seven	4
骑	qí	to ride	22
气温	qìwēn	air temperature	25
签证	qiānzhèng	visa	27
前	qián	ahead, front, forward	23
钱	qián	money	14
巧克力	qiǎokèlì	chocolate	24
青菜	qīngcài	green vegetable	19
青岛	Qīngdǎo	Qingdao (city name)	20
青岛啤酒	Qīngdǎo píjiǔ	Tsingtao beer	20
请	qǐng	please	2
请	qǐng	to invite, to treat	6
请问	qǐngwèn	may I ask, excuse me	2
秋（天／季）	qiū (tiān / jì)	autumn	25
去	qù	to go	4
然后	ránhòu	then, after	18

R

让	ràng	to let, to allow	14
热	rè	hot	25
人	rén	person, people	3

人民币	Rénmínbì	Chinese currency (RMB)	14
认识	rènshi	to recognize, to know	2
容易	róngyì	easy	24
肉	ròu	meat	11

S

三	sān	three	4
嗓子	sǎngzi	throat	28
商店	shāngdiàn	shop, store	5
上班	shàngbān	to go to work, to start work	5
上车	shàng chē	to get on (a vehicle)	23
上海话	Shànghǎihuà	Shanghai dialect	6
上网	shàngwǎng	to surf the internet	10
什么	shénme	what	2
什么时候	shénme shíhou	when (question)	11
什么事	shénme shì	what's happening	11
生日	shēngrì	birthday	4
十	shí	ten	4
十字路口	shízì lùkǒu	crossroads	23
时间	shíjiān	time	11
市中心	shì zhōngxīn	city centre, downtown	24
试	shì	to try	16
是	shì	to be	2
事	shì	things, matter, business	11
事业	shìyè	career	30
收	shōu	to accept, to receive	15
手	shǒu	hand	28
手机	shǒujī	mobile phone	7
手套	shǒutào	gloves	17
受伤	shòushāng	be injured, be wounded	28
书	shū	book	10
书店	shūdiàn	book shop	15
书法	shūfǎ	calligraphy	18
舒服	shūfu	comfortable	22
摔坏	shuāihuài	to drop and break	28
摔破	shuāipò	to injure (break into pieces) in a fall	28
涮羊肉	shuàn yángròu	lamb hotpot (a famous Beijing dish)	11
双	shuāng	(measure word for shoes, socks)	17
谁	shéi / shuí	who, whom	2
顺利	shùnlì	smooth	30

说	shuō	to speak, to say	3
四	sì	four	4
素菜	sùcài	vegetable dish	19
素食者	sùshízhě	vegetarian	19
虽然……但是……	suīrán...dànshì...	although...but...	18
岁	suì	year (of age)	8

T

他	tā	he, him	1
太	tài	too, very, extremely	11
太……了	tài...le	extremely..., too...	11
太太	tàitai	Mrs., lady, wife	2
汤	tāng	soup	19
疼	téng	ache, pain, hurt	28
天	tiān	day	4
天安门	Tiān'ānmén	Tian'anmen	21
天气	tiānqì	weather	25
条	tiáo	(measure word)	16
听说	tīngshuō	it is said, heard	24
听音乐	tīng yīnyuè	to listen to music	10
停	tíng	to stop	23
头	tóu	head	28
头疼	tóu téng	headache	28
退休	tuìxiū	to retire	9

W

外国	wàiguó	foreign country	12
外语	wàiyǔ	foreign language	12
完	wán	finish, end	24
玩儿	wánr	to have fun, to enjoy, to play	24
晚上	wǎnshang	evening	5
碗	wǎn	bowl, measure word	24
网址	wǎngzhǐ	website	7
往	wǎng	towards	23
微信	wēixìn	WeChat	7
位	wèi	(measure word for person-polite)	13
味道	wèidào	taste	20
喂	wèi	hello, hey	13
问	wèn	to ask	2
问题	wèntí	problem, question	19

我	wǒ	I, me	1
无线网	wúxiàn wǎng	Wi-Fi	21
五	wǔ	five	4

X

西	xī	west	23
西北	xīběi	northwest	23
西城区	Xīchéng Qū	Xicheng District	7
西瓜	xīguā	water melon	15
喜欢	xǐhuan	to like, to enjoy	10
虾	xiā	prawn, shrimp	19
下班	xiàbān	to finish work	5
下雪	xià xuě	to snow	25
下雨	xià yǔ	to rain	25
夏（天／季）	xià (tiān / jì)	summer	25
先	xiān	first	18
先生	xiānsheng	Mr., gentleman, husband	2
现金	xiànjīn	cash	15
现在	xiànzài	now, at the moment	5
想	xiǎng	would like, to think	14
向	xiàng	towards	23
小	xiǎo	small, little	17
小姐	xiǎojie	Miss., young lady	2
小时	xiǎoshí	hour	23
小说	xiǎoshuō	novel	26
小学	xiǎoxué	primary school	9
些	xiē	some	14
鞋	xié	shoes	17
写	xiě	to write	29
写书	xiě shū	to write a book	9
谢谢	xièxie	thank you	1
新春	Xīnchūn	Chinese New Year	30
新闻	xīnwén	news	10
信用卡	xìnyòngkǎ	credit card	15
星巴克	Xīngbākè	Starbucks	26
星期	xīngqī	week, day of the week	4
幸福	xìngfú	happiness	30
行	xíng	all right, OK	15
姓	xìng	surname, be surnamed	2
姓名	xìngmíng	full name	13

修	xiū	to repair, to mend	28
需要	xūyào	to need, to require	27
学生	xuésheng	student	9
雪	xuě	snow	25

Y

鸭	yā	duck	11
牙疼	yá téng	toothache	28
严重	yánzhòng	serious, critical	28
颜色	yánsè	colour	16
羊肉	yángròu	lamb	11
样子	yàngzi	style	17
药	yào	medicine	28
要	yào	to want, to need, will	14
也	yě	also, too, either	1
一	yī	one	4
一边……一边……	yìbiān...yìbiān...	at the same time	26
一点儿	yìdiǎnr	a little	10
一定	yídìng	definitely, certainly	13
一共	yígòng	altogether	15
一刻	yí kè	a quarter (time)	5
一起	yìqǐ	together	11
一下	yíxià	a bit, briefly	3
一样	yíyàng	same	25
一直	yìzhí	straight	23
医生	yīshēng	doctor	9
医院	yīyuàn	hospital	9
已经	yǐjīng	already	27
椅子	yǐzi	chair	19
阴天	yīntiān	cloudy	25
因为	yīnwèi	because	12
银行	yínháng	bank	9
英镑	Yīngbàng	Pound sterling	14
英国	Yīngguó	Britain	3
英汉词典	YīngèHàn cídiǎn	English-Chinese dictionary	15
英航	Yīngháng	British Airways	27
英语	Yīngyǔ	English language	3
用	yòng	to use	15
游泳池	yóuyǒngchí	swimming pool	21
有	yǒu	to have, there be	8

有名	yǒumíng	famous	20
有时候	yǒushíhou	sometimes	10
又……又……	yòu...yòu...	both...and...	18
右	yòu	right	23
鱼	yú	fish	19
愉快	yúkuài	happy, joyful	30
雨	yǔ	rain	25
语	yǔ	language	3
远	yuǎn	far	22
月	yuè	month	4
运动	yùndòng	sport, exercise	10

Z

再见	zàijiàn	good-bye	1
在	zài	(continuous particle)	26
在	zài	to be at, to be located, in, on	7
早上	zǎoshang	(early) morning	5
怎么卖	zěnme mài	how to sell?	15
怎么样	zěnmeyàng	How are things? How are you?	1
炸	zhá	to fry	24
炸薯条	zháshǔtiáo	chips	24
站	zhàn	station, stop	22
张	zhāng	(measure word for flat objects)	15
找	zhǎo	to look for, to find	13
这	zhè / zhèi	this	2
这么	zhème	such, so, like this	29
真	zhēn	really, truly	17
真的	zhēnde	really, truly	10
正	zhèng	just	17
正在	zhèngzài	in process of	26
只	zhǐ	only	15
知道	zhīdào	to know	5
直飞	zhífēi	direct flight	27
质量	zhìliàng	quality	18
中	zhōng	medium, middle	17
中药	zhōngyào	Chinese medicine	28
种	zhǒng	type	17
周末	zhōumò	weekend	10
猪肉	zhūròu	pork	19
住	zhù	to live, to stay	7

祝	zhù	to wish	29
转	zhuǎn	to change to (extension), to pass on	13
撞	zhuàng	to hit, to run into, to meet by accident	28
桌	zhuō	(measure word, table of [dishes])	24
桌子	zhuōzi	table	19
自行车	zìxíngchē	bicycle	22
字	zì	Chinese characters	18
字画	zìhuà	Chinese painting	18
走	zǒu	to walk, to leave, to go	22
走路	zǒulù	to walk, to go on foot	22
最	zuì	most	17
最好	zuìhǎo	best, It's better...	18
最后	zuìhòu	the last, finally	24
最近	zuìjìn	recently, lately	27
昨天	zuótiān	yesterday	4
左	zuǒ	left	23
左右	zuǒyòu	(after a numeral) about, or so	25
作家	zuòjiā	writer	9
坐	zuò	to sit, by	22
做	zuò	to do, to make	6
做饭	zuòfàn	to cook	10
做运动	zuò yùndòng	to do exercises	10
……的时候	...de shíhou	when, while	26

INDEX IV
ENGLISH-CHINESE VOCABULARY LIST

English	Pinyin	Character	Lesson
A			
a bit, briefly	yíxià	一下	3
a bottle of (measure word)	píng	瓶	20
a cup of, a glass of (measure word)	bēi	杯	20
a little	yìdiǎnr	一点儿	10
a quarter (time)	yí kè	一刻	5
a shopping centre name	Guómào zhōngxīn	国贸中心	26
(a traditional unit of weight, equal to 0.5 kg)	jīn	斤	15
accept, to receive	shōu	收	15
accountant	kuàijì	会计	9
ache, pain, hurt	téng	疼	28
add in	jiā	加	19
address	dìzhǐ	地址	7
(after a numeral) about, or so	zuǒyòu	左右	25
after, behind	hòu	后	28
age	niánjì	年纪	8
ahead, front, forward	qián	前	23
Air China	Guóháng	国航	27
air temperature	qìwēn	气温	25
airplane	fēijī	飞机	22
all kinds of alcohol drinks	jiǔ	酒	20
all right, OK	xíng	行	15
already	yǐjīng	已经	27
already, as early as	jiù	就	18
also, as well	hái	还	12
also, too, either	yě	也	1
although...but...	suīrán...dànshì...	虽然……但是……	18
altogether	yígòng	一共	15
and	hé	和	8

answer the phone, to pick up somebody	jiē	接	13
apartment	gōngyù	公寓	26
apple	píngguǒ	苹果	15
approximate, about	dàgài	大概	23
arm	gēbo	胳膊	28
ask	wèn	问	2
at the same time	yìbiān...yìbiān...	一边……一边……	26
Austria	Àodìlì	奥地利	3
autumn	qiū (tiān / jì)	秋（天／季）	25
avenue	dàjiē	大街	7

B

bank	yínháng	银行	9
be at, to be located, in, on	zài	在	7
be injured, be wounded	shòushāng	受伤	28
be sold out	màiwán	卖完	27
be windy	guā fēng	刮风	25
be	shì	是	2
bean curd, tofu	dòufu	豆腐	19
beautiful, pretty	měi	美	30
because	yīnwèi	因为	12
beef	niúròu	牛肉	19
beer	píjiǔ	啤酒	20
below zero	língxià	零下	25
best, It's better...	zuìhǎo	最好	18
bicycle	zìxíngchē	自行车	22
birthday	shēngrì	生日	4
black	hēi	黑	16
blog	bókè	博客	10
blue	lán	蓝	16
boat, ship	chuán	船	22
book shop	shūdiàn	书店	15
book	dìng	订	27
book	shū	书	10
borrow, to lend	jiè	借	27
both, all	dōu	都	3
both...and...	yòu...yòu...	又……又……	18
bowl, measure word	wǎn	碗	24
Britain	Yīngguó	英国	3
British Airways	Yīngháng	英航	27
broadband	kuāndài	宽带	21
business card	míngpiàn	名片	7

busy	máng	忙	1
but	dànshì	但是	6
buy	mǎi	买	6

C

cake	dàngāo	蛋糕	24
call back	huí diànhuà	回电话	13
call, to be called	jiào	叫	2
calligraphy	shūfǎ	书法	18
can, be able to	huì	会	10
canteen	cāntīng	餐厅	21
career	shìyè	事业	30
cash	xiànjīn	现金	15
chair	yǐzi	椅子	19
Chang'an Avenue	Cháng'ān Dàjiē	长安大街	7
change into	huànchéng	换成	27
change to (extension), to pass on	zhuǎn	转	13
change, to exchange	huàn	换	14
chat	liáotiān	聊天	21
cheap	piányi	便宜	15
check	chá	查	21
cheers	gānbēi	干杯	29
chicken	jī	鸡	19
Chinese character	Hànzì	汉字	29
Chinese characters	zì	字	18
Chinese currency (RMB)	Rénmínbì	人民币	14
Chinese medicine	zhōngyào	中药	28
Chinese New Year	Xīnchūn	新春	30
Chinese painting	zìhuà	字画	18
chips	zháshǔtiáo	炸薯条	24
chocolate	qiǎokèlì	巧克力	24
city centre, downtown	shì zhōngxīn	市中心	24
close, to turn off	guān	关	5
cloudy	yīntiān	阴天	25
coffee	kāfēi	咖啡	20
Coke	kělè	可乐	20
cold	lěng	冷	25
colour	yánsè	颜色	16
come from...	cóng...lái	从……来	3
come	lái	来	3
comfortable	shūfu	舒服	22
company	gōngsī	公司	9

compare, than (preposition)	bǐ	比	25
(complement marker)	de	得	29
computer	diànnǎo	电脑	21
(continuous particle)	zài	在	26
cook	zuòfàn	做饭	10
cooked rice	mǐfàn	米饭	19
correct	duì	对	3
cough	késou	咳嗽	28
country, state	guó	国	3
credit card	xìnyòngkǎ	信用卡	15
crossroads	shízì lùkǒu	十字路口	23

D

dad / father	bàba	爸爸	8
date	hào	号	4
daughter	nǚ' ér	女儿	8
day	tiān	天	4
deal with, to manage, to tackle	bàn	办	27
definitely, certainly	yídìng	一定	13
degree	dù	度	25
delicious, tasty	hǎochī	好吃	19
dictionary	cídiǎn	词典	15
difficult	nán	难	17
direct flight	zhífēi	直飞	27
dish, vegetable	cài	菜	19
do exercises	zuò yùndòng	做运动	10
do, to make	zuò	做	6
doctor	yīshēng	医生	9
Dongcheng District	Dōngchéng Qū	东城区	7
door	mén	门	5
drinks party	jiǔhuì	酒会	11
drive (a car)	kāichē	开车	22
drop and break	shuāihuài	摔坏	28
dry	gānzào	干燥	25
duck	yā	鸭	11

E

each, every	měi	每	5
(early) morning	zǎoshang	早上	5
easy	róngyì	容易	24
Edinburgh	Àidīngbǎo	爱丁堡	22
eight	bā	八	4

elder brother	gēge	哥哥	8
elder sister	jiějie	姐姐	8
e-mail	diànzǐ yóujiàn	电子邮件	21
embassy	dàshǐguǎn	大使馆	7
English language	Yīngyǔ	英语	3
English-Chinese dictionary	YīngèHàn cídiǎn	英汉词典	15
enter, to come in	jìn	进	26
Euro	Ōuyuán	欧元	14
evening	wǎnshang	晚上	5
every day	měi tiān	每天	5
everybody	dàjiā	大家	24
exchange rate	huìlǜ	汇率	14
(exclamatory particle)	a	啊	6
expensive	guì	贵	15
extremely	jí	极	20
extremely..., too...	tài...le	太……了	11

F

famous	yǒumíng	有名	20
far	yuǎn	远	22
father	fùqin	父亲	8
film, movie	diànyǐng	电影	6
finish work	xiàbān	下班	5
finish, end	wán	完	24
first	xiān	先	18
fish	yú	鱼	19
fit, suitable	héshì	合适	17
five	wǔ	五	4
floor, building	lóu	楼	21
fluent	liúlì	流利	29
foreign country	wàiguó	外国	12
foreign language	wàiyǔ	外语	12
four	sì	四	4
France	Fǎguó	法国	3
free time	kòng	空	11
French language	Fǎyǔ	法语	3
fried rice	chǎofàn	炒饭	19
friend	péngyou	朋友	2
from (in giving distances)	lí	离	22
from	cóng	从	3
fruit juice	guǒzhī	果汁	20
fry	zhá	炸	24

| full name | xìngmíng | 姓名 | 13 |

G

Germany	Déguó	德国	3
get on (a vehicle)	shàng chē	上车	23
gift, present	lǐwù	礼物	6
give a hand, to do a favour	bāngmáng	帮忙	27
give, for	gěi	给	13
gloves	shǒutào	手套	17
go to work, to start work	shàngbān	上班	5
go	qù	去	4
good, well	hǎo	好	1
good-bye	zàijiàn	再见	1
(grammar particle)	bǎ	把	27
Great Wall Hotel	Chángchéng fàndiàn	长城饭店	7
green (colour)	lǜ (sè)	绿（色）	16
green tea	lǜchá	绿茶	20
green vegetable	qīngcài	青菜	19
Guanghua Road (road name)	Guānghuá Lù	光华路	7
Guangzhou (a city in China)	Guǎngzhōu	广州	25
guest	kèrén	客人	13
gym	jiànshēnfáng	健身房	10

H

half	bàn	半	5
Hamburg	Hànbǎo	汉堡	3
hand	shǒu	手	28
happiness	xìngfú	幸福	30
happy	kuàilè	快乐	29
happy, glad	gāoxìng	高兴	2
happy, joyful	yúkuài	愉快	30
have a fever / temperature	fāshāo	发烧	28
have a cold	gǎnmào	感冒	28
have a good time, enjoy	kāixīn	开心	30
have a holiday or vacation	fàngjià	放假	27
have bad luck, be out of luck	dǎoméi	倒霉	28
have ever done (verbal suffix)	guò	过	20
have fun, to enjoy, to play	wánr	玩儿	24
have made reservation	dìnghǎo	订好	27
have, there is, there are	yǒu	有	8
he, him	tā	他	1
head	tóu	头	28

headache	tóu téng	头疼	28
healthy	jiànkāng	健康	30
hello	nǐ hǎo	你好	1
hello, hey	wèi	喂	13
help	bāng	帮	27
hit, to run into, to meet by accident	zhuàng	撞	28
home, family	jiā	家	7
honored, noble, expensive	guì	贵	2
hospital	yīyuàn	医院	9
hot	rè	热	25
hotel	fàndiàn	饭店	7
hour	xiǎoshí	小时	23
How are things? How are you?	zěnmeyàng	怎么样	1
how long	duō jiǔ	多久	27
how long	duōcháng shíjiān	多长时间	23
how many, how much	duōshao	多少	7
how many, what (date, time)	jǐ	几	4
how much is it?	duōshao qián	多少钱	15
how old	duō dà	多大	8
how to sell?	zěnme mài	怎么卖	15
hundred	bǎi	百	14

I

I, me	wǒ	我	1
ice	bīng	冰	20
immediately, right now	mǎshàng	马上	19
in process of	zhèngzài	正在	26
in that case, then	nàme	那么	22
injure (break into pieces) in a fall	shuāipò	摔破	28
inside	lǐ	里	21
introduce	jièshào	介绍	3
invite, to treat	qǐng	请	6
it doesn't matter	méi guānxi	没关系	5
it is said, heard	tīngshuō	听说	24
it seems, it looks as if	kànlái	看来	17

J

Jianguomen (place name)	Jiànguómén	建国门	7
journey, trip	lǚtú	旅途	30
jumper, sweater	máoyī	毛衣	16
junction, crossing	lùkǒu	路口	23
just now	gāngcái	刚才	21

just	jiù	就	19
just	zhèng	正	17

K

keep in touch	bǎochí liánxi	保持联系	7
kitchen	chúfáng	厨房	24
know	zhīdào	知道	5
kung fu	gōngfu	功夫	10

L

lamb hotpot (a famous Beijing dish)	shuàn yángròu	涮羊肉	11
lamb	yángròu	羊肉	11
language	yǔ	语	3
large	dà	大	17
lawyer	lùshī	律师	9
left	zuǒ	左	23
less, to (for time)	chà	差	5
let, to allow	ràng	让	14
like, to enjoy	xǐhuan	喜欢	10
listen to music	tīng yīnyuè	听音乐	10
live, to stay	zhù	住	7
living room, sitting room	kètīng	客厅	24
London	Lúndūn	伦敦	3
long	cháng	长	17
look for, to find	zhǎo	找	13
love, to love	ài	爱	10

M

Maotai (a kind of baijiu)	Máotái	茅台	20
map	dìtú	地图	15
may I ask, excuse me	qǐngwèn	请问	2
may, can, to have the permission to	néng	能	16
(measure word for books)	běn	本	15
(measure word for chairs)	bǎ	把	19
(measure word for family members)	kǒu	口	8
(measure word for flat objects)	zhāng	张	15
(measure word for painting)	fú	幅	18
(measure word for person-polite)	wèi	位	13
(measure word for shoes, socks)	shuāng	双	17
(measure word)	jiā	家	12
(measure word)	jiàn	件	16
(measure word)	tiáo	条	16

(measure word, table of [dishes])	zhuō	桌	24
meat	ròu	肉	11
medicine	yào	药	28
medium, middle	zhōng	中	17
meet	(kàn) jiàn	（看）见	26
meeting	huì	会	11
menu	càidān	菜单	19
milk	niúnǎi	牛奶	20
minute (duration)	fēnzhōng	分钟	23
minute	fēn	分	5
Miss., young lady	xiǎojie	小姐	2
mobile phone	shǒujī	手机	7
Modern standard Chinese	Pǔtōnghuà	普通话	6
money	qián	钱	14
month	yuè	月	4
most	zuì	最	17
mother	mǔqin	母亲	8
Mr., gentleman, husband	xiānsheng	先生	2
Mrs., lady, wife	tàitai	太太	2
mum / mother	māma	妈妈	8
museum	bówùyuàn / bówùguǎn	博物院／博物馆	21

N

name	míngzi	名字	2
near, close	jìn	近	22
nearby	fùjìn	附近	22
need, to require	xūyào	需要	27
New York	Niǔyuē	纽约	3
news	xīnwén	新闻	10
next year	míngnián	明年	4
nine	jiǔ	九	4
no problem	méi wèntí	没问题	19
no, not	bù	不	1
north	běi	北	23
northwest	xīběi	西北	23
not bad, pretty good	búcuò	不错	1
not have, there is not	méiyǒu	没有	8
novel	xiǎoshuō	小说	26
now, at the moment	xiànzài	现在	5
number	hào	号	7
nurse	hùshi	护士	9

O

o'clock	diǎn	点	5
of course	dāngrán	当然	16
often	cháng / chángcháng	常／常常	10
often	jīngcháng	经常	22
oh	ò	哦	9
one	yī	一	4
only	zhǐ	只	15
open, to start, to operate (a machine, a car)	kāi	开	5
or (only used in questions)	háishì	还是	19
or	huòzhě	或者	19
order dishes	diǎncài	点菜	19
other	bié de	别的	16
out	chū	出	23
overcoat	dàyī	大衣	16

P

painting, drawing	huà	画	18
Paris	Bālí	巴黎	3
park	gōngyuán	公园	24
(particle for following up question)	ne	呢	1
(particle)	le	了	9
pass, to go through, to celebrate	guò	过	29
(passive grammar particle)	bèi	被	28
passport	hùzhào	护照	21
password	mìmǎ	密码	21
person, people	rén	人	3
pink	fěn	粉	16
place	dìfang	地方	3
plain rice	báifàn	白饭	19
plan	dǎsuàn	打算	27
plan, to plan	jìhuà	计划	27
play (in a sport or game), to hit	dǎ	打	10
play ball	dǎqiú	打球	29
play tennis	dǎ wǎngqiú	打网球	10
please	qǐng	请	2
pork	zhūròu	猪肉	19
Pound sterling	Yīngbàng	英镑	14
practice	liàn	练	29
prawn, shrimp	xiā	虾	19

presence, to be here	guānglín	光临	19
pretty, beautiful	piàoliang	漂亮	17
primary school	xiǎoxué	小学	9
problem, question	wèntí	问题	19
public bus	gōnggòng qìchē	公共汽车	22

Q

Qingdao (city name)	Qīngdǎo	青岛	20
quality	zhìliàng	质量	18
(question particle)	ma	吗	1

R

rain	xià yǔ	下雨	25
rain	yǔ	雨	25
reach, to arrive	dào	到	23
read a book	dú shū	读书	9
read	kàn shū	看书	10
really, truly	zhēn	真	17
really, truly	zhēnde	真的	10
recently, lately	zuìjìn	最近	27
recognize, to know	rènshi	认识	2
red	hóng	红	16
repair, to mend	xiū	修	28
retire	tuìxiū	退休	9
return	huán	还	27
return	huí	回	13
ride	qí	骑	22
right	yòu	右	23
road	lù	路	7
roast duck	kǎoyā	烤鸭	11
room	fángjiān	房间	7
run	pǎobù	跑步	10

S

same	yíyàng	一样	25
satisfied	mǎnyì	满意	24
say hello to somebody	gēn...dǎ zhāohu	跟……打招呼	26
seafood	hǎixiān	海鲜	19
secretary	mìshū	秘书	9
see a doctor	kàn bìng	看病	28
seem, to be like	hǎoxiàng	好像	26
sell	mài	卖	15

send	fā	发	21
serious, critical	yánzhòng	严重	28
settle the bill	jiézhàng	结账	19
seven	qī	七	4
Shanghai dialect	Shànghǎihuà	上海话	6
shoes	xié	鞋	17
shop, store	shāngdiàn	商店	5
short	duǎn	短	17
sick, ill	bìng	病	28
side	biān	边	23
singing and dancing performance	gēwǔ	歌舞	21
sit, by	zuò	坐	22
six	liù	六	4
size	hào	号	17
small, little	xiǎo	小	17
smooth	shùnlì	顺利	30
snow	xià xuě	下雪	25
snow	xuě	雪	25
some	xiē	些	14
sometimes	yǒushíhou	有时候	10
sorry	duìbuqǐ	对不起	5
so-so	mǎmǎhūhū	马马虎虎	1
soup	tāng	汤	19
speak, to say	shuō	说	3
spicy (or strong for alcoholic drinks)	là	辣	20
spinach	bōcài	菠菜	19
sport, exercise	yùndòng	运动	10
Spring Festival (Chinese New Year)	Chūn Jié	春节	4
spring	chūn (tiān / jì)	春（天／季）	25
spring	chūntiān	春天	18
Starbucks	Xīngbākè	星巴克	26
station, stop	zhàn	站	22
still	hái	还	17
stop	tíng	停	23
straight	yìzhí	一直	23
street	jiē	街	7
structural particle	de	的	4
student	xuésheng	学生	9
style	yàngzi	样子	17
subway station	dìtiě zhàn	地铁站	22
successful	chénggōng	成功	30
such, so, like this	zhème	这么	29

(suggesting particle)	ba	吧	11
summer	xià (tiān / jì)	夏（天／季）	25
supermarket	chāoshì	超市	22
surf the internet	shàngwǎng	上网	10
surname, be surnamed	xìng	姓	2
swimming pool	yóuyǒngchí	游泳池	21

T

table	zhuōzi	桌子	19
tablet, pill	piàn	片	28
taste	wèidào	味道	20
tea	chá	茶	20
teacher	lǎoshī	老师	9
telephone	diànhuà	电话	7
tell	gàosù	告诉	13
ten	shí	十	4
thank you	xièxie	谢谢	1
that	nà / nèi	那	2
the Forbidden City, the Palace Museum	Gùgōng	故宫	21
the Great Wall	Chángchéng	长城	7
the last, finally	zuìhòu	最后	24
theatre	jùyuàn	剧院	21
then, after	ránhòu	然后	18
things	dōngxi	东西	10
things, matter, business	shì	事	11
this	zhè / zhèi	这	2
three	sān	三	4
throat	sǎngzi	嗓子	28
Tian'anmen	Tiān'ānmén	天安门	21
ticket	piào	票	27
tie	lǐngdài	领带	16
time	shíjiān	时间	11
times	cì	次	28
tired	lèi	累	1
today	jīntiān	今天	4
together	yìqǐ	一起	11
tomorrow	míngtiān	明天	4
too, very, extremely	tài	太	11
toothache	yá téng	牙疼	28
towards	wǎng	往	23
towards	xiàng	向	23
train station	huǒchē zhàn	火车站	22

train	huǒchē	火车	22
travel	lǚyóu	旅游	27
trousers	kùzi	裤子	17
try	shì	试	16
Tsingtao beer	Qīngdǎo píjiǔ	青岛啤酒	20
turn	guǎi	拐	23
two	liǎng	两	5
two	èr	二	4
type	zhǒng	种	17

U

underground, tube	dìtiě	地铁	22
understand	(kàn) dǒng	（看）懂	26
US dollar	Měiyuán	美元	14
USA	Měiguó	美国	3
use	yòng	用	15
username	dēnglùmíng	登录名	21

V

vegetable dish	sùcài	素菜	19
vegetarian	sùshízhě	素食者	19
vehicle	chē	车	22
very	hěn	很	1
very well, very good	hěn hǎo	很好	1
very, extremely	fēicháng	非常	10
visa	qiānzhèng	签证	27
visit	cānguān	参观	21

W

wait	děng	等	13
waiter / waitress	fúwùyuán	服务员	19
walk, to go on foot	zǒulù	走路	22
walk, to leave, to go	zǒu	走	22
want, to need, will	yào	要	14
watch film	kàn diànyǐng	看电影	10
watch, to see, to look at	kàn	看	6
water melon	xīguā	西瓜	15
way, means, method	bànfǎ	办法	29
wear, to put on	chuān	穿	17
weather	tiānqì	天气	25
website	wǎngzhǐ	网址	7
WeChat	wēixìn	微信	7

week, day of the week	xīngqī	星期	4
weekend	zhōumò	周末	10
welcome	huānyíng	欢迎	19
well-known liquor	míngjiǔ	名酒	20
west	xī	西	23
what	shénme	什么	2
what's happening	shénme shì	什么事	11
What's your surname? (polite)	nín guìxìng	您贵姓	2
when (question)	shénme shíhou	什么时候	11
when, while	...de shíhou	……的时候	26
where	nǎr	哪儿	3
which	nǎ / něi	哪	3
white	bái	白	16
who, whom	shéi / shuí	谁	2
Wi-Fi	wúxiàn wǎng	无线网	21
will, be about to	jiāng	将	27
wind	fēng	风	25
winter	dōng (tiān / jì)	冬（天／季）	25
wish	zhù	祝	29
with, and	gēn	跟	12
work, job	gōngzuò	工作	9
would like, to think	xiǎng	想	14
write a book	xiě shū	写书	9
write	xiě	写	29
writer	zuòjiā	作家	9

X

Xicheng District	Xīchéng Qū	西城区	7

Y

year (of age)	suì	岁	8
year	nián	年	4
yesterday	zuótiān	昨天	4
you	nǐ	你	1
you're welcome	bú kèqi	不客气	5
younger brother	dìdi	弟弟	8
younger sister	mèimei	妹妹	8
yuan (informal)	kuài	块	14